INTERNATIONAL DEVELOPMENT IN FOCUS

Making Devolution Work for Service Delivery in Kenya

ABDU MUWONGE, TIMOTHY STEPHEN WILLIAMSON,
CHRISTINE OWUOR, AND MURATHA KINUTHIA

Contents

Figures

Acknowledgments

This report was prepared by a World Bank team led by Abdu Muwonge, Muratha Kinuthia, Christine Owuor, and Timothy Stephen Williamson under the guidance of Paolo Belli, Meskerem Brhane, Helene Carlsson Rex, Allen Dennis, Peter Ellis, Robin Mearns, and Nicola Smithers. The study took place under the Country Director for Kenya, Rwanda, Somalia, and Uganda, Keith Hansen, and his predecessors, Carlos Felipe Jaramillo and Diarietou Gaye. The core members of the study team included James Muli Musinga (Agriculture), Ruth Charo (Education), Keziah Muthembwa (External Affairs), Diana Nzioki and Joel A. Turkewitz (Governance), Jane Chuma (Health), Lucy Musira (Human Resource Management), Utz Pape (Poverty and Equity), Samuel Thomas Clark and Annette Omollo (Public Participation), Sheila Kamunyori and Davison Muchadenyika (Urban), and Chris Heymans and Pascaline Ndungu (Water). Roderick M. Babijes, Michelle Lisa Chen, Evelyn Kagwanjah, Elizabeth Karuoya, Angelina Musera, and Caroline Odicko were program assistants at various stages of the study. Mary Kalerwa Muyonga coordinated the study under the overall stewardship of the core team led by Abdu Muwonge.

Work on the report was underpinned by a series of background papers prepared by consultants, including Julius Kinyungu and Timothy Njagi (Agriculture); Moses Abiero, Phelesia Akasa, and Donvan Amenya (Education); Jamie Boex and Patrick Chege (Fiscal); Diana Nzioki (Governance); Dr. Benjamin Tsofa (Health); Kithinji Kiragu (Human Resource Management); Professor Karuti Kanyinga (Politics and Accountability); Keziah Mwanga and Tom Odongo (Urban); Rolfe Eberhard and Dr. Dan Juma (Water); Tom Hart, Sierd Hardley, Gundula Loeffler, and Rebecca Simson from the Overseas Development Institute (Human Resources, Politics, and Public Financial Management); Mathew Benson, Alistair Haynes, and Carol Onsomu (Poverty and Equity); and Mike Winter (overall study).

The team gratefully acknowledges the valuable comments provided by the peer reviewers at the concept note, technical review, and decision-review meeting stages, which have contributed greatly to informing this report. Maitreyi B. Das, Deborah Hannah Isser, Ruth Kagia (external peer reviewer, senior adviser to the Office of the President, Kenya), Ayah Mahgoub, and Salim Rouhana served as peer reviewers at the concept stage. Samuel Thomas Clark, Deborah Hannah Isser, Roland White, and Serdar Yilmaz were peer reviewers at the technical and decision-review stages. Additional comments were received at the concept stage from Judy Baker, Peter D. Ellis, Utz Johann Pape, Margarita Puerto Gomez, and Kimberly Vilar.

The study was conducted jointly by the World Bank and the government of Kenya institutions represented through a study task force comprising representatives from the Commission on Revenue Allocation; Council of Governors; County Assemblies Forum; Intergovernmental Budget and Economic Council; Intergovernmental Relations Technical Committee; Ministry of Agriculture; Ministry of Devolution and the Arid and Semi-Arid Lands; Ministry of Education; Ministry of Health; Ministry of Public Service, Youth and Gender Affairs; Ministry of Water and Sanitation; National Assembly; National Gender and Equality Commission; National Treasury and Planning; Office of the Auditor General; Office of the Controller of Budget; and the Senate. The team acknowledges the participation of County Executive and County Assembly officials from the core counties that informed the case studies for this volume—namely, Garissa, Kisumu, Makueni, Nairobi, and Nyandarua.

In preparing the report, the team has benefited from discussions with members of the Country Management Unit, notably Carlos Felipe Jaramillo, as well as Trichur K. Balakrishnan, Xavier Furtado, Peter Isabirye, and Camille Lampart Nuamah. The team is thankful for the support provided by Ede Jorge Ijjasz-Vasquez, Bernice K. Van Bronkhorst, and Sameh Naguib Wahba. Jay Sewell was the principal editor of the report.

Finally, the team acknowledges the financial resources provided under the Kenya Accountable Devolution Program (KADP) managed by the World Bank and funded by the European Union and the governments of Denmark, Finland, Sweden, the United Kingdom, and the United States. Additional resources were provided by the Agile and Harmonized Assistance for Devolved Institutions (AHADI) program funded by the governments of the United Kingdom and the United States.

Executive Summary

INTRODUCTION

Kenya adopted a new constitution and began the process of devolution in 2010. The Constitution of Kenya of 2010 was the institutional response to long-standing grievances over the centralization of state powers and public sector resources as well as regional disparities in service delivery and development outcomes. This radical restructuring of the Kenyan state had three main objectives: (1) decentralizing political power, public sector functions, and public finances; (2) ensuring a more equitable spatial distribution of resources among regions; and (3) promoting more accountable, participatory, and responsive government at all levels.

The first elections under the new constitution, in 2013, established 47 new county governments. A new bicameral parliament was also elected, in which the National Assembly plays an oversight role regarding the national executive, while the Senate protects and promotes the interests of the county governments. Each county government is made up of a County Executive, headed by an elected governor, which works under the oversight of an elected County Assembly. County governments fulfill their constitutionally mandated responsibilities, financed by annually prescribed shares ("equitable shares") of national revenues; their own sources of revenues (own-source revenues); and various conditional grants from the national government and development partners.

Devolution has led to the establishment of institutions and systems for delivery of devolved services, but the stability of these institutions and systems will be critical for the reform to be assessed as a success. The basic institutional framework stipulated in the Constitution of Kenya of 2010 has largely been put into place. County governments are now well established. Two rounds of national and county elections, held in 2013 and 2017, resulted in successful transitions of political power. Kenyans associate devolution with certain dividends brought about by the constitution; however, the next phase will require stable, enabled, and effective institutions and systems to deliver more and better services to citizens and to further reduce regional disparities.

The constitution laid out a strong foundation for sharing responsibilities and resources between the national and county governments. Counties are assigned significant frontline service delivery functions, with the national government typically assuming a central mandate around policy, standards, and norms. With a constitutional guarantee of unconditional transfers from the national government, county governments are expected to have the means and the autonomy to address local needs. Moreover, constitutional provisions ensure that transfers to counties are designed to address regional disparities and to favor historically disadvantaged counties.

Seven years after the "devolution train" left the station, this report takes stock of how devolution has affected the delivery of devolved basic services to Kenyan citizens. Whereas devolution was driven by political reform, the ensuing institutions and systems were expected to deliver greater socioeconomic equity through devolved service delivery. This study, Making Devolution Work for Service Delivery (MDWSD), is the first major assessment of Kenya's devolution reform. The study provides key messages regarding what is working, what is not working, and what could work better to enhance service delivery based on currently available data. It provides an independent assessment of service delivery performance in five sectors (health, education, agriculture, urban, and water services) and includes an in-depth review of the main pillars of devolved service delivery: public financial management (PFM), intergovernmental finance, human resource management (HRM), politics, and accountability. The study was a jointly coordinated effort by the government of Kenya and the World Bank, carried out under the guidance of a study task force comprising officials from the National Treasury, line ministries, independent commissions, the Council of Governors, and county governments.

The study is largely based on a set of background papers and policy briefs, prepared for key sectors and for cross-cutting dimensions. Background papers were based on a standard set of analytical issues and research questions and relied on a triangulation of various data sources: surveys, administrative data, available literature, and interviews. Initial findings and recommendations of the MDWSD sector studies have been validated and fine-tuned through follow-up consultations and discussions. Based on these background papers, the study has put together a series of sector-specific and cross-cutting policy briefs, providing practitioners in both the government and the broader development community with key findings, in-depth assessments, and policy options on specific aspects of devolution and service delivery.

MAJOR ACHIEVEMENTS AND CHALLENGES

Overall, this study concludes that the contribution of devolution to service delivery is mixed, but there are promising signs. The *glass is half full* because devolution enabled the establishment of institutions and systems to support the delivery of devolved services and provided for a platform that is expected to enhance equity in Kenya. However, the *glass is still half empty* because of ambiguities in financing and service provision. The national government is still heavily involved in the delivery of many devolved services, governance, and coordination—challenges that impede frontline service delivery. As for the level and quality of devolved services that have been achieved, the *picture is mixed* since some sectors show positive trends in a few indicators but others do not.

Moreover, it is not clear whether overall inequities have decreased across the country, in part because a lack of disaggregated data constrains the measurement of impacts. There is a general shortage of data on service delivery outcomes, outputs, and inputs. Without regular and routine sector administrative data on service delivery and periodic and consistent surveys, the management, decision-making, and accountability processes to make devolution work for service delivery will become even more challenging.

A *promising sign* is that in the years since the "devolution train" left the station, the new county governments have been evolving and becoming more responsive and accountable for delivering the devolution dividends to Kenyans. Indeed, this study includes several examples of counties that have delivered transformative, world-class services in which a high quality of county leadership is making the difference. Despite the challenges of rapid transition to largely new county governments, devolution has not led to major disruption of service delivery. Counties have maintained—and, in many cases, significantly expanded—the levels of, and access to, services in health, education, and water. In the health sector, access to facilities has been expanded, deliveries attended by qualified birth attendants have increased, and immunization rates have stabilized. In the agriculture and urban sectors, however, the picture is mixed. Core agriculture extension services appear to have declined since devolution, although counties have provided farmers with access to input subsidies. The newly created urban institutions are still weak, and many counties are slow to empower them to function as envisaged by the Urban Areas and Cities Act of 2019.

Counties have invested substantially in infrastructure for service delivery. For example, counties built 1,419 dispensaries and 821 early childhood development and education (ECDE) centers between 2013 and 2018. To underpin growth, counties have invested in rural water supply schemes and agriculture infrastructure such as irrigation, markets, and rural roads. Urban investments have focused on drainage, street lighting, and solid waste management following renewed reform efforts to reestablish municipalities. However, across all sectors, many counties are grappling with issues of infrastructure quality, paying limited attention to issues of proper project appraisal processes and maintenance.

Counties have also invested in their human resources by recruiting staff to deliver services, and the numbers of health workers and teachers for ECDE establishments have increased significantly. For example, the number of trained ECDE teachers increased by 54 percent, from 73,012 in 2010 to 112,703 in 2018. In the health sector, the number of workers increased between 2013 and 2018 by 72 percent in Kilifi, 42 percent in Kwale, 28 percent in Makueni, 13 percent in Kisumu, and 5 percent in Nyeri.

Despite these increases, staffing shortages continue to be an issue, compounded by high rates of absenteeism (especially in the health sector) and sometimes low staff motivation as well as misallocation. The number of agriculture technical staff has declined, and extension services have suffered. In urban areas, technical staff such as planners, surveyors, economists, and municipal engineers are in short supply in some counties, or they are misplaced and not working in departments relevant to their expertise. For instance, as of 2019 in the planning and development control sections, the percentage of filled posts stood at 24.5 percent in Nairobi, 50 percent in Makueni, and 38.9 percent in Kisumu. The overall allocation of staff by counties is also inefficient because of the large share and growth of staffing in administrative departments and of administrative staff within service sectors. Counties spend 60–70 percent of operating expenses on labor, presumably in part because of inherited labor from the administrations of now-defunct local authorities. In short, human resource management remains a major challenge to county service delivery.

Despite improvements, disparities in economic and educational outcomes persist in Kenya, and addressing inequities remains a long-term task. Poverty rates in 2016, by county, range from 17 percent to 78 percent. Gross domestic product (GDP) in 2017, by county, ranged from K Sh 48,000 to K Sh 350,000 per capita. Remote, largely rural counties tend to have higher poverty and lower GDP, while the more urbanized and more populous counties have higher per capita GDP. Inequalities persist in health and educational outcomes after devolution between poorer and richer, and rural and urban counties. For example, the percentage of pupils able to read a story varies from 21 percent to 67 percent. Similar degrees of disparity can be seen in ECDE, with enrollment rates lower in poorer and more rural areas. However, these disparities in preprimary gross enrollment rates have been decreasing since devolution. For the water, agriculture, and urban sectors, lack of data makes it difficult to identify tendencies and patterns with respect to disparities between counties.

Large disparities persist in health service delivery. Poorer and more rural counties continue to have access to fewer and lower-quality services than wealthier and more urban counties; for example, deliveries in health facilities vary from 33 percent to 100 percent of births; maternal mortality varies from 187 to 3,795 per 100,000 live births; health worker density varies from 3.4 to 24 per 10,000 population; and the proportion of fully immunized children varies from 46 percent to 100 percent. Across many health outputs, there has been limited convergence between facilities in poorer and richer counties, with inequalities persisting. Facilities in rural counties have worse availability than more urban counties for over half of the listed essential drugs and suffer from higher staff absentee rates. For some essential equipment (such as thermometers, stethoscopes, and sphygmomanometers), facilities in poorer counties fall behind those in richer counties. Likewise, facilities in poorer and more rural counties tended to have fewer vaccines than wealthier and more urban counties in 2018.

However, health services are improving, and disparities, such as access to vaccines and deliveries, are shrinking in some areas. Overall levels and disparities in skilled birth attendance have improved after devolution. The availability of measles vaccines has increased across all geographic areas since 2012; the same positive trend appears in the availability of polio vaccines. Essential drug availability has also improved, with one-third of these drugs increasingly available in facilities in poorer counties.

FINANCING SERVICE DELIVERY

A notable achievement of devolution is that Kenya has put in place a fiscal framework for sharing national revenues between the national government and the county governments. At the apex is the Division of Revenue Act (DORA), which stipulates how national government and county governments share national revenues. Among county governments, revenue sharing is through the County Allocation of Revenue Act (CARA). Both DORA and CARA are enacted annually, but the amounts are set in a complex, often heated, negotiation process—with protests and disputes settled (with sometimes significant delays) by the National and County Government Coordinating Summit ("The Summit"). As a result, this framework has resulted in significant interruptions to the smooth flow of funds to support devolved service delivery, which in turn affects quality and outcomes.

The constitution assigns significant functional responsibilities to county governments, but they currently only account for 13 percent of total public spending, down from a peak of 16 percent in fiscal year (FY) 2014/15. County spending has increased from an initial K Sh 229 billion in FY2014/15 to K Sh 327 billion per year by FY2017/18—an increase of 49.3 percent in nominal terms over the first four years of devolution. This significant increase has contributed to the observed increases in service delivery levels and investments. In contrast, however, national spending nearly doubled, from K Sh 1.094 trillion in FY2013/14 to K Sh 1.960 trillion in FY2017/18. This increase has been driven not only by significant increases in debt servicing over time (a major driver of Consolidated Fund Services) but also by growth in the national government's recurrent and development expenditures. Therefore, overall, the counties' share of total government spending has declined. And the national government retains a higher share of fiscal resources even in sectors where functions have been devolved.

The basic framework for county-level allocation and use of their financial resources is in place and functional. The Public Finance Management Act 2012 provides counties with a comprehensive framework for planning and budgeting—which is, by and large, used by counties. The national Integrated Financial Management Information System (IFMIS) has been progressively improved and has been rolled out to all counties. These have been significant achievements in ensuring minimum PFM standards; however, some counties use IFMIS half-heartedly and often in parallel with old systems.

County performance in planning and budgeting, however, has been suboptimal and has undermined the quality and sustainability of services. Plans and budgets do not focus sufficiently on service delivery, and budgets cannot answer simple questions such as how much is being spent where in the county on different levels of services. Budgets tend not to show allocations to subcounties or facilities. Budgets also tend to use input-linked results indicators rather than service delivery outputs or outcomes. This makes it difficult to link spending to services. In addition, operational expenditures are underbudgeted. Operating budgets for service delivery are also squeezed by high payroll costs and high administrative expenditures. As noted earlier, counties use 60–70 percent of operating expenses for labor, which crowds out the spending on service delivery.

Although counties are executing their budgets, execution rates are volatile and very low for development budgets. Some of these low development budget execution rates may result from late releases of transfers by the National Treasury, although that would still not explain why some counties do a much better job than others. To better understand the underlying reasons, there is a need for better systems to monitor, track, and analyze spending at the county level.

One aspect of county expenditure management that may be compromising service delivery is the unreliable flow of budgeted funds to sector departments and frontline facilities. In some counties where county treasuries operate in a very centralized way, hospitals and health centers often do not receive a predictable flow of funds, which constrains their operations. In other cases, however, county treasuries have found ways of "decentralizing" operations spending to frontline service delivery units.

CITIZEN ENGAGEMENT IN SERVICE DELIVERY

Devolution has established electoral, horizontal, and direct accountability mechanisms at the county level that have enabled citizens to exercise some degree of oversight of counties' service delivery performance. County-level elections—for both the County Executive and the County Assembly—have been competitive and enjoyed good voter turnout, averaging about 85 percent in 2013 and 78 percent in 2017. The performance of incumbents has been reported as one key factor in the 2017 elections, which saw a notable turnover in governors and members of county assemblies (MCAs). However, the MCAs tend to be more accountable to their ward electorates—focusing more on supporting ward-specific projects than on improving countywide service delivery.

Horizontal accountability, however, has been weak. The MCAs reportedly have limited oversight and scrutiny of their respective county executives, partly because of capacity constraints among the MCAs and their staff relative to the executive. In addition, as noted above, the MCAs' oversight and scrutiny in many counties is often focused on ward-level investments and the funds allocated for ward-based projects rather than on broader measures of countywide service delivery.

Direct citizen accountability of county service delivery, through project management committees (PMCs), has also sometimes focused on the implementation of individual investment projects rather than on service delivery in a wider sense. The PMCs offer opportunities for citizen engagement during the construction phase, but during postconstruction there is less opportunity for continued citizen feedback on the delivery of services from that facility.

Counties are legally bound to ensure that citizens participate in a range of planning and budgeting activities—and all counties have tried to ensure that they do consult with local citizens in one way or another. That said, citizen participation in county-level planning processes has been poorly coordinated and inadequately facilitated by county governments. Moreover, citizens have tended to participate by advocating for particular local investment projects.

The normative framework for intergovernmental consultation, cooperation, and coordination is in place, with The Summit at the apex, supported by a range of sectoral and cross-cutting intergovernmental forums. This framework is intended to ensure that the national government and counties work together to resolve the many issues that cannot be addressed unilaterally—such as functional assignments; PFM norms; HRM systems; and sector-specific guidance, norms, and standards. However, analysis of this aspect of devolution is beyond the scope of this study, and further analysis is needed to identify constraints and make recommendations.

CALL FOR ACTION

This study shows that the future of devolution is promising, as the new county governments are functioning and are becoming more responsive and accountable for delivering devolution dividends to the Kenyan citizens.

Achieving this promise will require both levels of government to play their parts. County governments will have to deliver to citizens on their devolved mandate. National government will need to nurture and provide commitment (political, financial, and technical) to the county governments to deliver on their devolved mandate. This study outlines a broad agenda for the future of devolution, which requires concerted action within, across, and among the spheres of government—their executives and legislatures as well as citizens.

The study concludes by proposing the development of a joint plan of action for making devolution work for service delivery and identifying the initial entry points where county and national governments can start. To those ends, the study recommends the following key policy actions:

- *Address residual ambiguities or disputes over functions.* Clarify the service-delivery responsibilities of various tiers of government and ensure that funding corresponds to those responsibilities.
- *Enhance the adequacy, efficacy, equity, and reliability of county revenues.* This will require, for example, a review of the share of county resources relative to devolved functions, enhancements to revenue allocation formulas, and measures to strengthen the mobilization of own-source revenues.
- *Improve intergovernmental coordination.* National and county governments need to cooperate, coordinate, learn, and build trust between and across levels of government and within sectors.
- *Promote devolution beyond county government headquarters* where it is feasible and practical to do so. Counties need to decentralize responsibility toward the point of service delivery and deliver predictable finances.
- *Adopt a strategic, results-oriented, and coordinated approach to HRM reforms* to support county governments.
- *Enhance structures for meaningful public participation.* Facilitate the participation of the public in decision-making and strengthen the accountability of local politicians for service delivery.
- *Enhance county planning, budgeting, and execution.* Realign resources within and across sectors to respond to local needs and national priorities for service delivery.
- *Invest in data to build the evidence base for devolved sectors* through increased focus on disaggregated sector data, development of service delivery norms and standards, disaggregated financial reporting norms, and strengthened devolution results monitoring.

Abbreviations

ADP Annual Development Plan
ALM asset and liability management
ASALs arid and semi-arid lands
CA County Assembly
CARA County Allocation of Revenue Act
CASB County Assembly Service Board
CBROP County Budget Review and Outlook Paper
CCI County Creditworthiness Initiative
CEC County Executive Committee
CPSB County Public Service Board
CRA Commission on Revenue Allocation
CRF County Revenue Fund
CSO civil society organization
DHIS District Health Information System
ECD early childhood development
ECDE early childhood development and education
FY fiscal year
GRM grievance redress mechanism
HMT health management team, hospital management team
HRM human resources management
IBEC Intergovernmental Budget and Economic Council
IFMIS Integrated Financial Management System
IGRTC Intergovernmental Relations Technical Committee
K Sh Kenya shilling
KDSP Kenya Devolution Support Program
KUSP Kenya Urban Support Program
M&E monitoring and evaluation
MCAs members of County Assemblies
MDAs ministries, departments, and agencies
MDWSD Making Devolution Work for Service Delivery
MP member of parliament
NALM National Assets and Liabilities Management (department)
NGO nongovernmental organization

O&M	operations and maintenance
OSR	own-source revenue
PBB	program-based budget
PFM	public financial management
PIM	public investment management
PIMIS	Public Investment Management Information System
PMs	performance measures
PMC	project management committee
PSC	Public Service Commission
TSC	Teachers Service Commission
WSP	water service provider
WWDA	Water Works Development Agency

1 Introduction and Analytical Framework

CONTEXT

Devolution in Kenya is an integral part of a major constitutional reform, the aims of which are to redistribute political power, establish a more inclusive political system, and share resources more equitably. The centerpiece of this devolution reform was the new Constitution of Kenya of 2010, adopted after a national referendum. It is widely accepted that in the wake of the 2007–08 post-election violence, improving Kenya's political settlement was the primary driver that led to the reintroduction of devolution after many previous attempts (World Bank 2012).

Although improving service delivery may have been implicit in this process, it was not the primary driver or point of discussion. The institutional reforms enshrined in the new constitution were intended to address a range of long-standing grievances—stretching over decades—related to the highly centralized distribution of political power and persistent regional imbalances in development (Boone 2012; D'Arcy and Nistotskaya 2019; Kanyinga 2016; Mueller 2008). Devolution was a key element of the constitutional response to these grievances and, along with other measures, was intended to share the power and authority of central government and an "imperial" presidency—by establishing self-governing county governments—and to reduce regional disparities in development.

A decade has now passed since the new constitution was enacted and kick-started a dramatic transformation of the Kenyan state. Implementing devolution as part of the new constitutional reforms has been immensely challenging. Moving away from a centralized and unitary state to a highly devolved and quasi-federal state has been a multidimensional paradigm shift, requiring major institutional reforms, huge changes in the management of public finances and human resources, and transformations in mindsets and behavior.

Guided by the provisions of the 2010 constitution, major political and institutional achievements and reforms have underpinned a radical restructuring of the Kenyan state, devolving significant powers and responsibilities from the national level to the counties.[1] County governments in all 47 counties are now well established and have become an entrenched feature of Kenya's political landscape. Consistent with constitutional provisions, county governments are now responsible for the delivery of many public goods and services. To ensure that counties had the means to deliver services, the constitution also provided for an equitable sharing of revenues between and among the national and county levels, weighted in favor of disadvantaged areas and groups.

In principle, the devolution of functions was intended to improve service delivery through enhanced local accountability and greater allocative efficiencies. In practice, it is less clear whether service delivery has improved or whether socioeconomic disparities have been reduced.

Devolution has involved the establishment of key institutions entrusted with delivery of key basic services, and the evidence suggests that the reform remains popular among citizens (Cheeseman et al. 2019; El Messnaoui et al. 2018). However, there has not been a major undertaking to assess the effects of devolution on service delivery. This study takes stock of what has worked well, what could work better, and what has constrained improvements in service delivery in selected devolved sectors. This study is underpinned by the analytical framework described in this chapter.

OBJECTIVES OF THE STUDY

The Making Devolution Work for Service Delivery (MDWSD) study was initiated in response to the government's request, endorsed by Kenya's Council of Governors, that the World Bank lead a stocktaking assessment of devolution and service delivery. MDWSD was accordingly designed to assess the contribution of devolution toward improving service delivery in Kenya and to identify policy options that address the identified challenges and opportunities. It is a joint government of Kenya and World Bank initiative to (1) understand *what has worked* and *what could work better* for service delivery since 2013, and (2) spell out what needs to be done to make devolution work better to improve service delivery.

MDWSD builds upon an earlier World Bank report, "Devolution without Disruption" (DWD), which looked at "the critical issues that Kenya's policy makers will need to address, as the country seeks to fulfill the constitutional promise of a more devolved government that is closer and more responsive to the people" (World Bank 2012). The forward-looking DWD report primarily focused on intergovernmental financial arrangements, public financial management, accountability, and a range of other issues (including public service) from a perspective of ensuring that service delivery was not disrupted during the transition to a devolved system and also improved over time.

MDWSD takes up the story of service delivery during and after the immediate transition to devolution and assesses what has happened to service delivery and how services have been devolved, financed, and managed since 2013. The study was driven by a set of research questions: How was devolution expected to improve service delivery, and how was this to be achieved? What has happened to sector outcomes and service delivery since devolution? How has the financing, management, and decision-making for service delivery inputs, systems, and processes changed (de facto)? How has this affected service delivery outcomes— or how is it *expected* to affect outcomes—in terms of the level, quality, and equity of service delivery across and within counties? What are the successes achieved, challenges faced, and opportunities for improving service delivery? And what are the potential options available to address these challenges and take advantage of these opportunities?

HOW WAS DEVOLUTION EXPECTED TO CHANGE SERVICE DELIVERY?

As noted above, devolution was intended to redistribute political and administrative powers from the center to the local level to enable a shift of resources away from the national to the subnational level. The 2010 constitution dismantled what had been (until then) a highly centralized state, sharing state powers between the national government and 47 new county governments. In doing so, devolution aimed to mitigate the outcomes of a "winner-takes-all" political system by ensuring that winners at the national level did not win everything. Constitutionally empowered to take on major public sector functions, to access a minimum share of national revenues, and to raise their own revenues, county governments were expected to provide citizens in all of Kenya's regions with access to services, irrespective of who held power at the national level. Although the national government would continue to be responsible for nationwide public goods (such as defense, foreign policy, and monetary policy), it would no longer exercise a monopoly on service delivery.

Devolution was also expected to ensure that national resources would be more equitably distributed across the country. As well as affirming the equality of all citizens, the constitution includes several provisions explicitly aimed at reducing disparities between counties as well as promoting equitable development and marginalized areas and groups.[2] Promoting equitable development and addressing regional disparities occupy an important place in the underpinning of devolution because of the long-standing nature and prevalence of spatial and social inequalities in Kenya. Combined, the devolution of functions and more equitable distribution of power and resources has the potential to reduce disparities in service delivery across Kenya.

By establishing elected county governments, giving them constitutionally mandated service delivery responsibilities, and providing them with financial resources, devolution has the potential to strengthen service delivery further in two ways: first, by reducing the gap between citizens and the state, which can bring decisions on service delivery closer to the public and enable the public to hold the officials more easily to account; and second, by providing county governments with the flexibility to deploy human and financial resources in ways that respond to local demands for service delivery. By establishing this shorter route, the expectation was that citizens would also be more able to hold officials accountable for their performance (World Bank 2003, 2012) and that county governments would provide better-quality services that are more responsive to local needs and priorities.

STUDY FRAMEWORK

The study developed a simple analytical framework to assess the impact of devolution on service delivery. The framework lays out the envisaged inputs to the devolution process, the potential effects of these inputs on service delivery processes within and across sectors, and the potential impact of these effects on service delivery outcomes (figure 1.1).

The effects of devolution are analyzed along four theoretical dimensions of devolution inputs, which are mutually reinforcing.

Functions. The devolution of functions takes place, accompanied by sectoral service delivery and intergovernmental coordination arrangements. County governments are given clear sector service delivery mandates based on subsidiarity principles, entailing management of services by the lowest competent authority within county governments.

FIGURE 1.1

Analytical framework for assessment of devolution

Level 1: Devolution Inputs	Level 2: Effects on Service Delivery Processes	Level 3: Service Delivery Outcomes
a. Devolution of functions accompanied by sectoral service delivery and intergovernmental coordination arrangements	• County governments have clear service delivery mandates based on subsidiarity principles. • There are sector-specific policies, county management arrangements, and information for service delivery. • Intergovernmental coordination mechanisms resolve issues and promote mutual accountability for service delivery performance.	*Increased and more equitable access to services* *Stronger, localized accountability for services*
b. Intergovernmental financing arrangements and local discretion in allocation and use of resources	• Adequate and equitable resources are available to counties to deliver services. • Counties are able to allocate resources in line with local service delivery needs and national objectives. • Financing is linked to the achievement of service delivery results.	*Quality services delivered in line with established sectoral norms and standards*
c. Devolved human resources to deliver functions and services	• Counties are able to hire and deploy staff within the counties and to the front line. • There are more motivated staff, working at the front line, with the required skills to do the job. • Closer and stronger management and oversight of service delivery staff	*Services that are more responsive to local needs*
d. Transparency, public participation, local political, and accountability arrangements	• Counties are transparent, making relevant information available to the public on service delivery. • Local public and political participation increases the decision-making for investments and service delivery. • Strong local accountability processes are established for service delivery.	*Greater public awareness and demand for services*

External factors, county and sector context

Source: World Bank.

Accompanying the devolution of functions, sector-specific policies and county management arrangements for service delivery are agreed upon between national and county governments, including service delivery norms, institutional arrangements, and systems accompanied by consistent management information. Intergovernmental coordination mechanisms are put in place to effectively resolve issues and promote mutual accountability for service delivery performance between and across levels of government.

The combination of clear mandates, strong and common systems for service delivery, and intergovernmental coordination are the foundation for strong local service delivery.

Financing. Intergovernmental financing arrangements that provide local discretion in allocation and use of resources are put in place. These arrangements make available adequate and equitable resources to counties that enable them to deliver services. Counties have the discretion to allocate resources in line with local service delivery needs while achieving national objectives. Financing for service delivery is linked to the achievement of service delivery results. This enables and provides incentives for county governments to deliver services that are equitable and efficient within and across counties.

Human resources. Counties can hire and deploy adequate staff across county governments and to the front line in a way that enables equitable delivery of services. There is closer and stronger management and oversight of service delivery staff, because county departments are closer than national government to subcounties and the front line. Staff working at the front line have the required skills for the job and are more motivated to perform their tasks.

Transparency, public participation, and local political accountability arrangements. County governance structures are transparent, citizens have access to information and opportunities to participate, and counties are accountable. The first element—transparency—relates to information transparency. To participate in decision-making and hold counties and service providers to account, citizens need reliable information about government programs, rules and standards, finances, and decision-making as well as service delivery performance relevant to citizens' needs and priorities.

The second element—public participation—relates to citizen participation in decision-making and service delivery oversight. Citizens need opportunities to participate in decisions, articulate their needs and priorities, and provide feedback on service delivery.

The third element—local political accountability arrangements—means that, ultimately, county governments and frontline service providers will respond to citizen priorities and feedback if citizens have meaningful opportunities to hold them to account for their decisions and actions as well as for their lack of action.

These four core dimensions provide an analytical framework for taking stock of progress to date. These inputs and effects of devolution on service delivery are by no means automatic. They require purposeful, consistent, and cooperative action by national and county government over the long term. This study starts by asking, *What has happened to service delivery in practice?* It then assembles and analyzes available evidence on the evolution of devolution inputs, the effects of those inputs on the service delivery process, and how they may have affected service delivery. From this framework, the study investigates the story of service delivery since the introduction of devolution.

The study is based on assessments of (1) service delivery across five key sectors; and (2) the main cross-cutting thematic areas that underpin devolution and service delivery. The five service delivery sectors selected are health, education, agriculture, water and sanitation, and urban development, which together account for most of the services that are directly provided by counties. In addition to these sector studies, MDWSD's cross-cutting assessments covered politics and accountability, equity, fiscal devolution, county financial management, human resource management, and intergovernmental frameworks.

The study concludes by assessing progress against the analytic framework overall. What are the successes achieved, challenges faced, and opportunities for improving service delivery? What are the potential options available to address these challenges and take advantage of these opportunities?

DATA AND LIMITATIONS

The study relied on various data sources: surveys, administrative data, available literature, and interviews. A wide range of data indicators (for example, inputs, outputs, process-oriented results, and outcomes where possible) were gathered and analyzed to provide insights into the questions outlined above. It is worth pointing out that the data were cross-sectional across 2013–18.

A major caveat for this study concerned the paucity of data on some of the indicators used. Another limitation relates to the attribution issue, especially regarding the assessment of devolution's impacts on sectoral outcomes that are influenced by several other factors that we could not control for.

The study did not set out to undertake a full impact evaluation of devolution, because of the limited data on outcomes (both before and after 2013). What the MDWSD study has done is much more of a stocktaking assessment to provide evidence to the government on what is working, what is not working, and what could work better to make devolution work for service delivery.[3] In addition, the study does not look at services being directly delivered by the national government under devolution. However, the study does examine the national government's role in enabling county governments to deliver on their devolved mandates.

Devolution in Kenya means that service delivery now depends on both county governments and the national government. Although counties are responsible for most frontline service delivery functions, the national government also continues to provide services in several sectors, the most important being education. These nationally delivered services were not included in the study.

However, strengthening devolution is not just a question of strengthening county governments and their frontline service delivery capabilities; it is also about strengthening the national government's ability to fulfill its constitutional role in the management of devolved services and improving the effectiveness of intergovernmental fiscal and other relations. MDWSD did look at these national-level responsibilities, even though it focused primarily on frontline service delivery at the county level.

Although the final stages of the MDWSD study were concluded during the ongoing COVID-19 pandemic and locust invasions, it was designed and undertaken before either had started. As a result, the study only briefly refers to them. Nonetheless, the pandemic and the locust invasions pose acute challenges to both the national and county governments and to devolution as a system.

It is recognized that all counties have had to adapt their health service delivery sectors to manage epidemiological responses on the ground, treat clinical cases, and deploy their agriculture services to control locust invasions. The national government, for its part, has undertaken nationwide health policy initiatives to contain the coronavirus and has needed to coordinate the implementation of national health measures with all 47 county governments; the same applies to pest control and management.

At the same time, the economic and fiscal consequences of the pandemic and the locust invasion are also significant challenges to both levels of government and require a good deal of intergovernmental coordination and collaboration if they are to be met effectively. The agenda for making devolution work for service delivery is made even more relevant by the recent and ongoing crises faced by Kenya.

STUDY COVERAGE AND PRODUCTS

MDWSD background papers have been prepared for each sector and for each dimension. These are based on a standard set of analytical issues and research questions, aimed at better understanding what has changed as a result of devolution in terms of outcomes, inputs, and processes. Each background paper relies on information and data collected from a variety of secondary sources, reviews of relevant documentation, and fieldwork conducted in several counties.[4]

Primary data were collected from selected core counties, based on sector-specific criteria. During field visits to counties, interviews were conducted with county government staff from various departments. MDWSD study teams also accessed supporting documents where possible. Secondary data were collected mainly from national datasets, surveys, and reports from ministries, departments, and agencies. Table 1.1 summarizes the core study counties and data

TABLE 1.1 **MDWSD methodology for county-level sector studies, by sector**

SECTOR	CORE STUDY COUNTIES	SECONDARY DATA SOURCES
Agriculture	Garissa, Kilifi, Kisumu, Makueni, Nairobi, Nyandarua, Uasin Gishu	BOOST database and other county reports
Education	Garissa, Kisumu, Makueni, Mombasa, Nairobi, Nyandarua, Samburu	Education sector analysis reports, statistical reports (economic survey and MoE statistical booklet), and World Bank's ECDE cost and financing study
Health	Garissa, Kilifi, Kisumu, Kwale, Makueni, Nyeri	District Health Information System 2 (DHIS2), Master Facility Listing (MFL), and integrated Human Resource Information System (iHRIS) databases
Urban	Kiambu, Kisumu, Makueni, Nairobi	County reports
Water	Kisumu, Mombasa, Nairobi, Nyeri	IFMIS, county reports, national sector reports, census data, and WSP reports

Source: World Bank.
Note: BOOST is a platform that provides user-friendly access to granular county budget data using different visualization tools; DHIS2 is an online health information management software platform. ECDE = early childhood education and development; IFMIS = Integrated Financial Management Information System; MoE = Ministry of Education; WSP = Water Service Provider; MDWSD = Making Devolution Work for Service Delivery.

sources used, by sector. At an early stage in MDWSD, a "solutions" workshop enabled national and county stakeholders to discuss methodological and emerging issues and to identify ways forward.

The initial findings and recommendations of the MDWSD sector studies have been validated and fine-tuned through follow-up consultations. During sector forum workshops, the findings and policy recommendations of the sector and cross-cutting background studies also were discussed and fine-tuned.

Finally, MDWSD has put together a series of policy briefs. The policy briefs provide practitioners in both the government and in the broader development community with key findings, in-depth assessments, and policy options on specific aspects of devolution and service delivery. Along with the background papers, the MDWSD policy briefs underpin this synthesis report.

The MDWSD process was overseen by a joint task force, comprising the government of Kenya and and the World Bank, which was established in May 2019. Task force members represent key government ministries and bodies, the Council of Governors, other Kenyan stakeholders, the devolution donor working group, and World Bank practice areas. Within the World Bank, sector units in a variety of practice areas had primary responsibility for drafting terms of reference, recruiting research teams, facilitating field visits, supervising work, and organizing follow-up workshops.

This synthesis report provides decision makers and senior officials in the national government, in county governments, and in Kenya's wider development policy community with a summary of the key findings and policy options from the MDWSD study. It is based on and highlights the findings of MDWSD's sector-based and cross-cutting studies.

STRUCTURE OF THE REPORT

The remainder of this synthesis report is structured around five main sections, as follows: Chapter 2 analyzes what has happened to service delivery in Kenya since devolution and focuses on outcomes, outputs, inputs, and expenditures. Chapters 3 through 6 assess the dimensions of devolution set out in the analytical framework. Chapter 7 concludes with an overall assessment of progress, challenges, opportunities, and sets of key policy options and recommendations in areas of action—all of which are aimed at improving service delivery under devolution. A more detailed series of matrixes are contained in appendix A with policy options for each of the thematic areas.

NOTES

1. The Transitional Authority and the Commission on the Implementation of the Constitution played important roles in guiding devolution in the early years of constitutional implementation.
2. See articles 174, 201, and 203 of the Constitution of Kenya of 2010.
3. In addition, this study has not explicitly tried to look at international comparative experience in assessing Kenya's devolution reforms and their effect on service delivery. This has largely been because of time and resource constraints and a need to focus on what has happened in-country. However, it will be important—in a future piece of analytical work—to put Kenya's devolution and service delivery experience into an international and

comparative perspective, not only to enrich in-country discussions but also to inform a more global understanding of the interface between devolution and service delivery.

4. In addition to a general review of devolution across the country, the study undertook deep-dive case studies in five counties: Garissa, Kisumu, Makueni, Nairobi, and Nyandarua. The deep-dive counties were selected by the task force, and they offer several dimensions that represent other counties. It is important to point out that the national government took over some of the functions of Nairobi City County, and the study did not look into this issue, given that it happened at the time when background work for the study was concluded. It is an important issue that future studies will have to look into.

REFERENCES

Boone, C. 2012. "Land Conflict and Distributive Politics in Kenya." *African Studies Review* 55 (1): 75–03.

Cheeseman, N., K. Kanyinga, G. Lynch, M. Ruteere, and J. Willis. 2019. "Kenya's 2017 Elections: Winner-Takes-All Politics as Usual?" *Journal of Eastern African Studies* 13 (2): 215–34.

D'Arcy, M., and M. Nistotskaya. 2019. "Intensified Local Grievances, Enduring National Control: The Politics of Land in the 2017 Kenyan Elections." *Journal of Eastern African Studies* 13 (2): 294–312.

El Messnaoui, A., D. Omowole, L. Mrewa, and R. F. Silvosa. 2018. "A Political Economy Analysis of Devolution in Kenya." Report, Institute of Economic Affairs, Nairobi.

Kanyinga, K. 2016. "Devolution and the New Politics of Development in Kenya." *African Studies Review* 59 (3): 155–67.

Mueller, S. D. 2008. "The Political Economy of Kenya's Crisis." *Journal of Eastern African Studies* 2 (2): 185–210.

World Bank. 2003. *World Development Report 2004: Making Services Work for Poor People.* Washington, DC: World Bank.

World Bank. 2012. "Devolution without Disruption: Pathways to a Successful New Kenya." Report No. 72297, World Bank, Washington, DC.

2 Trends in Service Delivery

KEY MESSAGES

- Service delivery performance from the first few years of devolution is mixed, with some positive developments along with continued challenges and some disruption.
- Devolution has *not* led to a collapse in service delivery.
- Counties have generally expanded and invested in services that were devolved to them.
- Challenges in the quality and efficiency in service delivery persist, although there have been some positive developments in some sectors. Staff absenteeism is a key challenge.
- Significant disparities in service delivery remain, although service delivery has improved in counties that lag behind. Disparities have been reduced in some areas, including elements of health and early childhood development and education delivery.
- There is a challenge of gathering data within and across sectors on service delivery outcomes, outputs, inputs, and financing.

INTRODUCTION

As discussed in the previous chapter, devolution is intended to meet several objectives with respect to service delivery. Devolution seeks to strengthen and reduce existing and long-standing regional disparities in public service delivery and poverty in Kenya. By decentralizing service delivery functions to county governments and units within county governments, devolution seeks to ensure services are more effectively managed. By making adequate resources available over time through the fiscal framework for those functions, devolution is expected to enable improvements in coverage and quality of services delivered. Through equitable sharing of financial resources and other mechanisms, devolution is intended to provide poorer, historically disadvantaged counties with relatively more resources per capita to finance improvements in service delivery.

Devolution was also intended to provide more opportunities for citizens at the grassroots level to have their say in how resources are allocated at the lowest levels and provide bottom-up accountability for how those resources are used. However, devolution is no silver bullet; it is not a substitute for sectoral policies, systems, and processes for service delivery or institutional capacity but rather an enabler of improved service delivery.

This chapter sets out a summary of available evidence on service delivery trends and disparities, in terms of outcomes, outputs, inputs, and financing available. The chapter starts by examining trends in the level and quality of devolved services overall and the financing of those services in health, early childhood education, agriculture, water, and urban services. It next examines disparities in the service delivery and financing of those services. It then highlights the challenge of gathering data; there are large gaps in the data on service delivery, which makes this analysis challenging. Nevertheless, the available information does provide important insights into the state of devolved service delivery in Kenya. Finally, the purpose of this chapter is to set out the trends and patterns—the *what*. Subsequent chapters explore the reasons behind them—the *why*.

LEVEL AND QUALITY OF DEVOLVED SERVICES

Devolution of service delivery has taken place in the context of sustained economic growth and reduction of poverty in Kenya and improving health and education outcomes. Real per capita gross domestic product (GDP) has increased from K Sh 104,242 to K Sh 173,272 over the five years between 2013 and 2018 (figure 2.1). Poverty and maternal mortality have been on a downward trend—from 47 percent to 36 percent, and from 115 to 52 per 1,000 live births, respectively (figure 2.2). Literacy rates have also improved, from 73 percent to 84 percent. These positive trends in outcomes, which predate devolution, set the backdrop for county delivery of services.

FIGURE 2.1

Per capita GDP in Kenya, 2012–18

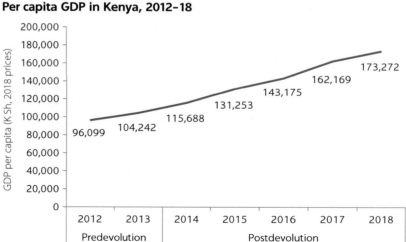

Sources: KNBS 2018a, 2018b; District Health Information System (DHIS) 2015 data; Ministry of Education, Science and Technology 2015.

FIGURE 2.2

Poverty, health, and education outcomes in Kenya, 2005 vs. 2015

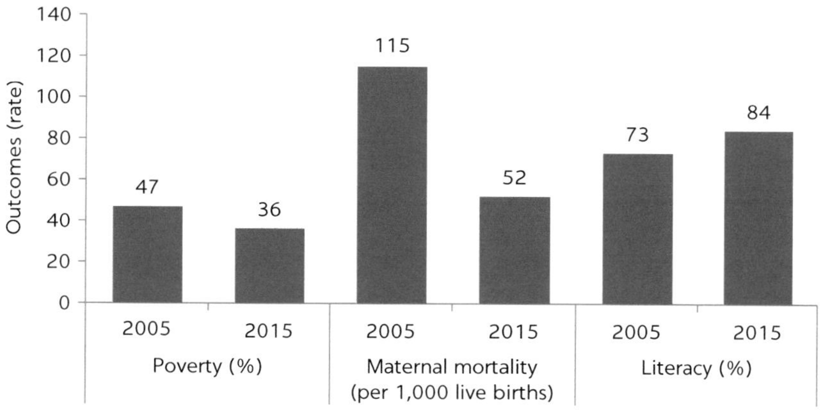

Sources: KNBS 2018a, 2018b; District Health Information System (DHIS) 2015 data; Ministry of Education, Science and Technology 2015.
Note: The poverty rate is the proportion of Kenyans living on less than the international poverty line (US$1.90 per day). The literacy rate is the proportion of school-going children age 3 and above who can read or write in at least one language.

Levels of devolved service delivery

Health, education, and water services

Counties have maintained and, in many cases, significantly expanded the levels of, and access to, service delivery in health, education, and water. For example, in health, outpatient visits to county hospitals, health centers, and dispensaries have increased from 9 to 13 per facility (per day) between 2013 and 2018, as the number of facilities has expanded (figure 2.3, panel b). The number and share of deliveries supervised by skilled attendants has increased from nearly 800,000 (59 percent) in 2013 to over 1.1 million (69 percent) in 2018 (figure 2.3, panel a). Immunization rates have fluctuated but had recovered to predevolution levels by 2018.

Enrollment in early childhood education has continued to increase at similar rates to those before devolution, with total enrollment increasing from 2.9 million in 2013 to 3.4 million in 2018 (figure 2.3, panel e). The net enrollment rate (NER) has also increased from 70.4 percent in 2013 to 77.2 percent in 2018.

In the water sector, estimates show access to basic drinking water facilities in rural areas increased from 47 percent in 2013 to 50 percent in 2017 (figure 2.3, panel d). Meanwhile, urban water coverage has remained flat at 85 percent, although piped water access declined from 63 percent in 2013 to 61 percent in 2015 (figure 2.3, panel c). Despite this, an additional 2.4 million people received piped water between 2014 and 2018 in urban areas.

Agriculture and urban sectors

There is an absence of quantitative data on service delivery in both the agriculture and urban sectors, and the qualitative information collected during this study paints a more mixed picture. While value addition in agriculture has continued to grow since 2017 (figure 2.3, panel f), counties have been active in a variety of ways. County agriculture departments have intervened in value chains by promoting standardization and helping farmers access export markets. Many have provided subsidies for seeds and fertilizers. Others have tried to make improved livestock breeds available.

FIGURE 2.3

Recent service delivery trends in Kenya

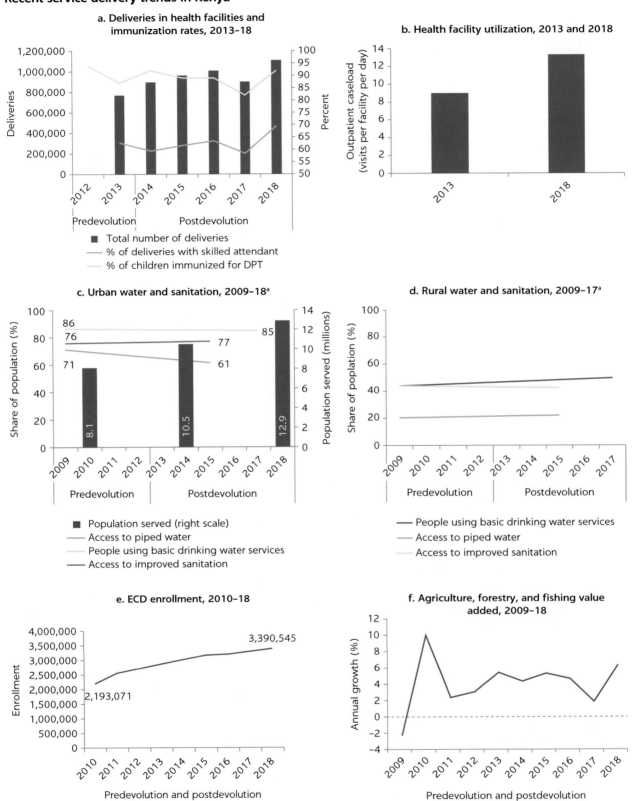

Sources: KNBS 2018a, 2018b; District Health Information System (DHIS) 2018 data; Ministry of Education, Science and Technology 2015; WHO and UNICEF 2019.
Note: DPT = diphtheria, pertussis, and tetanus; ECD = early childhood development.
a. Water access data were available only through 2015, the period captured by the 2015/16 Kenya Integrated Household Budget Survey (KNBS 2018a).

TABLE 2.1 **Examples of completed municipal service investments under Kenyan urban support program**

SERVICE INFRASTRUCTURE INVESTMENT TYPE	COMPLETED
Roads constructed or rehabilitated (km)	32
Drainage systems (km)	13
Footpaths and bicycle lanes (km)	12
Footbridges (km)	2
Streetlights	1,299
Parking lots constructed	400
Markets	4
Public parks and green urban spaces rehabilitated	2
SWM vehicles (skip loaders, tippers, etc.)	24
Skips	475

Source: World Bank 2020.
Note: km = kilometers; SWM = solid waste management.

However, core agriculture services in the sector have suffered following devolution, particularly extension services. Interviews with staff and farmers in Garissa, Kilifi, Nairobi, and Uasin Gishu Counties suggest that farmers are less likely to receive extension services postdevolution.

The picture is similarly mixed in urban services. Counties have continued to provide core municipal services, such as solid waste management, and to maintain urban infrastructure. Some counties highlighted the challenges of maintaining solid waste management services with aging equipment and a lack of operational inputs. Meanwhile, waste collection in some urban areas appears to have improved through county delegation of solid waste management responsibilities to neighborhoods (including through greater privatization in solid waste collection) and increased public awareness (table 2.1).

County investment levels

Counties have made significant investments in service delivery infrastructure, which has affected access. The number of health facilities has increased by 34 percent, with 1,497 built between 2013 and 2018 (figure 2.4, panel a). Health facilities now serve an average of 8,000 people, down from 8,300 in 2013. Counties have also invested heavily in new (and sometimes high-end) medical equipment. By and large, county health departments have ensured a steady supply of essential medicines.

In the education sector, 821 early childhood development and education (ECDE) centers have been built across the country between 2013 and 2018 (figure 2.4, panel b). In the water sector, underpinning the growth in access to rural water, there has been significant investment in rural supply schemes. Counties have also invested in agriculture sector infrastructure, such as irrigation schemes, the construction of markets, and investments in rural road networks (figure 2.4, panel c). In the early years of devolution, investments in urban services were limited, but they have picked up since FY2018/19.

FIGURE 2.4

Kenyan investments in facilities and expansion of access, selected sectors

a. Number of primary health facilities and hospitals, 2013–18

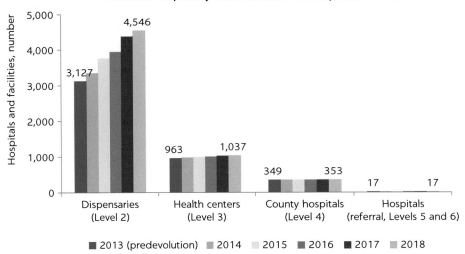

b. Number of ECDE facilities, 2012–18

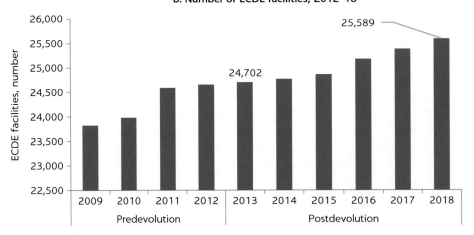

c. Composition of investments in agriculture, FY2013/14–FY2017/18

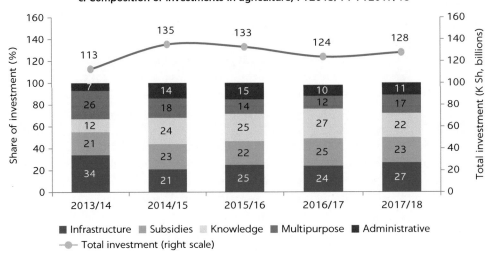

Sources: KNBS 2018b; District Health Information System (DHIS) 2018 data; Ministry of Education, Science and Technology 2015.
Note: ECDE = early childhood development and education.

After a hiatus in many counties, investments have been made in drainage, street lighting, and solid waste management following the establishment of urban institutions. Street lighting is one popular area of investment. In Makueni and Kisumu Counties, street and public lighting has increased from below 10 percent coverage to 30 percent and from 20 percent to 35 percent, respectively. Coverage has increased, with Nairobi County rising from 26,000 street-lights (about 30 percent) coverage to over 50,000 (about 45 percent) between 2013 and 2019.

Counties have also invested in human resources, recruiting staff to deliver services (figure 2.5, panel d). In 2015, the total number of county government employees was estimated at 130,000 following the Capacity Assessment and Rationalization of the Public Service (CARPS) exercise (Ministry of Public Service 2016). Later, in 2017, the Office of the Auditor General estimated the number at 150,000 based on regular payrolls (COB 2017).

Health workers and teachers for early childhood establishments increased significantly, although staffing in agriculture has decreased. Overall, the number of employees working in health in the counties grew by 46 percent between 2013

FIGURE 2.5

Recent trends in service delivery staffing in Kenya

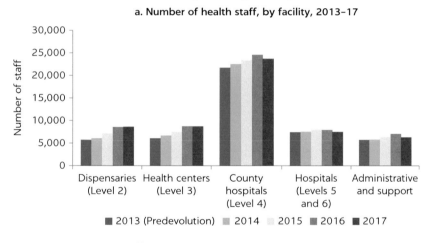

a. Number of health staff, by facility, 2013–17

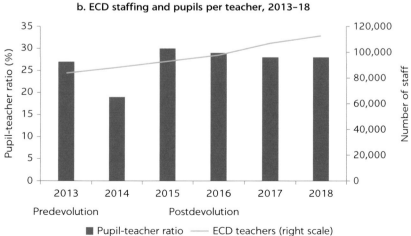

b. ECD staffing and pupils per teacher, 2013–18

(continued next page)

FIGURE 2.5, *continued*

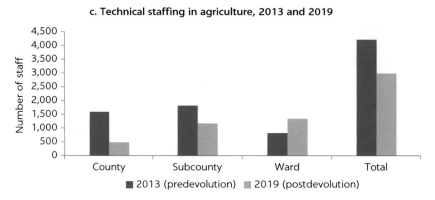

c. Technical staffing in agriculture, 2013 and 2019

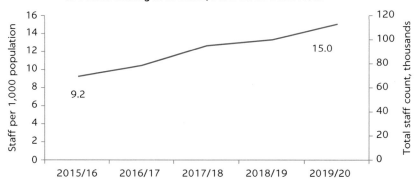

d. Overall staffing in counties, FY2015/16–FY2019/20

Sources: Kenya National Bureau of Statistics (KNBS); Kenya Economic Surveys, 2010–19; District Health Information System (DHIS) 2018 data.
Note: ECD = early childhood development.

and 2017 (figure 2.5, panel a)—from 46,259 to 67,740 (Ministry of Health 2018). This has culminated in improved health worker density in the public health sector, from 5.0 core health workers[1] per 10,000 residents in 2014 to the current 8.3 per 10,000 inhabitants.[2]

In the education sector, the number of trained teachers in early childhood development and education (ECDE) institutions increased from 88,154 in 2014 to 112,703 in 2018 (figure 2.5, panel b). Since 2015, the pupil-to-teacher ratio in ECDE centers has fallen from 30:1 to 28:1, while enrollment has increased. Conversely, in agriculture, overall staffing has declined significantly, from 4,218 workers in 2003 to 2,987 in 2019 (figure 2.5, panel c).

Despite increases in staffing, shortages and absenteeism persist, especially in the delivery of health services. Combined with staff motivation, these are critical challenges. Hospitals are relatively well staffed, with county Level 4 hospitals having over 70 percent of professional staff relative to norms, while Levels 5 and 6 are staffed above norms. However, primary health facilities are poorly staffed (figure 2.6). The increases in staff have been allocated evenly across Level 2, 3, and 4 facilities, even though many of the new facilities constructed have been dispensaries (Level 2). Dispensaries only have on average one nurse or midwife relative to a norm of four, and most of them lack a public health officer. Health centers have 34 percent of the recommended health professional staff. Staffing levels remain well below the World Health Organization's

FIGURE 2.6

Professional staffing shortages or surpluses in Kenyan primary health facilities, by level

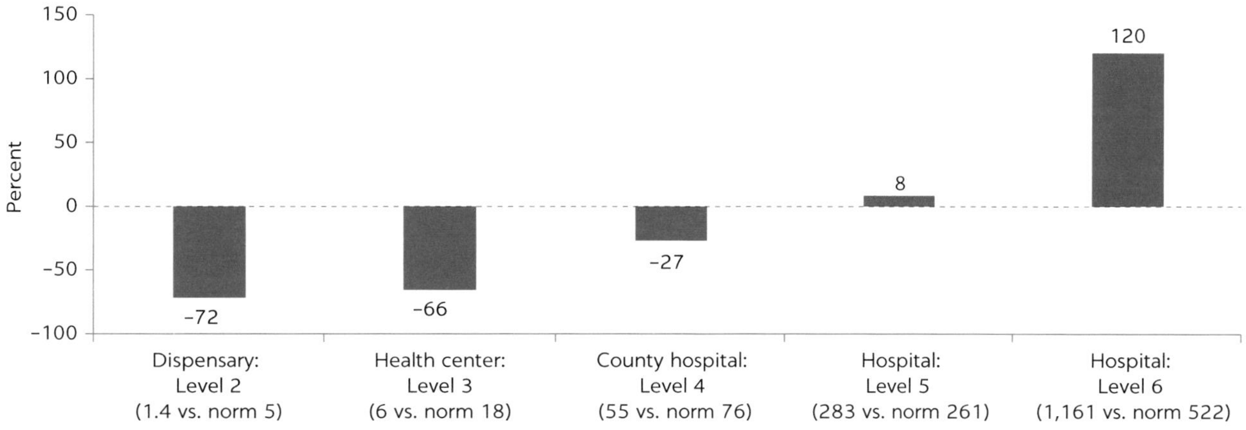

Source: Ministry of Health 2019.
Note: Staffing shortages or surpluses are relative to 0, which designates the staffing norm.

simulated threshold of 44.5 per 10,000 for universal health care (UHC) and the Sustainable Development Goals (SDGs) by 2030.

Although staffing levels in county agriculture departments have been declining, a more substantial proportion of technical staff is now posted to the ward level, which is a positive development that provides the opportunity to strengthen links between citizens or farmers and service delivery staff. Staff shortages are compounded by high rates of absenteeism, especially in health, where more than 50 percent of staff are away from a facility at any time—a significant deterioration from 2012, when absenteeism was nearer to 30 percent. Although most absenteeism among health professionals is authorized for extended training and other reasons, this undoubtedly has a significant impact on the quality of services available, especially at lower-level units, which already have skeletal staff.

Quality of devolved services

Counties have continued to face challenges in delivering quality health care. Complicated by increases in staff absenteeism in the health sector, the overall quality of care remains poor. Adherence to clinical guidelines overall, and with respect to maternal and neonatal cases, remains well below 50 percent, while drug and equipment availability continue to hover around 50 percent (figure 2.7). Nevertheless, there have been some improvements. For example, diagnostic accuracy has improved significantly, from 45 percent in 2012 to 68 percent in 2018, and the availability of infrastructure has also increased markedly, from below 50 percent to more than 70 percent.

In ECDE, water, agriculture, and urban development, there is a lack of quantitative data available on quality; however the evidence from the case study counties is mixed. In education, county governments had made efforts to procure teaching guides and learner workbooks as well as other learning materials. However, quality assurance systems and resources are still underdeveloped and

FIGURE 2.7

Metrics of health service delivery quality in Kenya, 2012 and 2018

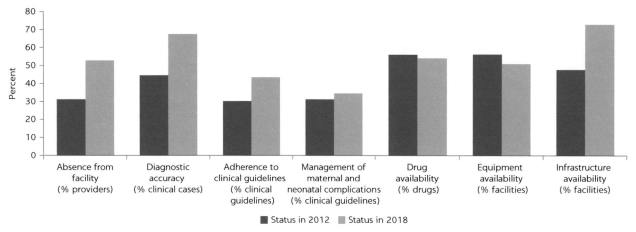

Source: Ministry of Health 2019.

inadequate, especially at the subcounty level. There is lack of enforcement of learner assessment guidelines and the basic education curriculum, and as a result some of the child development assessment practices are inappropriate.

In the water sector, there has been a reduction of the share of population accessing piped systems, which implies an increased reliance on more-basic sources. In agriculture, stakeholders expressed concern that the demand-driven extension model was not functioning and that disease control interventions were weak. In urban development, the consistency of enforcement and standards of development control are variable. Unreliable operational budgets are likely to adversely affect solid waste management and the maintenance of urban infrastructure.

The overall allocation of staff by counties is inefficient because of the large share and growth of staffing in administrative sectors. In one of the focal counties for the Making Devolution Work for Service Delivery (MDWSD) study, for example, the county health management team consisted of more than 70 staff, not all of whom had clear roles. In agriculture, the number and share of nontechnical staff, although high, has decreased both in total and relative to technical staff. Staffing the oversight and management of service delivery needs to be adequate, but it should not be inflated.

Although services continue to function, there are also concerns about inefficiency and sustainability in the water sector. In the urban water sector, the performance of water companies in 2017 was better than in 2009, although there is some evidence that performance, in aggregate, declined in the postdevolution period (2013–17). There is a wide variation in performance between the best and worst performing utilities, as well as different trends in performance, with some improving and some declining. On the one hand, water companies have proved to be reasonably resilient to the changes in governance as a result of the robust institutional setup (a regulator and corporatized companies), together with protective policies and legislation. On the other hand, there has been a concerning decline in the financial viability of the sector, with water companies experiencing declining tariffs (in real terms) and reducing operating cost-coverage ratios. In the rural water sector, there is little available data on performance; however, concerns related to the functionality and reliability of rural water infrastructure exist. For example, it has been reported that "almost one-third of rural water systems are dysfunctional while the other two-thirds start malfunctioning within 3–5 years of construction" (Kwena 2015).

TRENDS IN EXPENDITURE ON DEVOLVED SERVICE DELIVERY

Since the introduction of county governments in 2013, county spending has increased from an initial K Sh 229 billion in FY2014/15 to K Sh 327 billion in FY2017/18 (figure 2.8). This represents an increase of 49.3 percent in nominal terms over the first four years of devolution—a significant increase that has contributed to the observed increases in service delivery levels and investment.

It is important to contrast this increase with that of national spending. Except for a slight contraction from FY2012/13 to FY2013/14—the first year the devolved fiscal framework came into force—national government expenditures have grown faster than county expenditures. They nearly doubled from K Sh 1,071.8 billion in FY2013/14 to K Sh 1,810.4 billion in FY2017/18. This increase has been driven not only by significant increases in debt servicing (a major driver of Consolidated Fund Services, which include debt payments, pensions, and some salaries for constitutional offices) but also by growth in national government recurrent and development expenditure. Therefore, the share of counties in overall spending has declined since FY2014/15.

In per capita terms, the average expenditure per county to deliver its mandated functions in health, education, water, and infrastructure increased from K Sh 5,694 in FY2013/14 to K Sh 8,630 in FY2017/18, or 29 percent (figure 2.9). Unsurprisingly, because it is the largest service delivery function

FIGURE 2.8

Composition of public expenditures in Kenya, FY2013/14–FY2017/18

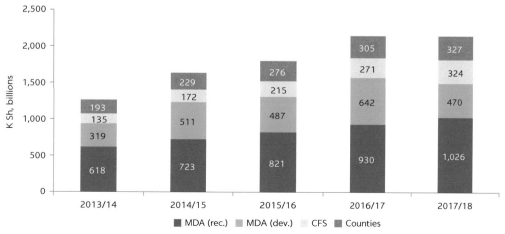

Source: World Bank based on Controller of Budget data (various years).
Note: CFS = Consolidated Fund Service; MDA (dev.) = ministry, department, agency (development); MDA (rec.) = ministry, department, agency (recurrent).

FIGURE 2.9
Total county per capita spending, FY2013/14–FY2017/18

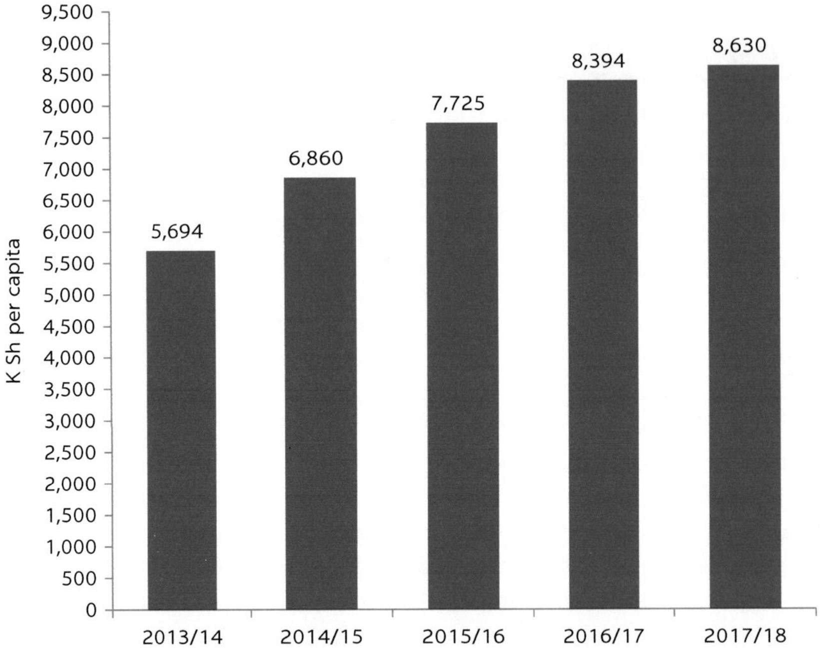

Source: World Bank calculations based on Controller of Budget data (various years).

devolved, health makes up the largest share: over 25 percent of total county expenditure. Per capita health spending increased by 64.5 percent over the first four years of devolution, from K Sh 1,572 in FY2014/15 to K Sh 2,427 in FY2017/18 (figure 2.10). Funding for agriculture, water, and education started at K Sh 400–500 per capita on average, with education increasing significantly by FY2017/18 to K Sh 796 per capita (58 percent), with more modest increases for water to K Sh 580 (32 percent) and for agriculture to K Sh 527 (26 percent).

These figures show a revealing picture of county preferences toward investing in health and education relative to water and agriculture. Administrative spending has also grown, with per capita spending in the Office of the Governor and other administrative services increasing from K Sh 2,683 in FY2014/15 to K Sh 3,385 (31 percent) in FY2017/18, while County Assembly spending per capita increased from K Sh 612 to K Sh 853 (39 percent) over the same period.

It is important to highlight the contributions of citizens and other sources of finance to service delivery in the counties. Annual revenue by the water companies was about K Sh 21 billion in 2017. This compares with total budgeted county expenditure of K Sh 27 billion that year. Out-of-pocket health expenditure by citizens was estimated at 27.7 percent of total health expenditure in the Kenya National Health Accounts FY2015/16 (Ministry of Health 2017). This approximates K Sh 2,000 per capita, roughly equivalent to the county health expenditure that year. The policy of universal health care is intended to address this in

FIGURE 2.10

County per capita spending, by sector, FY2014/15–FY2017/18

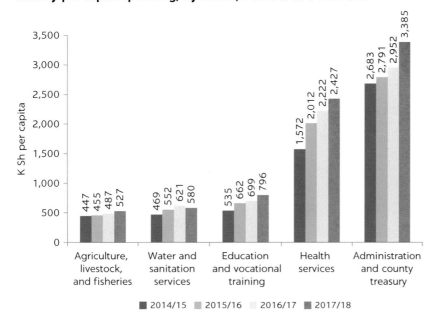

Source: World Bank calculations based on Controller of Budget data (various years).

public facilities. Furthermore, as discussed later in the report, there is also substantial funding, outside of county budgets, that continues to finance service delivery—for example, via Water Works Development Agencies (formerly Water Service Boards) or national government projects.

DISPARITIES IN SERVICE DELIVERY

Disparities in economic, health, and education outcomes persist in Kenya, and addressing inequities is a long-term task. In 2018, the poverty headcount ranged, by county, from 17 percent to 78 percent (map 2.1, panel a; figure 2.11, panel a). The gross county product (GCP) ranged from K Sh 48,000 to K Sh 350,000 per capita (map 2.1, panel c; figure 2.11, panel a). It is remote, rural areas that tend to have higher poverty and lower GCP, while urbanized and more populous counties have higher per capita GCP.

Inequalities persist in health outcomes after devolution across both poorer and richer as well as rural and urban counties. Maternal mortality varies from 187 to as high as 3,795 per 100,000 births (figure 2.11, panel b), with counties with higher proportions of poor people persistently showing higher numbers (map 2.1, panel b). Likewise, predominately rural counties continue to have higher maternal mortality rates than predominantly urban counties.

Literacy and numeracy rates also vary. For example, the percentage of pupils able to read a story varies from 21 percent to 67 percent (map 2.1, panel d; figure 2.11, panel b). A key objective of devolution is to address these

MAP 2.1

Disparities in poverty, health, and education outcomes across Kenya, by county

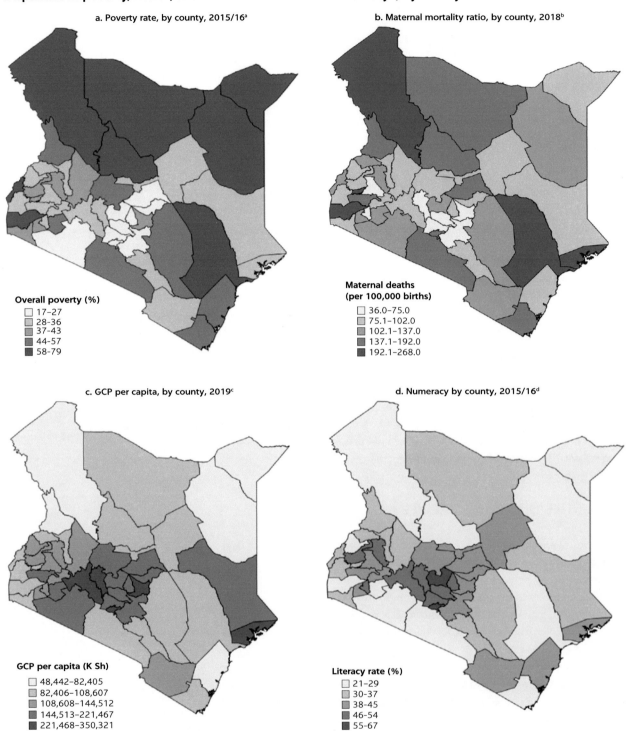

a. Poverty rate, by county, 2015/16[a]

Overall poverty (%)
- 17–27
- 28-36
- 37-43
- 44-57
- 58-79

b. Maternal mortality ratio, by county, 2018[b]

Maternal deaths (per 100,000 births)
- 36.0–75.0
- 75.1–102.0
- 102.1–137.0
- 137.1–192.0
- 192.1–268.0

c. GCP per capita, by county, 2019[c]

GCP per capita (K Sh)
- 48,442–82,405
- 82,406–108,607
- 108,608–144,512
- 144,513–221,467
- 221,468–350,321

d. Numeracy by county, 2015/16[d]

Literacy rate (%)
- 21–29
- 30-37
- 38-45
- 46-54
- 55-67

Sources: KNBS 2018a; Kenya National Bureau of Statistics (KNBS) gross county product (GCP) data. ©World Bank. Further permission required for reuse.

a. The poverty rate is measured as the proportion of Kenyans living on less than the international poverty line (US$1.90 per day).

b. The maternal mortality ratio is measured as the number of maternal deaths per 100,000 live births.

c. The per capita gross county product (GCP) is in Kenyan shillings.

d. Literacy is measured as the percentage of school-going children age 3 and older who can read or write in at least one language.

FIGURE 2.11

Overall poverty, per capita GCP, literacy, and maternal mortality outcomes in Kenya

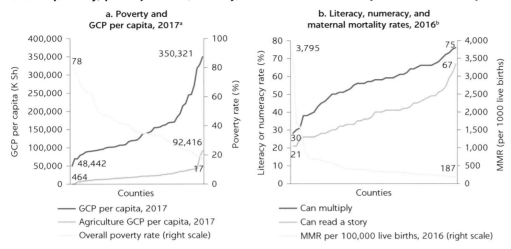

Sources: KNBS 2018a, 2018b; District Health Information System (DHIS) 2018 data; Ministry of Education, Science and Technology 2015; World Bank 2020.
Note: Graphs show the minimum and maximum values, providing an overall picture of the counties.
GCP = gross county product.
a. The poverty rate is measured as the proportion of Kenyans living on less than the international poverty line (US$1.90 per day).
b. The maternal mortality ratio (MMR) is measured as the number of deaths per 100,000 live births. Literacy is measured as the percentage of school-going children age 3 and older who can read or write in at least one language. Numeracy is measured as the percentage of school-going children age 3 and older who can divide or multiply.

longstanding inequities that persist across Kenya and make service delivery more responsive to local needs.

There remain large disparities in health service delivery. Poorer and more rural counties continue to access fewer and worse-quality services than wealthier and more urban counties. Deliveries attended by skilled health personnel in health facilities in counties vary from 33 percent to 122 percent (map 2.2, panels a and c). The proportion of children fully immunized varies from 46 percent to 109 percent (map 2.2, panels b and d).[3]

While continued disparities should be no surprise, there are signs of improvement in health services in poorer and more rural areas, and disparities are being reduced in areas such as vaccine availability and deliveries. Overall levels and disparities in skilled birth attendance and child immunization have improved postdevolution, as demonstrated by higher and flatter distribution across counties in 2018 than in 2013 (figure 2.12). The county with the lowest immunization rate has improved from 20 percent to 46 percent, and the county with the lowest proportion of attended deliveries increased from 11 percent (Mandera) to 34 percent (Narok). In 2018, Narok was lowest, as Mandera increased its birth-attendance rate to 38 percent.

MAP 2.2

Improvements and reduced disparities in skilled birth attendance and child immunization in Kenya, by county

a. Share of deliveries by skilled birth attendant, by county, 2013

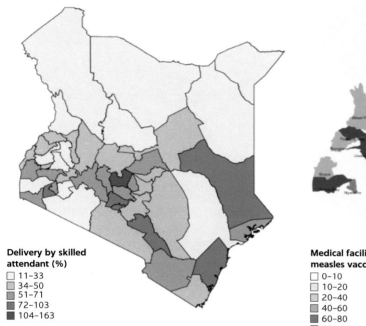

Delivery by skilled attendant (%)
- [ ] 11–33
- [ ] 34–50
- [ ] 51–71
- [ ] 72–103
- [ ] 104–163

b. Measles vaccine availability, 2012

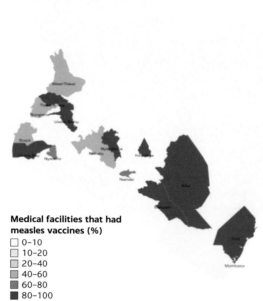

Medical facilities that had measles vaccines (%)
- [ ] 0–10
- [ ] 10–20
- [ ] 20–40
- [ ] 40–60
- [ ] 60–80
- [ ] 80–100

Counties with missing data are coded as 0

c. Share of deliveries by skilled birth attendant, by county, 2018

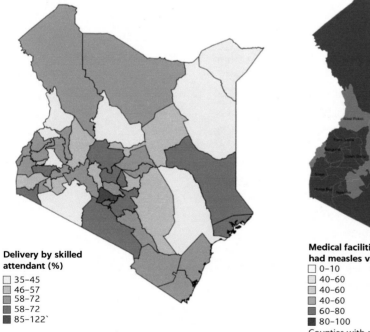

Delivery by skilled attendant (%)
- [ ] 35–45
- [ ] 46–57
- [ ] 58–72
- [ ] 58–72
- [ ] 85–122`

d. Measles vaccine availability, 2018

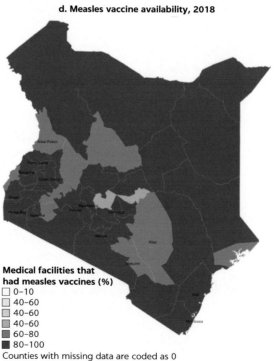

Medical facilities that had measles vaccines (%)
- [ ] 0–10
- [ ] 40–60
- [ ] 40–60
- [ ] 40–60
- [ ] 60–80
- [ ] 80–100

Counties with missing data are coded as 0

Source: Kenya District Health Information System (DHIS) data, 2013–18.

FIGURE 2.12

Recent trends in deliveries by skilled birth attendants and measles vaccination across Kenya

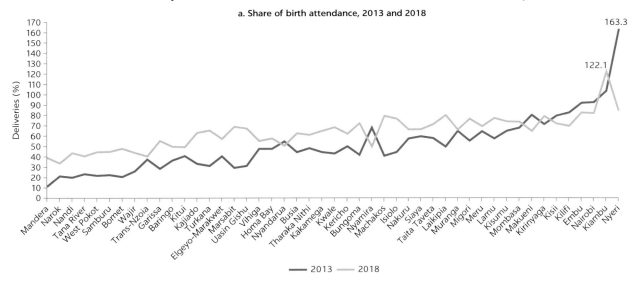

a. Share of birth attendance, 2013 and 2018

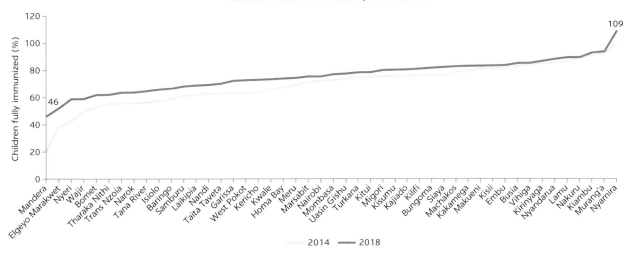

b. Share of children immunized, 2014 and 2018

Source: Kenya District Health Information System (DHIS) data, 2013–18.

In addition, health worker density ranges from 3.4 to 24 per 10,000 population (figure 2.13, panel d). Absenteeism varies significantly across counties and is not related to health worker density (figure 2.13, panel e). Inequalities persist in facilities in poorer and more rural counties, which have less availability of more than half of the listed essential drugs, for example. For some essential equipment, facilities in poorer counties fall behind those in richer counties. Facilities in more rural counties display higher staff absentee rates than those in more urban counties. Likewise, facilities in poorer and more rural counties continue to have less vaccine availability than wealthier and more urban counties in 2018. Although the number of health facilities has significantly increased, the distribution of facilities by population varies widely across counties (figure 2.13, panel a).

FIGURE 2.13

Disparities in health facility access, skilled health worker density, and health staff absenteeism across Kenya

a. Population per health facility, by county, 2018

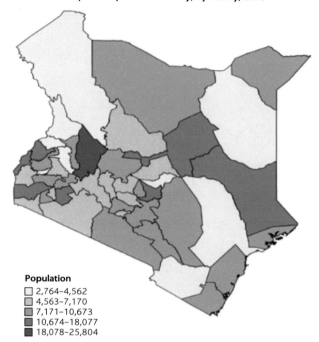

Population
- ☐ 2,764–4,562
- 4,563–7,170
- 7,171–10,673
- 10,674–18,077
- 18,078–25,804

b. Population per health facility, by county, 2018

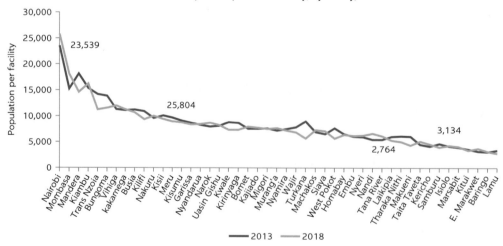

(continued next page)

FIGURE 2.13, *continued*

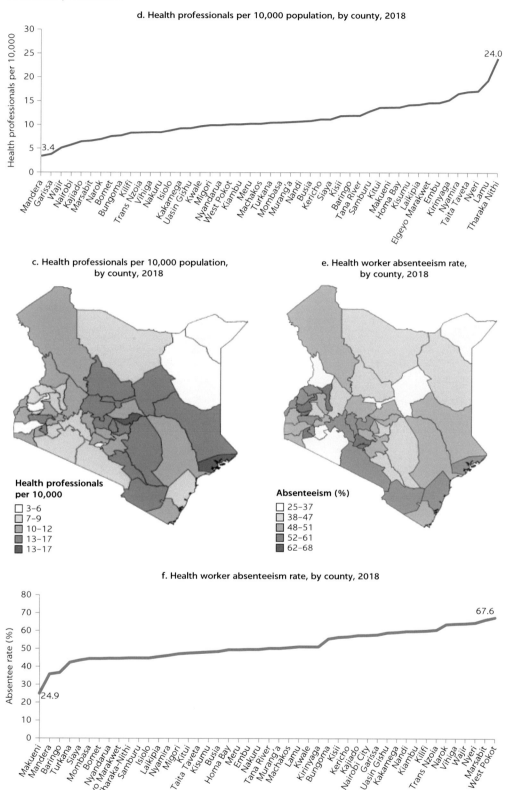

d. Health professionals per 10,000 population, by county, 2018

c. Health professionals per 10,000 population, by county, 2018

Health professionals per 10,000
- 3–6
- 7–9
- 10–12
- 13–17
- 13–17

e. Health worker absenteeism rate, by county, 2018

Absenteeism (%)
- 25–37
- 38–47
- 48–51
- 52–61
- 62–68

f. Health worker absenteeism rate, by county, 2018

Source: Kenya District Health Information System (KDHIS) data 2013–18.

Disparities in education and water across Kenya

a. ECDE gross enrollment rate, by county, 2018

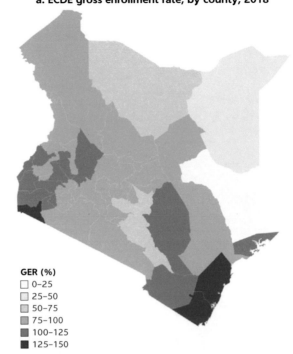

GER (%)
- 0–25
- 25–50
- 50–75
- 75–100
- 100–125
- 125–150

b. ECDE gross enrollment rate, by county, 2014 and 2018

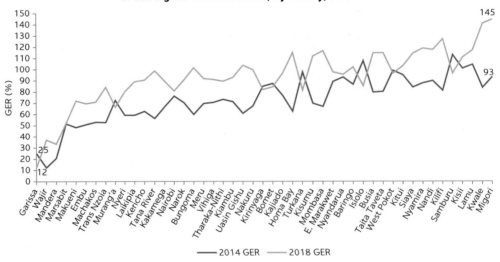

— 2014 GER   — 2018 GER

(continued next page)

FIGURE 2.14, *continued*

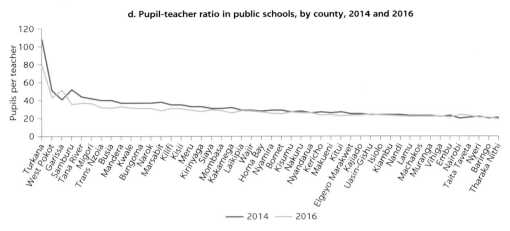

d. Pupil-teacher ratio in public schools, by county, 2014 and 2016

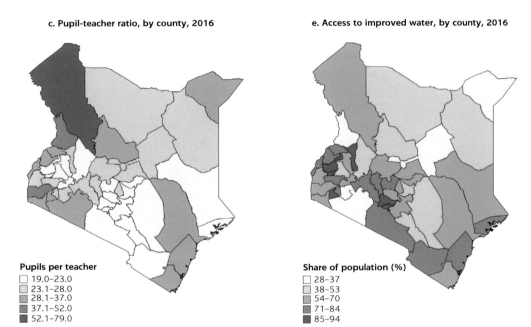

c. Pupil-teacher ratio, by county, 2016

e. Access to improved water, by county, 2016

Pupils per teacher
- 19.0–23.0
- 23.1–28.0
- 28.1–37.0
- 37.1–52.0
- 52.1–79.0

Share of population (%)
- 28–37
- 38–53
- 54–70
- 71–84
- 85–94

f. Access to improved water, by county, 2016

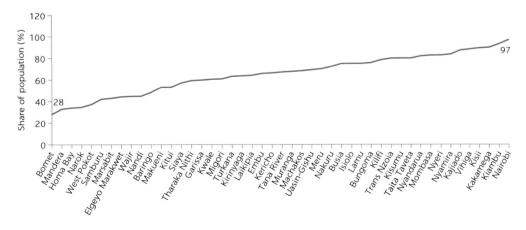

Sources: KNBS 2018b; Ministry of Education, Science and Technology 2015; WASREB 2016.
Note: ECDE = early childhood development and education; GER = gross enrollment ratio.

Essential drug availability has also improved, with one-third of these drugs having greater availability in facilities in poorer counties. The rural county with the fewest health facilities relative to population, Mandera, has reduced the average population each one serves from 21,033 to 14,590 through the construction of new facilities—and this is likely to be an important factor in improving skilled birth attendance rates.

Similar disparities can be seen in ECDE, but again disparities in preprimary gross enrollment rates have been reduced postdevolution. Gross enrollment rates varied between 12 percent and 113 percent in 2018 (figure 2.14, panels a and b). Those counties with enrollment rates below 70 percent in 2013 increased enrollment by an average of 27 percent. Those counties with enrollment rates above 70 percent increased enrollments by a far lower average of 15 percent—illustrating a significant reduction in disparities. However, this reduction has not been entirely equitable. While there was little difference between average enrollment rates of poorer and wealthier counties and rural and urban counties before devolution, disparities have emerged since. The change between 2014 and 2018 was worse for poorer counties than for richer counties, indicating a divergence of preprimary net enrollment in the years following devolution. The pupil-to-teacher ratio ranged from a low of 19:1 in Tharaka Nithi County to a high of 79:1 in Turkana County, showing the disproportional distribution of ECDE teachers across counties (figure 2.14, panels c and d).

There are also significant disparities in water access, which varied from 28 percent to 93 percent in 2016 (figure 2.14, panels e and f). Beyond this, the paucity of data means that it has been challenging to assess trends in disparities in water, agriculture, or urban development. It is likely that disparities in access to water in rural areas will have begun to be addressed: as described below, counties with lower water coverage have tended to invest more.

DISPARITIES IN COUNTY EXPENDITURE ON DEVOLVED SERVICES

There are large variations in per capita expenditure by counties overall and within sectors alongside the large variations in the scope and levels of services and investments being delivered by counties (figures 2.15–2.18). Overall per capita expenditure varies between K Sh 5,200 (Kiambu County) and K Sh 21,000 (Lamu County). Overall, it is the poorer, larger, and least populated counties that have higher per capita expenditures, which is a feature of the formula for the equitable share. Those counties with higher expenditure need to spend more; some populous and urbanized counties have relatively low per capita expenditures.

Sectoral shares of expenditures also vary significantly across counties, implying different service delivery priorities in different counties as well as the legacy of the scope and level of services provided before devolution (map 2.3). In health, per capita spending varies from K Sh 1,181 (Kakamega) to K Sh 6,505 (Lamu) (map 2.3, panel b). In water and agriculture, the degree of variability is similar. Agriculture spending per capita varies from K Sh 92 (Nairobi) to K Sh 1,500 (Lamu) (map 2.3, panel e); and education spending per capita varies from K Sh 166 (Nyeri) to K Sh 1,300 (Kwale) (map 2.3, panel c). The variation in water expenditure is even greater, varying from near zero investment (K Sh 17 in Murang'a) to K Sh 2,500 (Isiolo) (map 2.3, panel d).

Total per capita spending, by major economic category and county, FY2017/18

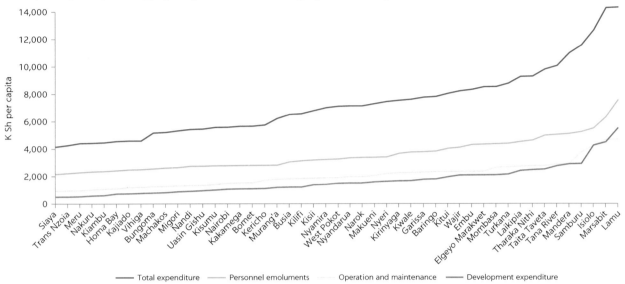

Source: Calculations based on Controller of Budget data (various years).

Per capita spending, by focus sector and county, FY2017/18

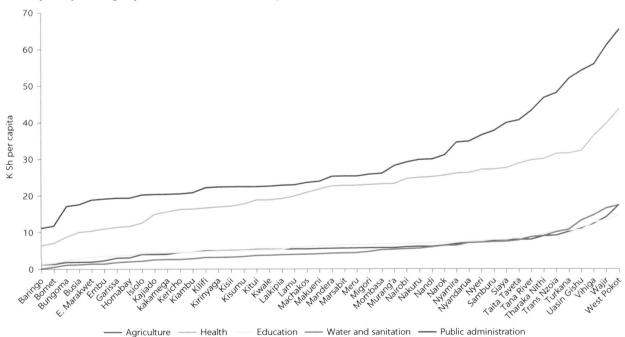

Source: Calculations based on Controller of Budget data (various years).

FIGURE 2.17
County variations in shares of economic category, FY2017/18

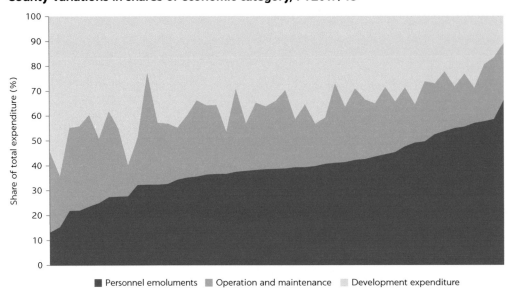

Source: Calculations based on Controller of Budget data (various years).
Note: Graph shows minimum and maximum values, providing an overall picture of the counties.

FIGURE 2.18
County variations in sector shares, FY2017/18

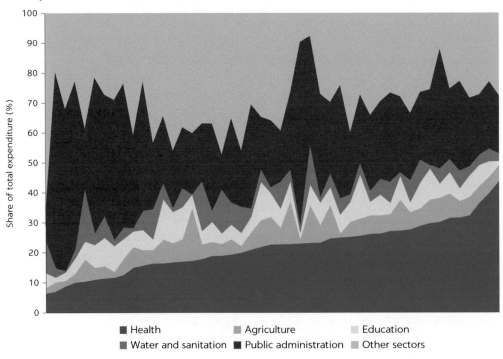

Source: Calculations based on Controller of Budget data (various years).
Note: Graph shows minimum and maximum values, providing an overall picture of the counties.

MAP 2.3

Per capita county spending in Kenya, overall and by sector, FY2017/18

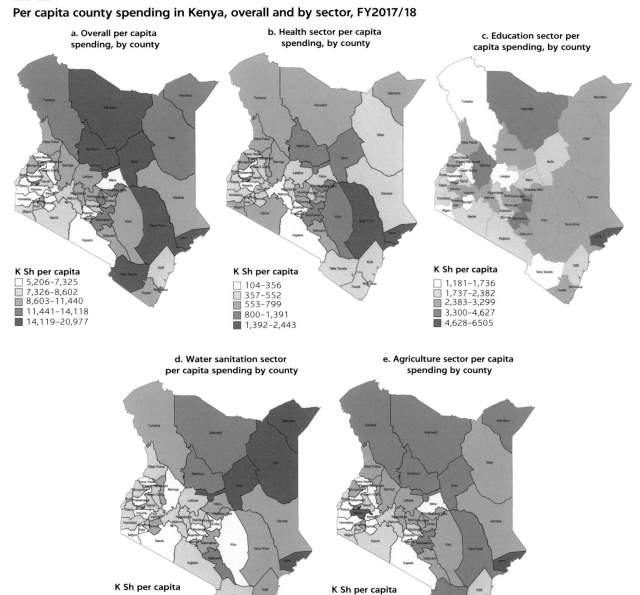

Sources: Calculations based on Controller of Budget data (various years); KNBS 2018b.

It is important to note that some of the variations may also result from mis-classification of some expenditures by counties in their use of the chart of accounts—especially personnel—as public administration, which may artifi-cially depress the level of sector expenditures and inflate administration expenditure.

Those counties with inferior services—which tend to be counties that are poorer and more sparsely populated—have been able to spend more per capita on service delivery than those in urban, wealthier, and more populous coun-ties. In general, the pattern of expenditure across counties is loosely and inversely correlated to service delivery outcomes. This has enabled counties that are lagging behind to at least expand services at similar rates to others, in some cases starting to close the gap. For example, in the water sector, some counties with lower water coverage tend to invest relatively more in water. Counties, across the board, have made the largest increases in expenditure in health and education, and these have shown substantial improvements in sector service delivery across counties. Nevertheless, across-the-board investments have enabled poorer, more remote counties to close the gap in areas such as maternal mortality.

THE DATA CHALLENGE

Although it has proved possible to assemble evidence on service delivery trends, disparities, and financing, there are significant gaps in the data on service delivery available to counties and the national government. There is little systematic data available on service delivery outcomes, outputs, and inputs, and whatever data *are* available are fragmented and inconsistent, making it difficult to compare progress over time.

In the health and education sectors, management information systems exist, but they do not appear to be used to systematically facilitate decision-making and accountability within counties or to compare performance across counties. In rural water, agriculture, and urban services, there is little or no routine administrative performance data. Multiple surveys are carried out, which are often one-offs and measure similar things in different ways, but few generate data that are comparable over time or are conducted regularly enough to ascertain trends.

Data on county revenues and expenditures are more readily available; however, the data are not without challenges. As is explained later in this report, county budget data are structured and presented in inconsistent ways and are not well linked to service delivery.

If devolution is to be made to work for service delivery, this data challenge must be met. Counties and the national government must have comparable data in the form needed to enable them to manage and monitor service delivery effectively and to make informed decisions on the allocation and use of resources. This involves having a combination of (1) routine service delivery information, collected regularly through functional sector management information systems; and (2) survey instruments that periodically consistently measure service delivery outcomes and quality. It also involves financial data that are structured such that information on service delivery performance can be linked to the resources deployed for those services.

CONCLUSIONS

Overall, the available evidence shows that the impact of devolution on service delivery has been mixed (table 2.2). There have certainly been improvements, but they have not been uniform or across the board. Although access to services (such as health and early childhood education) does appear to have improved, the quality of services does not seem to have improved a great deal and, in a few

TABLE 2.2 **What has worked and what could work better in public service delivery, by sector**

SECTOR	WHAT HAS WORKED	WHAT COULD BE WORKING BETTER
Health	• Expanded health facilities and equipment • Increased staffing of health facilities • Increased budget allocations • Reduced disparities in service delivery access and levels in some areas	• Staff absenteeism, motivation, and deployment of existing human resources • Balance between investment in infrastructure and equipping and operating existing services • Balance in provision of preventive and curative care • Quality of care • Availability of consistent and standard service delivery performance information over time
Agriculture	• More frontline staff • Investments in agriculture infrastructure	• Disruption and decline in frontline agricultural extension services • Overall decline in staffing, which remain inadequate and poorly motivated • Absence of information on agriculture service delivery
Early childhood education	• Improved enrollment rates • Reduced disparities in enrollment • Increased spending • More trained teachers • More ECDE centers	• Reduction in disparities not equitable • More teachers needed to reduce teacher-to-student ratio • Availability of management information on quality of ECDE services
Water	• Increased investments and coverage in rural water • Increased urban population served	• Urban water investments inadequate for population growth • Functionality of rural water supply schemes • Absence of management information in rural water service delivery
Urban services	• Increased level of investments, later supported by conditional grants	• Availability of funding for urban services and investments • Absence of management information on urban services

Source: World Bank.
Note: ECDE = early childhood development and education.

cases, may have deteriorated (particularly in the immediate post-2013 period). But devolution has *not* led to a collapse in service delivery, which was a concern before the first national and county elections were held after the adoption of the new 2010 constitution. In the post-2013 period immediately following the establishment of county governments, there were undoubtedly challenges and some confusion and disruption; yet most counties have been able to take on their service delivery functions in a short space of time.

Counties have generally expanded and invested in services that were devolved to them. Access to, and use of, county services has increased in health and other sectors that had previously been neglected, such as rural water and ECDE. County governments have increased expenditure on investments, equipment and supplies, and staff in the service delivery sectors for which they are responsible. This has not been universal; staffing in agriculture and consequently extension services have suffered. Investments in piped water have not kept pace with population growth in urban and rural areas.

The quality and efficiency in service delivery represent more significant challenges, although there have been some positive trends. Human resources are inadequate, and issues of absenteeism and staff motivation, especially in health, represent major constraints to service delivery quality and efficiency. The quality of services being delivered is limited by a lack of adherence to guidelines and norms, such as the educational curriculum and clinical standards. Challenges in the maintenance and sustainability of investments undermine both their quality and value. This points to the need to strengthen the management of service delivery.

Significant disparities in service delivery remain, although service delivery has improved in counties that lag behind, and disparities have been reduced in some areas. Counties with inferior services, which tend to be counties that are poorer and more sparsely populated, have been able to spend more per capita on service delivery than those in urban, wealthier, and more populous counties. There are early signs of reduction in disparities in some areas of health and ECDE service delivery, but this is not uniform.

There is a challenge of data within and across sectors on service delivery outcomes, outputs, inputs, and financing. Without regular and routine sector administrative data on service delivery and periodic and consistent surveys, it will prove even more challenging for the management, decision-making, and accountability processes to make devolution work for service delivery.

In conclusion, service delivery performance has been mixed during the first five years of devolution, with some positive developments, continued challenges, and some disruption. The following chapters explore the underlying reasons for these developments and identify what has worked well and what could work better to make devolution work for service delivery.

NOTES

1. Core health workers include doctors, nurses, midwives, and clinical officers.
2. The health worker density figure is for counties, excluding private sector and national referral hospitals.
3. County sources indicate that some counties have recorded a rate exceeding 100 percent for a number of years.

REFERENCES

COB (Office of the Controller of Budget). 2017. "Annual County Governments Budget Implementation Review Report for Fiscal Year." COB, Nairobi.

KNBS (Kenya National Bureau of Statistics). 2018a. *2015/16 Kenya Integrated Household Budget Survey (KIHBS): Basic Report*. Nairobi: KNBS.

KNBS (Kenya National Bureau of Statistics). 2018b. *Economic Survey 2018*. Nairobi: KNBS.

Kwena, Ronald. 2015. "Determinants of Sustainability of Rural Water Projects in Kenya: A Case Study of the Netherlands Development Organisation (SNV) Supported Water Schemes in Kajiado County." *Strategic Journal of Business & Change Management* 2 (2): 2025–77.

Ministry of Education, Science and Technology. 2015. "2014 Basic Education Statistical Booklet." Government of Kenya, Nairobi.

Ministry of Health. 2017. "Kenya National Health Accounts FY2015/16." Statistical report, Government of Kenya, Nairobi.

Ministry of Health. 2018. "Kenya Health Sector Human Resources (KHSHR) Strategic Plan, End Term Review." Government of Kenya, Nairobi.

Ministry of Health. 2019. "Kenya Harmonized Health Facility Assessment (KHFA) 2018/2019: Annex Tables, Questionnaires, and Footnotes." Book 2 of the KHFA 2018/2019, Ministry of Health, Government of Kenya, Nairobi.

Ministry of Public Service. 2016. "Capacity Assessment and Rationalization of the Public Service (CARPS): An Inter-Governmental Steering Committee Report to the National Summit." Government of Kenya, Nairobi.

WASREB (Water Services Regulatory Board). 2016. Impact Report. WASREB, Nairobi.

WHO and UNICEF (World Health Organization and United Nations Children's Fund). 2019. "WHO UNICEF Immunization Coverage Estimates 2018 Revision." Data report, WHO, Geneva; and UNICEF, New York.

World Bank. 2020. "Urban Sector Background Study." Unpublished Background Sector Study for this volume, World Bank, Nairobi.

3 Functions, Management, and Intergovernmental Relations

KEY MESSAGES

Overall

- Overall, county governments have effectively taken up the management of the devolved functions to the extent that the national government has permitted.
- In varying degrees across sectors and counties, there remain significant gaps and weaknesses in the structures and systems for managing service delivery.
- Statutory mechanisms for intergovernmental coordination at both national and sectoral levels are in place, but they are not yet effectively operational.

Priority Interventions

- Streamline and strengthen systems for monitoring and evaluation (M&E) in county governments as well as for the exchange of data, information, and knowledge between counties and national ministries, departments, and agencies (MDAs) at the sectoral level.
- Develop the capacity of the technical backups to the intergovernmental sectoral forums.

INTRODUCTION

This chapter looks at the ways in which service delivery functions have been devolved, how counties have handled sector management functions, and how the national and county governments have worked together to manage the devolution of service delivery. All of these underpin the extent to which devolution works for service delivery.

Devolution in Kenya means that service delivery functions are distributed between the national government and county governments. Clearly assigning these functions is important to determine accountability, to ensure that finance follows function, to minimize duplication and inefficiency, and to avoid conflicts between levels of government over who does what. Although frontline service delivery functions for which county governments are largely responsible are hugely important, it is also important to ensure that national responsibilities for policy, regulatory, and support functions are met.

County management of sectoral service delivery functions needs to be effective to ensure that services are accessible and of good quality. While each service delivery sector has its specificities, all of them rely on key management processes (such as information and quality control), and all of them need to operate based on systems and structures (such as integrated hierarchies and delegation). If sector departments are poorly organized, do not monitor services, neglect to provide regular on-the-job support and supervision, and the like, then local services will suffer.

Intergovernmental consultation, cooperation, and collaboration are fundamentally important to making devolution work for sector service delivery in a quasi-federal system such as Kenya's. Effective service delivery is a joint national and county responsibility, and many of the challenges that have arisen (and will continue to arise) cannot be addressed "unilaterally." The national and county levels need to work together to meet the many challenges of service delivery under devolution—a lot of "what could work better" (as described and discussed in this report) depends on counties and the national government taking decisions together. Strengthening intergovernmental *consultation*, *cooperation*, and *collaboration* is key to

- Improving the organization of service delivery functions;
- Identifying the most appropriate ways in which frontline county-level service delivery is supported by the national government;
- Ensuring that national and county functions (for example, agricultural research and extension as well as primary and early childhood education) in the same sector are linked up;
- Reducing overlap and duplication;
- Maximizing informational synergies; and
- Ensuring that national policies, regulations, and standards are appropriate and meaningful.

For service delivery "chains" to result in solid outcomes, they need to be linked properly. The same goes for cross-cutting dimensions, such as public financial management and human resources management (HRM), which require that both national and county levels work together to agree on and use common frameworks and processes.

DEVOLUTION OF FUNCTIONS

Service delivery functions have largely been devolved to counties that have taken over the management of these services. The de jure assignment of functions and expenditure responsibilities between the national government and the county governments largely conforms to the subsidiarity principle, and the de facto functional assignment generally matches this de jure assignment. Table 3.1 summarizes the constitution's assignment of functions to the national and county levels of government. Kenyan counties have taken on responsibilities for delivering many of the functions they were assigned in the constitution, including

TABLE 3.1 **Distribution of functions between national and county governments in Kenya**

NATIONAL GOVERNMENT	COUNTY GOVERNMENTS
1. Foreign affairs and policy; international trade 2. Use of international waters and water resources 3. Immigration and citizenship 4. Relationship between religion and state 5. Language policy 6. National defense 7. Police services 8. Courts 9. National economic policy and planning 10. Monetary policy, currency, banking 11. National statistics and data 12. Intellectual property rights 13. Labor standards 14. Consumer protection and social security standards 15. Education policy, standards, curricula, examinations 16. Universities, tertiary educational institutions, primary schools, secondary schools, and special education institutions 17. Promotion of sports and sports education 18. Transport and communications, including national trunk roads, roads standards 19. National public works 20. Housing policy 21. General principles of land planning and coordination of county planning 22. Protection of the environment and natural resources 23. National referral health facilities 24. Disaster management 25. National historical monuments 26. National elections 27. Health policy 28. Agricultural policy 29. Veterinary policy 30. Energy policy and regulation 31. Capacity building and technical assistance to the counties 32. Public investment 33. National betting, casinos, and gambling 34. Tourism	1. Agriculture, including (a) crop and animal husbandry, (b) livestock sale yards, (c) county abattoirs, (d) plant and animal disease control, and (e) fisheries 2. County health services, including (a) county health facilities and pharmacies; (b) ambulance services; (c) promotion of primary health care; (d) licensing and control of food; (e) veterinary services (excluding regulation of the profession); (f) cemeteries, funeral parlors, and crematoria; and (g) refuse removal and dumps, solid waste disposal 3. Control of pollution and other public nuisances 4. Cultural activities 5. County transport, including (a) county roads, (b) street lighting, (c) traffic and parking, (d) public road transport, and (e) ferries and harbors 6. Animal control and welfare 7. Trade development and regulation, including markets, trade licenses, local tourism, cooperative societies 8. County planning and development, including (a) statistics, (b) land survey and mapping, (c) boundaries and fencing, (d) housing, and (e) electricity and gas reticulation and energy regulation 9. Preprimary education, village polytechnics, homecraft centers. and childcare facilities 10. Implementation of specific national government policies on natural resources and environmental conservation 11. County public works and services, including (a) storm water management systems in built-up areas, and (b) water and sanitation services 12. Fire-fighting services and disaster management 13. Control of drugs and pornography 14. Ensuring and coordinating the participation of communities in governance at the local level and assisting communities

Source: Fourth Schedule, Constitution of Kenya 2010.

agriculture, early childhood development and education (ECDE), health, water, and urban development. In many sectors and subsectors, the distribution of service delivery and related functions has unfolded relatively smoothly.

Human and financial resources have been devolved to counties alongside administrative decision-making powers (as discussed in detail in other sections of this report). Counties are provided with a significant share of national revenues through the equitable share, and over 100,000 national and former local authority civil servants were transferred to counties to deliver services. Although counties have only limited revenue-raising powers, they have autonomy to allocate the equitable share across sectors according to local priorities.

However, there continue to be areas of dispute over service-delivery functions between national and county governments, especially relating to infrastructure investment. As shown in table 3.2, while the Fourth Schedule of the Constitution provides overall normative guidance on the two-tiered distribution of service-delivery responsibilities, there are areas where responsibility for service delivery between national and county governments is not carried out in

TABLE 3.2 **Disputes over, and lack of clarity about, functions and finance: Sector perspectives**

SECTOR	AREAS OF CONTENTION, OVERLAP, AND CONFUSION
Agriculture	Despite the devolution of most sector functions to counties, the national government has retained about two-thirds of finance functions for the sector.
	Both the national government and counties have continued to provide similar types of services in the finance sector. The lack of clarity or misinterpretation of the Fourth Schedule of the Constitution appear to be a key reason for this.
	Examples:
	Input subsidies: Fertilizer is a key input to reversing low productivity. Before devolution, the government had initiated a fertilizer subsidy program to help improve access and utilization. Subsidized fertilizer was distributed through National Cereals and Produce Board (NCPB) depots. This posed a challenge for smallholder farmers because the NCPB depots are about 25 kilometers from farming households (Njagi et al. 2015). When county governments took office in 2013, some of them initiated parallel subsidy systems, while others organized farmers in groups and subsidized their transport to the NCPB depots, thereby increasing access to the fertilizer subsidy. However, it is not clear whether county governments can sustain input subsidy programs based on their budgets. In addition, although the national government retained the subsidy function, replicating or doubling up on it at the county level (without having addressed the challenges associated with input subsidy programs) amounts to a poor investment choice and ineffective expenditure.
	Extension and other services: In the agriculture sector, semiautonomous government agencies (SAGAs), which are national government agencies, have continued to function. The functions allocated to SAGAs largely overlap with those of county governments. In addition, multipurpose projects implemented by the national government also have mandates that overlap with those of county governments.
Health	The national government is providing significant additional financing for its policy priorities in the health sector, but there have been disputes around the degree of county involvement in the design of conditional grants, especially the managed medical equipment scheme through which the national government has financed additional equipment for two hospitals in each county.
Urban	The national government's mandate (as defined in the Fourth Schedule of the Constitution) is to provide policy direction and coordination in the urban development and service delivery sector. However, national development policies (such as the National Slum Upgrading and Prevention Policy) continue to place national ministries, departments, and agencies (MDAs) at the center of urban development, despite the provisions of the constitution. Key national MDAs, such as the State Department of Housing and Urban Development (SDHUD), continue to perform devolved functions—such as urban planning, housing, and provision of infrastructure and services (urban roads, street lighting, and drainage works)—through national government and donor-financed programs. Ideally, these federal departments and directorates should only provide policy direction and capacity support to counties to implement these programs.
ECDE and education	In the early childhood development and education (ECDE) sector, there is one worrying ambiguity about who is responsible for what: It is unclear whether the national government or counties are responsible for ensuring (and financing) the training of ECDE teachers in Competency-Based Curriculums (which is a national policy initiative). As it stands, this aspect of teacher training appears to have been put on the back burner.
	In the wider education sector, county governments provide substantial finance from their budgets for scholarships and bursaries in the secondary and tertiary subsectors. The Making Devolution Work for Service Delivery (MDWSD) study shows that 11 counties allocated 22 percent of their total education sector budgets to scholarships and bursaries, even though secondary and tertiary education are national government functions.
Water	County governments have taken ownership of urban water companies, but responsibility for urban water infrastructure investment remains disputed. The Water Act 2016 made this the responsibility of national Water Works Development Agencies, but counties are challenging the constitutionality of this Act in the courts. This issue is looked at in more detail in box 3.1.

Source: World Bank 2020a, 2020b, 2020c, 2020d.

accordance with the constitutional mandates or where responsibilities are unclear or disputed. This risks duplication or service delivery gaps, which may arise when neither national government nor counties assume responsibility for a function for which responsibility is mistakenly assumed to lie elsewhere. It can also lead to conflict between the two tiers of government.

The most fundamental dispute is in the urban water supply sector, where both national and county governments lay claim to the responsibility for urban water infrastructure development. Box 3.1 provides further details on this problem.

BOX 3.1

The distribution of functions and finance in the urban water supply sector

Institutional arrangements in the urban water sector are complex, and some context is necessary to understand what could work better in the sector. The Water Act 2016 provides the overarching legal framework for postdevolution institutional arrangements in the sector, as summarized in table B3.1.1.

As envisaged by the Water Act 2016, water service providers (WSPs) are local utilities that provide piped water to urban areas on a largely commercial basis. WSPs are owned by their respective county governments (who appoint WSP boards) and are regulated by the Water Services Regulatory Board (WASREB), a national government regulator.

Water Works Development Agencies (WWDAs), on the other hand, are *nationally* owned regional utilities, which (on behalf of the *national* government) are responsible for implementing large infrastructure projects in the urban water supply sector. Such water supply projects are intended to be eventually handed over (as assets) by the WWDAs to county-owned

WSPs, with the latter assuming the responsibility for repaying any loans used to finance the infrastructure. The WWDAs access (grant and local) financing for urban water supply infrastructure from both the national government and Kenya's development partners.

There is clearly some degree of dissonance here: the 2016 Water Act's assertion that the WWDAs (national water utilities) play a significant role in the development of urban water supply infrastructure does not sit easily with the constitutional responsibility of counties to manage water supply services.

These arrangements have led to a duplication of planning and asset creation functions, with counties and WWDAs carrying out identical functions with little or no coordination. Planning between the county WSPs and the WWDAs is not aligned. The WWDAs (because they continue to enjoy privileged access to national government and development partner funding) are nonetheless the main players in the planning

TABLE B3.1.1 **Institutional arrangements in the urban water and sanitation sector under the Water Act 2016**

INSTITUTION	OWNERSHIP LEVEL	NO. OF ENTITIES	FUNCTION
Department of Water and Irrigation	National government	1	Oversee urban and rural water and sanitation policy, national planning and reporting, finance investments in water and sanitation.
Water Services Regulatory Board (WASREB)	National government	1	Set national standards, evaluate and recommend tariffs, set license conditions and accredit water service providers; monitor, regulate, and enforce license conditions; monitor compliance with standards.
Water Works Development Agencies (WWDAs)—previously Water Services Boards (WSBs) Regional public utilities	National government	8	"Undertake the development, maintenance and management of the national public water works" and "operate the waterworks and provide water services as a water service provider, until such a time as responsibility for the operation and management of the waterworks are handed over to a county government." The national government is currently an asset holder.
Licensed water service providers (WSPs) Local commercially oriented urban providers (water companies)	County governments	86	Undertake urban water supply operations on behalf of county governments. WSP boards are appointed by county governments and subject to national legislation.

Source: World Bank 2020d.

(continued next page)

Box 3.1, *continued*

and creation of urban water supply assets—processes that largely exclude counties, even though the assets are eventually supposed to be transferred to county-owned utilities and eventually paid for by counties. The envisaged comprehensive planning framework is not working.

As a result, counties have contested postdevolution institutional and financing arrangements for the urban water supply sector, claiming that the Water Act 2016 is unconstitutional. Given this, the current approach to sector financing is not sustainable, particularly regarding loan financing through the WWDAs. The financing model for the urban water supply sector is fragile and appears to be broken. Counties are not passing on repayments of sector loans for water infrastructure to the national government, which has accumulated considerable debt for these investments, estimated at between K Sh 105 billion and K Sh 180 billion in 2019.

This tension—between the national government and the counties—is at the heart of what currently troubles the urban water supply sector. Both government and development partner financing for urban water supply and sanitation has continued to follow this model, which is unsustainable.

Source: World Bank 2020d.

In the agriculture, health, and urban sectors, the disputes are not fundamentally over which functions are held by counties but how these are financed. Although those sectors' functions are the counties' responsibility, the national government continues to spend significant funds on specific inputs and projects. In areas where there is a lack of clarity in functions, or in areas of national policy priority, sector ministries tend to retain budgets rather than devolve to counties. Counties argue that these funds (and the functions they finance) should be devolved rather than goods and infrastructure being provided to counties in kind. The lack of a clear framework for conditional grants, whereby sector-specific funding can be transparently managed, has been an important factor in this situation. This is shown clearly in health, where the dispute has been around the design of an in-kind conditional grant whereby the national government has provided hospital equipment through the medical equipment scheme.

Responsibilities over shared functions could be better defined. In several areas, responsibilities are held jointly by the national and county governments. The COVID-19 crisis has especially highlighted this regarding public health, disaster management, and emergency response. The lack of detailed unbundling and division of responsibilities within shared functions has caused conflicts between the national government and county governments.

Several underlying factors explain many of these conflicts and disputes over functional responsibilities for service delivery:

- Most obviously, it is likely that national ministries or county governments are protecting or seeking to expand institutional turf as well as the fiscal resources that come with that turf.
- There is almost certainly a degree of bureaucratic or institutional inertia, particularly on the part of national ministries, departments, and agencies (MDAs), that slows down or even impedes any devolution of functions and resources to counties. Handing over functions that—for a long time—have

been fulfilled by national MDAs (such as the Kenya Urban Roads Authority) is never easy and often slow.

- The constitution's provisions regarding functional responsibilities are not always crystal clear and thus subject to different (and competing) interpretations. For example, in the urban water supply sector, infrastructure planning has been retained at the national level under the Water Act 2016 on the basis of the national government's constitutional responsibility for "national public works." (See box 3.1, which shows how the Fourth Schedule of the Constitution assigns functions across the national and county levels.)
- Finally, national MDAs have long worked in a predevolution paradigm that gave them operational responsibilities. In many cases, this is their default modus operandi, and shifting away from it to a more "federal" government modus operandi has required skills, knowledge, and mindsets that have yet to develop.

Whatever the reasons for continued conflict or confusion over functional responsibilities in sectors, the lack of functioning and effective frameworks for sector coordination between national government structures at the county level and the county governments has hampered clarification over the devolution of service delivery functions (box 3.1).

COUNTY MANAGEMENT OF SECTOR SERVICE DELIVERY

The basic institutional framework for service delivery is in place and has been improving. Counties have established the essential management structures for providing services. Public financial management systems have enabled them to spend funds, planning and monitoring systems are in place, HRM systems have enabled them to manage and recruit staff, citizens have been able to engage with their county governments, and basic social and environmental management policies have been set up.

As discussed in box 3.2, the State Department for Devolution's annual capacity and performance assessments (ACPAs) show that county performance across a range of core dimensions (financial management, planning, HRM, civic education and participation, investment implementation, and social and environmental management) has steadily improved since fiscal year (FY) 2016/17.

All counties have put into place basic management arrangements for their devolved service delivery sectors, although these may vary from county to county. County health sectors, for example, have continued to operate based on health management teams (HMTs) at county and subcounty levels. In the agriculture sector, county management arrangements vary from one county to another, but all have established core units (crops, livestock, veterinary services, and fisheries) and a service delivery hierarchy (counties, subcounties, and wards).

County institutions have overseen a continuation and expansion of services, which demonstrates a degree of management capacity. County institutions have maintained and, in some areas, expanded service delivery within sectors. This means they have established a decision-making capacity.

The ECDE sector has seen a significant increase in gross enrollment rates over the last decade, the number of trained teachers has increased, and counties have invested in the construction of new ECDE centers. Counties have also

BOX 3.2

Improvements in county performance since FY2016/17

The Kenya Devolution Support Program (KDSP)—
implemented by the State Department for Devolution
(in the Ministry of Devolution and the Arid and Semi-
Arid Lands [ASALs]) and financed by the World
Bank—has made capacity-building and performance
grants available to all 47 counties on the basis of their
compliance with a range of minimum conditions
(MCs) and scores on performance measures (PMs).
The KDSP grants incentivize counties to comply with
the MCs and to improve their performance.

Annual capacity and performance assessments
(ACPAs), undertaken by third-party consulting firms,
measure county performance across the five Key
Result Areas (KRAs) included in the National Capacity
Building Framework (NCBF):

- *KRA1:* Public Financial Management
- *KRA 2:* Planning and Monitoring and Evaluation
  (M&E)
- *KRA 3:* Human Resource Management

- *KRA 4:* Civic Education and Participation
- *KRA 5:* Investment Implementation and Social
  and Environmental Management.

For each KRA, the ACPAs measure and score county
performance across a range of indicators.

The first ACPA examined county performance in
FY2016/17. Since then, two ACPAs have been undertaken. Average county performance has improved
steadily across all five KRAs (figure B3.2.1), thus
enabling counties to access more and larger KDSP
grants.

The ACPA results make clear that counties have
improved their performance across all KRAs. Although
KDSP performance-based grants have undoubtedly
provided counties with incentives to do so, it is also
likely that county governments have simply become
more experienced and strengthened their management capacities over time and as a result of
capacity-building inputs.

FIGURE B3.2.1

Improvement in county government ACPA scores, FY2016/17 through FY2018/19

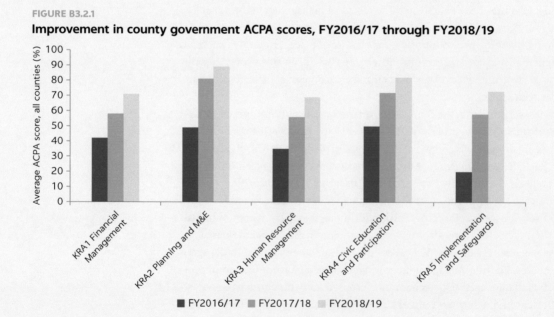

Sources: Annual capacity and performance assessments (ACPA) reports 2018–20, Ministry of Devolution and the ASALs.
Note: KRA = Key Result Area; M&E = monitoring and evaluation.

invested massively in health facilities, which have increased by 34 percent, and improved the availability of essential commodities. Staffing numbers have also increased, but with large variations across counties, and a number of counties have improved HRM processes. Prompt salary payment, promotions, redesignations, and so on were reported to have improved postdevolution. Progress in access to rural water appears to have accelerated under devolution, as a result of increased investments by counties, and the number of people with access to a piped water supply has increased in both urban and rural areas.

All of these results attest to the progress that counties have made in setting up the structures and processes for service delivery, including staff structures, planning and budgeting processes, systems for prioritizing projects, and allocating resources and processes for public participation.

Despite this progress, poor management structures within counties may be undermining service delivery. Before devolution, many sectors had sought to overcome the disadvantages of the centralized structure by decentralizing significant managerial responsibility to deconcentrated offices—typically to the district but also to constituency-based mechanisms and to facilities themselves. For example, the district office was the key focus of service delivery in the agriculture, education, and health sectors. The equivalent of the district office is now the subcounty. However, in many counties, the decentralized management of service delivery appears to have weakened since devolution.

Centralized management structures within counties concentrate decision-making and resources at county headquarters, undermining service delivery. The management relationships between frontline providers, subcounty (former district) offices, and the county department headquarters have not been well specified. As a result, subcounty offices have not had sufficient autonomy to effectively manage service delivery. This means that investment decisions are often not linked to human resource or operational funding, as discussed in chapter 5 of this report. Box 3.3 highlights some of the ways in which counties have structured the management of their health sectors.

In the urban sector, there has been limited delegation of functions and responsibilities to newly created city and municipal boards. They have not been given the intended delegated powers and have little financial autonomy (see box 3.4).

Excessive political interference in the management of county services

In the urban water sector, some water service providers (WSPs) have faced management challenges as a result of excessive interference on the part of county government "principals." WSPs, which are commercially oriented companies (by law), have been transferred to county government ownership since devolution, although they continue to be regulated by the national regulator.

WSP board members are appointed by county governments and act as agents to county principals. In some cases, county ownership and control over WSP board appointments has not led to encouraging results (box 3.5) and in some cases may have compromised utility performance.

Weak information and monitoring and evaluation (M&E) systems

Information and performance monitoring systems are not functioning effectively. The national government's policy-making function is being undermined

BOX 3.3

County health sector management

The organizational structures of county departments of health are quite varied. In one of the case counties (County A), for example, the top county leadership decided to operate a lean County Health Management Team (CHMT) of fewer than 10 members, all charged with strategic leadership and management roles, while operational management functions were decentralized to Sub-County Health Management Teams (SCHMTs), hospital management teams (HMTs), and primary facility management committees (FMCs):

> You see even by the look of our office block . . . , we have a very lean management team at the county level made of key directors who are in charge of strategic functions of their respective directorates, [and] all other day-to-day management functions have been decentralized to SCHMTs, HMTs, and the primary facility committees. (senior health manager, county A)

In contrast, in another case study county (County B), it was said that the CHMT was being used to reward people with political appointments. In this county, a participant reported that the CHMT had over 70 members, most of whom had no specific management portfolio. This they felt was confusing for the mid-level managers (SCHMTs and HMTs) because they did not know whom to link with at the CHMT level for specific management issues:

> I think the CHMT in this county is more than seventy members, even if you ask some of the members themselves, they don't even know how many they are. . . . [T]his usually gives us lots of problems; when you go there with an issue from the sub-county, you don't even know which officer you should talk to. (subcounty health sector manager, county B)

Though all the case study counties had set up subcounty-level management units, in some of the counties the subcounty teams did not have clear roles and were not provided with facilitative resources. This results in confusion and a lack of proper allocation of roles for subcounty health management teams.

Source: Adapted from World Bank 2020b.

BOX 3.4

Urban governance and management arrangements under devolution

The Urban Areas and Cities Act (UACA), enacted early in 2011, and revised and approved in 2019, provides a legal framework for urban governance and management under devolution. Although the UACA has limitations as an institutional framework, it has the considerable virtue of underlining the need to address the particularities of urban governance and management by establishing specific arrangements within the broad framework of devolution. However imperfectly, the UACA articulates the need for cities to be managed by dedicated urban institutions (urban boards).

Many counties have indeed followed the UACA's provisions by establishing municipal boards for their larger cities and for their county capitals, encouraged by the Kenya Urban Support Program (KUSP), which has provided them with major fiscal incentives for doing so. To date, over 60 municipal boards have been established by 45 county governments.[a] At the same time, counties have also appointed municipal administrations, supervised by their respective municipal boards, that have a range of responsibilities for managing the delivery of urban infrastructure and services.

Counties have been slow to establish and empower urban boards in secondary cities and county capitals. Although the fiscal incentives offered through KUSP have indeed encouraged most counties to set up municipal boards, few counties appear to have delegated significant responsibilities to them. In many cases, municipal boards have been limited to

(continued next page)

Box 3.4, *continued*

overseeing the implementation of investment projects out of KUSP urban development grants and have not been entrusted with the responsibility for managing urban services in general. This underlines some likely deficiencies in the UACA, which does little to spell out how counties (as principals) and urban boards (as agents) are expected to work effectively to manage cities and urban areas.

At the same time, the UACA's institutional "model" does not fully address urban management challenges in city-counties and in those counties (such as Kiambu) where clusters of urban areas exist. In short, it can be argued that the UACA is not fully consistent with the range of urban areas and their different requirements (and opportunities) in terms of urban management.

Source: World Bank 2020c.
a. The two city-counties of Nairobi and Mombasa were not beneficiaries of infrastructure grants under KUSP. However, they are expected to put in place the enabling urban management institutions and systems under various governing legislations.

Water service providers: utility governance and management performance under devolution

The quality of utility governance (as exercised by some counties) has been a concern in the urban water sector. Performance varies widely between the best and worst performing WSPs (utilities), all of which are county-owned. These utilities have operated within the same policy, legislative, and institutional environment, suggesting that the key differentiating factor is the quality of the management—which appears to have suffered (in cases such as Garissa, Mombasa, and Nairobi) from governance instability linked to county politics and political economy.

Governance interventions by some counties have negatively affected the performance of water companies. Frequently mentioned concerns are political interference in WSP board appointments, in appointments of managerial and other staff, and in routine operational decisions, which has weakened accountability and the capacity to make technically informed operational decisions.

The evidence shows a strong relationship between the soundness of the corporate governance and water company performance.

Governance performance has been mixed. The Water Service Providers Association (WASPA) is a strong advocate for creating governance conditions for keeping shareholders at arm's length from operations and for appointing competent management on performance contracts that are evaluated quarterly.

in several sectors by the lack of routine monitoring data to compare county performance—for example, as follows:

- *In the health sector,* the District Health Information System (DHIS) existed before devolution and could be better adapted to changes since the time that the counties came into existence, as well as to collect more comprehensive data to better inform decision-making processes (box 3.6).
- *In ECDE,* key data are not being collected, and the data that are collected are not being fed into the national information system (box 3.7).
- *In the water sector,* there is no reliable system for monitoring the performance of rural water systems.
- *In agriculture,* data systems for commodities and for HRM collapsed.

BOX 3.6

Information management in the devolved health sector

Kenya adopted the District Health Information System (DHIS) for comprehensive management of health information within the sector before devolution. However, over the years, this tool has only been used as a one-way conduit for the transmission of data with minimal analysis, data use, and feedback at the subnational level. In addition, the DHIS was set up primarily to manage health service delivery data, with minimal capacity for managing other routine management data. These data include health inputs data—such as budget allocations, human resources for health (HRH), and health products and commodities—that are necessary for strategic and operational planning and management. Clearly, the DHIS itself needs an upgrade to make it better suited to devolution.

General data and record keeping at the county level have been poor and ill-coordinated. For example, there were multiple sources of human resource data in the case study counties, each of which significantly varied from the others. This also applied to data on health products and commodities. A look at the DHIS shows that county monthly reporting rates decreased around 2013–15 (in the early days of devolution). This led to a general picture of perceived low coverage of essential health services across counties. This reporting trend has, however, shown significant improvement since 2016.

Source: World Bank 2020b.

It is also an issue for fiscal data, where there is no standard sector or program classification that would enable comparisons of how much counties are spending on sector functions—something that is also an issue in the ECDE and health sectors.

Weak county information management capacities have been further stretched by the existence and use of multiple, fragmented monitoring systems as well as a plethora of project-based M&E systems. Poor information management is a threat to service delivery; it makes it impossible to judge whether existing policies are working and whether they need to be adjusted or new policies introduced. Poor management information weakens the basis for decision-making, programming, and resource allocation; makes it difficult or impossible to assess service delivery results; and undermines intracounty and intergovernmental coordination. Conversely, good information management underpins good service delivery.

Counties do not always appear to ensure enough in the way of oversight, supervision, quality assurance, and on-the-job support for frontline service delivery units. These "meso-level" (or "back-up") functions appear to be poorly assured by many county departments. This weakens their ability to track performance and thus to ensure quality.

This is of particular importance in sectors such as health, ECDE, and agriculture. In the health sector, the benefits of this support to frontline facilities is clear: County A, which shows better performance across all quality indicators, operates an "institutionalized integrated facilitative supervision mechanism" for all levels of care, which provides opportunities for health managers and senior (more experienced) health workers to support frontline junior health workers. However, County A appears to be the exception rather than the rule in this regard. Box 3.8 illustrates the challenge of providing quality assurance in the ECDE sector.

BOX 3.7

Deficiencies in ECDE information management

Most of the counties visited for the Making Devolution Work for Service Delivery study lacked updated gross enrollment rates and net enrollment rates data as well as retention and transition rates. Early Childhood Development and Education (ECDE) data are not adequately captured in the National Education Management Information System (NEMIS). Ministry of Education officers reported that whereas primary and secondary education data are approximately 70 percent and 100 percent captured in NEMIS, respectively, data for the ECDE subsector have not been integrated into the system. In addition, though the Controller of Budget reports captured data on county budgets and expenditure on ECDE services, there is inadequate information on the financing for the ECDE subsector by subprogram across the 47 counties.

Source: World Bank 2020a.

Inadequate management agreements and coordination

Management arrangements are not simply a county issue, since national policies are being implemented locally, and Kenya would benefit from greater consistency in the management service delivery across counties. There is a lack of clarity in all sectors as to how services should be delivered and managed. This needs to be resolved through intergovernmental coordination. Policies, standards, institutional arrangements, and systems for service delivery (including HRM, public financial management [PFM], and M&E) need to be agreed upon between counties and the national government for each sector. These arrangements affect how management structures are operationalized within counties and how national and county governments work together.

Finally, poor operational coordination between county-level national government structures and county governments weakens the performance of shared functions. Coordination between county governments and county commissioners is not smooth in all places. Conflicts persist between the national government units and the county governments. And even where there are no disputes, the mechanisms for enhancing relations between the national units and county government units are not effectively used. In some counties, county commissioners ensure that national government sector ministries consult with county governments where there are related or shared functions, such as between national government responsibility for primary education and county government responsibility for ECDE. However, in other areas, national and county government institutions operate in parallel without coordination or collaboration.

The extent of collaboration is inevitably affected by political factors such as whether the county governor is from the dominant and ruling party coalition, by local bureaucratic factors such as competition for office space, and by human relationships. However, there is no clear guidance or standards for how the relationship between county commissioners and county governments should operate, not only at the county headquarters level but also down to the subcounty and ward level.

BOX 3.8

Quality assurance in the ECDE sector

The national preprimary education policy mandates that the Ministry of Education collaborate with county governments in providing quality assurance to enforce standards. The quality standards relate to curriculum and pedagogy, learning materials, physical facilities, health and nutrition, quality of teachers, role of stakeholders, children's rights, inclusivity, safety, and protection.

For quality assurance, the standard guidelines provide assessment tools and procedures to support the process. The policy mandates that quality assurance officers assess physical facilities in all preprimary schools, supervise teachers and learning, and document and disseminate their findings to stakeholders to improve the quality of services provided to all children, including those with disabilities. The officers are also expected to follow up on the quality assurance reports and ensure effective implementation of curricula for learners and teachers.

Though quality assurance is a critical component in improving educational outcomes, the Making Devolution Work for Service Delivery study revealed that county governments have given it little attention. County governments have recruited field officers and assigned them responsibilities to ensure that all Early Childhood Development and Education (ECDE) services adhere to the established quality standards.

However, focus group discussions with field officers in the counties visited revealed weak quality assurance structures at the subcounty level. For example, while County A assigned an ECDE field officer to more than 200 ECDE centers spread across two subcounties, County B had assigned only one officer per subcounty, with some subcounties having as many as 98 ECDE centers.

The study also revealed that the officers' ability to undertake quality assurance was further strained by their assignment to other administrative duties. This lack of facilitation was mentioned as a major challenge in the monitoring and supervision of ECDE centers, especially in rural and hardest-to-reach areas, thus limiting most quality assurance visits to urban centers and centers located closer to their offices. In County C, the study revealed significant duplication of efforts, with ECDE, social protection, and quality assurance officers assigned almost identical roles without clarity in their terms of reference.

Finally, the capacity of field officers to carry out the quality assurance mandate was also cited as a challenge. The subcounty coordinators interviewed indicated that though they are aware of the ECDE assessment and monitoring tools, they have not sensitized the center managers and head teachers to them, thus affecting center-based supervision.

Source: World Bank 2020a.

Weaknesses in county management of service delivery have several likely explanations:

- *Starting from scratch.* County governments (themselves created in 2013) have had to establish entirely new sector departments. In some cases (for example, health), this has been facilitated by the preexistence of deconcentrated service delivery units and facilities that could be adapted to new county requirements. In other sectors (for example, rural water supply), counties inherited little and have had to start from scratch—inevitably taking time to set up sector management structures that can take on all necessary activities. In the urban sector, the dissolution of municipal governments left counties with an institutional vacuum, resulting in an initial deterioration in urban service delivery that is only gradually being filled.
- *Building capacity.* Under devolution, county sector departments have taken on "meso-level" or middle management functions (such as information management, quality assurance, or procurement) that were previously the prerogative of national MDAs and for which staffing and systems have been

lacking at the county level. In the health sector, for example, managing a countywide health service requires many more skills and systems than managing a single health facility.

- *Lacking guidance.* Effective county-level management of service delivery has been hampered by the absence of sector guidance. In the absence of comprehensive sector management norms, standards, and guidelines, newly established county sector departments have been left to their own devices far more often than necessary. This has inevitably led to management failures or shortfalls.

INTERGOVERNMENTAL RELATIONS

The 2010 constitution envisages that devolution would involve cooperation between levels of government, and legislation sets up a series of intergovernmental fora to achieve this. The Constitution of Kenya, Article 189 ("Cooperation between national and county governments"), states that "Government at either level shall . . . assist, support and consult. . . the other level of government" and that "Government at each level, and different governments at the county level, shall cooperate in the performance of functions and exercise of powers."

The Intergovernmental Relations Act 2012 provided an institutional framework for precisely this purpose. Since 2013, how have the national government and the county governments worked together in ways that ensure good service delivery? While many of the substantive issues that should be tackled through intergovernmental coordination, collaboration, and cooperation are examined in other sections of this report, this section looks at the established mechanisms for accomplishing this and the extent to which they have been functional.

Intergovernmental forums

The intergovernmental forums set out in legislation are in place. The National and County Government Coordinating Summit, the Council of Governors, and the Intergovernmental Relations Technical Committee—all prescribed by the Intergovernmental Relations Act 2012—have been established. The Intergovernmental Budget and Economic Council prescribed by the Public Finance Management Act 2012 has also been established. These forums meet regularly to undertake the functions set out for them in legislation and have established subcommittees on sector or thematic lines to further their work.

In addition, an Intergovernmental Consultative Sectoral Forum has been established for each sector as envisaged under the Intergovernmental Relations Act 2012. Some sectors have tried to use this as a basis for establishing mechanisms to facilitate coordination and cooperation (box 3.9). Development partners have also organized themselves to better support national and county government coordination—establishing, for example, the PFM Donor Working Group and the Devolution Donor Working Group.

The Council of Governors has also proven to be an active and energetic voice for the counties. It has established various technical committees along sector lines that act as caucuses for the respective County Executive Committee (CEC) members.

BOX 3.9

Intergovernmental coordination in the agriculture sector

The agriculture sector has set up four coordination mechanisms:

- A ministerial-level Intergovernmental Forum on Agriculture
- A Joint Agricultural Steering Committee to replicate the ministerial-level forum but comprising technical teams

- The Joint Agricultural Sector Consultation and Coordination Mechanism, which brings together all stakeholders in the sector, including the private sector, civil society, and development partners
- The Agriculture County Executive Committee Members Caucus to enable counties to coordinate.

Role of the judiciary

The judiciary has played an effective role in settling disputes between levels of government. Although the judiciary is not part of the devolved structure of government, the courts play an important role in the implementation of devolution. The constitution vests the supreme court with advisory powers to provide guidance when there are conflicts between various entities. The other courts also have jurisdiction to determine matters concerning disputes between various agencies, including disputes over mandates.

Disputes between the two levels of government and between the county assemblies and their executives have been reaching the courts for arbitration. In some instances, the courts have prevented disputes from paralyzing service delivery in the counties. These have included disputes between the National Assembly and the Senate over their respective roles in the division of the revenue bill; disputes between the national and county governments over the division of health functions; or disputes over the responsibility for roads in the counties.

In most cases, the courts have rendered judgments that by and large favor devolution. Some of the filed cases have challenged the national government's actions in continuing to retain functions intended for the counties or establishing new or parallel institutions to carry out functions assigned to the counties. The role the courts have played in resolving these disputes has thus effectively safeguarded devolution and helped to further its objectives.

Weaknesses and recommendations

Coordination and cooperation between the national government and county governments can be strengthened. The operations of both cross-sectoral and sector forums have had mixed results. For example, although the Intergovernmental Budget and Economic Council (IBEC) functions effectively, it is almost solely focused on crisis management during the division-of-revenue process and does not effectively cover the broader range of fiscal and PFM issues that need discussion across national and county governments, including the design of conditional transfers. The failure to effectively agree on how to manage conditional grants has led counties to complain of inadequate and inconsistent communication on the purpose of conditional grants, undermining the contribution of this funding for service delivery.

Although some of the sector and other forums have been functional, they have frequently been unable to facilitate constructive dialogue. Sector coordination mechanisms could work more effectively in many sectors. Ineffective coordination means that a range of challenges and problems (which require both national and county levels to work together) are not adequately addressed or resolved. Many of the service delivery problems identified in the Making Devolution Work for Service Delivery (MDWSD) study could have been resolved through properly functioning sector or cross-cutting intergovernmental forums. Examples include ambiguities or conflicts related to the devolution (or nondevolution) of functions (such as in the urban water sector); links between national and county functions in sectors (such as the supply of medical equipment in the health sector); the design and implementation of conditional grants (where IBEC could facilitate consultations and discussions); HRM deficiencies; and the implementation of national policies and regulations (such as in the health sector).

However, there have been encouraging cases of intergovernmental dialogue, such as in the agriculture sector as discussed above. The National and County Government Co-ordinating Summit (comprising the president and all 47 county governors) needs to be underpinned by greater technical-level coordination. Each political-level forum should be underpinned by a technical-level forum (table 3.3). Political decision-making can only be effective where technical discussions have identified key issues and options for addressing them. Both the IBEC and sector forums have clear technical-level counterparts. These technical committees need to meet regularly to prepare the ground for political-level meetings. There also needs to be a smooth flow of information from sector committees to the more-general committees.

In addition, sector coordination has been undermined by intergovernmental competition and by slow changes in behavior. At the start of devolution, county suspicion of the national government may have played a key role. Now a critical issue is that national MDAs are finding it difficult to make the transition from a former "command-and-control" line ministry modus operandi to a quasi-federal model. National government line ministries have not found it easy to adapt to devolution and the need to coordinate and cooperate with subnational (county) health authorities (as opposed to controlling them). They are accustomed to ordering the introduction of policy or standards rather than acting as national custodians who need to "negotiate" policy implementation and regulation with semiautonomous county governments. National government policy and regulatory functions need to become effective through intergovernmental mechanisms.

TABLE 3.3 **Intergovernmental coordination mechanisms in Kenya, by level**

LEVEL	GENERAL	FISCAL	SECTOR
Political	National and County Government Co-ordinating Summit	Intergovernmental Budget and Economic Council (IBEC)	Sector intergovernmental consultative forums
Technical	Meetings of county secretaries convened by the Intergovernmental Relations Technical Committee	IBEC subcommittees on Budget, Loans and Grants, Legal and Economic Policy	Joint Sector Steering Committees

Source: World Bank.

Where intergovernmental coordination structures have worked at a technical level, implementation of measures that have been jointly identified, discussed, and agreed upon has not been effective. The recommendations and resolutions from these coordination mechanisms or structures are often not implemented or complied with by either the national government or county governments. For example, the Intergovernmental Sectoral Forum for Public Service Management has met regularly to discuss issues and identified approaches for tackling some of the HRM deficiencies. Despite this, few agreed-upon actions have been rolled out or complied with.

Finally, the potential of regional economic blocs is not yet realized. This is still a nascent and somewhat neglected dimension of intergovernmental (inter-county) relations. Regional economic blocs potentially provide the framework for greater collaboration between neighboring counties on areas of mutual interest, but their potential to do so has not been realized. Potential areas where gains could be realized include rationalizing the referral process to Level 5 (former provincial) hospitals and allowing Level 4 hospitals across counties to focus on different specializations. In agriculture, regional economic blocs have the potential to support improved policy coordination, given the common agroclimatic zones covered by the blocs, and to improve coordination on transboundary issues, such as pest and disease control.

In sum, intergovernmental coordination, collaboration, and cooperation have not worked as effectively as needed for several reasons. As already mentioned, part of this can be attributed to the novelty of Kenya's new state structure in which the national government and county governments are constitutional peers rather than hierarchical partners. National MDAs have not found it easy to see or communicate with their subnational counterparts as governmental peers. There is also an underlying dynamic of intergovernmental competition over fiscal resources, which has encouraged counties to sometimes take an aggressive position toward the national government and make intergovernmental interactions more about conflict resolution or intergovernmental crisis management—and much less about finding solutions to problems. Finally, coordination and collaboration cost time and money, and intergovernmental frameworks and mechanisms have not been operationalized because of a lack of resources and organizational inputs.

CONCLUSIONS

The first element in the framework for assessing devolution and service delivery in Kenya shows a negative-to-mixed outcome (table 3.4). In all three areas—functions and responsibilities, sector management, and intergovernmental relations—there have been achievements that have contributed to making service delivery work:

- Many service delivery functions have been devolved and taken on by counties.
- Counties have established core sector management structures and processes and have gradually improved their performance over time.
- Intergovernmental frameworks have been put into place.

On the other hand, the distribution of some functional responsibilities (and the resources that go with them) has been contested and conflictual;

TABLE 3.4 **Assessment of the devolution of functions, management of devolved sectors, and intergovernmental relations**

AREA	WHAT HAS WORKED	WHAT IS NOT WORKING
Functions and responsibilities	• Devolution of key service delivery sectors (health, ECDE) to counties without major problems	• Conflict between national government and counties in urban water supply sector • Duplication in some sectors (agriculture, urban, education) but not leading to conflict
Sector management	• Counties' assumption of core management functions • General improvement in county performance over time • Establishment of sector departments in counties • Expansion of facilities in key service delivery sectors (health, ECDE)	• Overcentralization of service delivery management by county-level departments (health) • Insufficient delegation to frontline facilities (health) or to agencies (urban, urban water) • Inadequate information management (health, ECDE) • Weak quality assurance and support (health, ECDE) • Inadequate sector-specific guidance, norms, and standards (all sectors)
Intergovernmental relations	• Establishment of basic frameworks and mechanisms	• Ineffective use of statutory frameworks

Source: World Bank.
Note: ECDE = early childhood development and education.

the county management of sectors has often been deficient; and intergovernmental coordination, collaboration, and cooperation have not worked well enough to find solutions to problems in the new structure of devolved service delivery.

REFERENCES

Njagi, T., L. Kirimi, K. Onyango, and N. Kinyumu. 2015. "The Status of the Agricultural Sector after Devolution to County Governments." Working Paper No. 68/2015, Tegemeo Institute, Nairobi.

WASREB (Water Services Regulatory Board). 2018. "WASREB Annual Report 2017/18." Annual report and financial statements for the financial year ended June 30, 2018, WASREB, Nairobi.

World Bank. 2020a. "Early Childhood Development and Education Sector Background Study." Background sector study for this volume, World Bank, Nairobi.

World Bank. 2020b. "Health Sector Background Study." Background sector study for this volume, World Bank, Nairobi.

World Bank. 2020c. "Urban Sector Background Study." Background sector study for this volume, World Bank, Nairobi.

World Bank. 2020d. "Water Sector Background Study." Background sector study for this volume, World Bank, Nairobi.

4 Finance, Resource Allocation, and Use

KEY MESSAGES

Overall

- The intergovernmental fiscal transfer framework and revenue-sharing process forms the backbone of fiscal devolution but needs a stronger link to county service delivery needs.
- County planning and budgeting processes do not answer four key questions: What services are resources being spent on? Where have the resources been spent? What resources have been allocated to service delivery facilities? What are the results?
- There is an absence of sectoral guidance on how to finance, budget, manage, monitor, and report on funds for service delivery (including generating and using assets).

Priority Interventions

- Sector budgeting and expenditure norms and standards need to be developed and implemented corresponding with clear county sector delivery objectives.
- Uniform processes and systems are needed to capture and monitor targeted and actual service delivery results from fiscal planning, budgeting, monitoring, evaluation, and reporting processes— ensuring capture of both financial and nonfinancial data in a consistent and comparable way over time (and integrated with national sectoral information management systems).
- Development of an incentive-based conditional grant framework is needed to provide additional results-oriented and qualified financing to counties in a harmonized way. The framework should be used by both development partners and government and tied directly to implementation of key reform steps that would enhance service delivery. These include increasing own-source revenue, improving cash management, decentralizing control and distribution of resources to service delivery units, and other reforms.

INTRODUCTION

This chapter assesses how devolution has ensured that (1) fiscal resources are adequately and equitably shared in ways that enable county governments to deliver services in line with their assigned functions; and (2) counties allocate and use their resources to improve the quality of, and access to, devolved services.

The intergovernmental fiscal system has a key role to play in ensuring that adequate resources are available at the county level to finance their subnational service delivery mandates. At the same time, it underpins a more equitable spread of resources across counties to ensure that existing socioeconomic disparities are reduced over time. How Kenya's intergovernmental fiscal system does or does not achieve these objectives is a major determinant of whether devolution works for service delivery and reduces disparities.

The potential benefits of devolution should operate through the allocation and use of public resources for service delivery in ways that are more responsive to local needs and accountable to citizens. County plans and budgets should allocate resources to better match the preferences of the residents of the county (improved allocative efficiency). And counties should better spend funds to deliver more and higher-quality public services for a given level of funding (improved technical efficiency).

FRAMEWORK FOR FINANCING SERVICE DELIVERY

The framework for financing devolved service delivery works along four "pillars" of fiscal decentralization:

- *Pillar 1:* Assignment and financing of expenditure responsibilities based on county functional responsibilities
- *Pillar 2:* Revenue assignments and county revenue administration
- *Pillar 3:* The intergovernmental fiscal transfer system
- *Pillar 4:* Alternative financing mechanisms, including subnational borrowing.

Funds following functions: Expenditure assignments and vertical sharing for devolved service delivery

The first pillar of the framework relates to the vertical sharing of resources, which first involves the assignment of expenditure responsibilities in line with functional responsibilities (discussed in more detail in chapter 3). Once expenditure responsibilities have been determined, it is the purpose of the three remaining pillars of intergovernmental finance to ensure that an adequate level and mix of funding sources are available to subnational governments to fulfill their expenditure responsibilities. Here we examine both expenditure assignments and the overall vertical sharing of resources.

The de jure assignment of functions and expenditure responsibilities in Kenya between the national government and the county governments largely conforms to the subsidiarity principle. In a few sectors, such as education and health, there is a broad match between the de jure situation and the de facto functional assignment, with counties generally spending the financial resources that are at their disposal in pursuit of their constitutional mandates. However, as discussed in chapter 3, there are several sectors where the assignment of functions has been disputed or appear to be inappropriate, such as in urban, water, and agriculture.

The division of revenue in Kenya is based on a recommendation from the Commission on Revenue Allocation (CRA), which in practice has ended up being subject to various negotiations between the national government and Council of Governors at the Intergovernmental Budget and Economic Council (IBEC) and ultimately the National Assembly and Senate, which have to pass the annual Division of Revenue Act (DoRA). The Senate also has the responsibility to approve the formula for allocating each county's share of revenue (based on the CRA's recommendation) and to pass the annual County Allocation of Revenue Act (CARA).

Whereas the division of revenue mechanisms and negotiations have seen prolonged delays and stalemates, arguably they have ensured that county governments receive a level of resources that enables them to function as subnational governments at a basic level. In addition, basic public expenditure management processes are being followed at both the national and county levels. In other words, basic intergovernmental fiscal systems and public expenditure processes are in place to ensure that counties can spend on the functional responsibilities that have been transferred to them.

In addition, horizontal expenditure patterns suggest that counties with higher expenditure needs (or counties deemed to have been historically disadvantaged) generally spend more per person than counties expected to have lower expenditure needs or in an economically stronger position. This underlines the extent to which resource allocation and use are addressing equity issues.

Despite the establishment of an intergovernmental fiscal system that enables counties to function at a basic level, the overall level of national government spending seems relatively high and is increasing despite the significant decrease in the de jure service delivery functions at the national level. Counties, on the other hand, account for a low (and declining) percentage of total spending, even though they have significant service delivery functions. The functioning of the national government seems to have changed relatively little. Whereas county governments have been assigned significant functional responsibilities by the constitution, they currently only account for 13 percent of total public spending, down from a peak of 14 percent in fiscal year (FY) 2014/15 (figures 4.1 and 4.2). An increasing share of fiscal resources has been allocated to national government in recent years.

Within some of the sectors where functions have been devolved, the national government retains a higher share of spending than one might expect. For example, 60 percent of spending in agriculture and 79 percent in water is undertaken by the national government (figure 4.2). In some sectors, this seems to be the result of national ministries retaining functions and resources that arguably—if not by the constitution, then by the subsidiarity principle—should now be respectively performed and used at the county level. In other cases, it appears that sector ministries (if and when given a choice) prioritize interventions and expenditures within the national ministry's remit in relation to devolved interventions or, in some cases, bypass county government structures to deliver devolved services. This is particularly evident in agriculture, water, and urban

FIGURE 4.1

National and county government shares of total public expenditure in Kenya, FY2013/14–FY2017/18

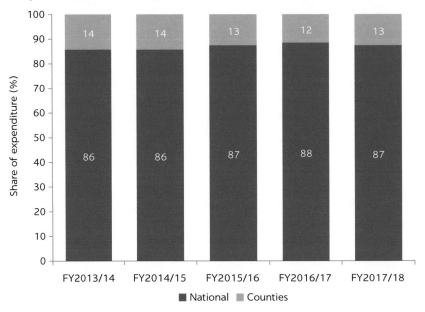

Source: Office of the Controller of Budget, annual national and county governments budget implementation review reports, FY2013/14–FY2017/18.

FIGURE 4.2

National and county government shares of public expenditure in Kenya, by sector, FY2017/18

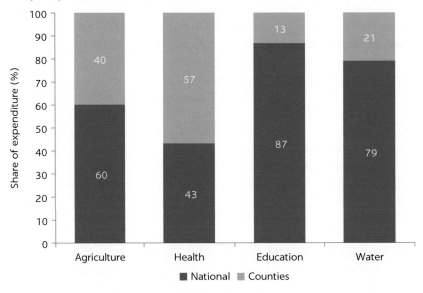

Source: Office of the Controller of Budget, annual national and county governments budget implementation review reports, FY2017/18.

services (as discussed in chapter 3). Many such cases have been the object of contention between county governments and the national government.

The three remaining pillars of a fiscally devolved system are now examined in turn.

Revenue assignments and the county revenue administration

Revenues from the counties themselves are just a minor part of the current narrative on intergovernmental finance of service delivery in Kenya, with only about 10 percent of county expenditures being funded from the county's own revenues (figure 4.3). Outside the main urban economic centers of the country, own-source revenue (OSR) generation is often a considerably smaller share of county total revenues.[1]

To a large extent, the limited dependence on OSR was by constitutional design, presumably to prevent horizontal fiscal imbalances from emerging between the economically more prosperous counties and those counties which have been historically disadvantaged in terms of economic activity and investment. To this extent, the limited allocation of OSR to the county level seems to have had the intended result of a relatively even distribution of OSR.

However, a consequence of the limited assignment of revenues to the county level—intended or not—is that counties are highly grant-dependent, creating a situation in which county leaders only have a weak political incentive to collect OSR. After all, in most counties, even if the elected county leadership could double the county taxes and revenues collected (which would no doubt be a politically difficult decision), the corresponding increase in total county funding would only allow for an increase in county spending of about 10 percent. The hesitance of county leaders to improve county revenue collection is further exacerbated by general weaknesses in county revenue administration (and possibly also in country revenue forecasting).

County OSR is of declining importance (figure 4.4). After an initial increase in volume to a high of 0.54 percent of gross domestic product (GDP) in FY2014/15, county OSR has fallen in both volume and as a smaller percentage of GDP (0.38 percent) as of FY2017/18. As a proportion of total county revenues, OSR has fallen from a high of 12.9 percent in FY2014/15 to 8.7 percent in 2017/18 (figure 4.3).

FIGURE 4.3

Composition of county funding sources in Kenya, FY2013/14–FY2017/18

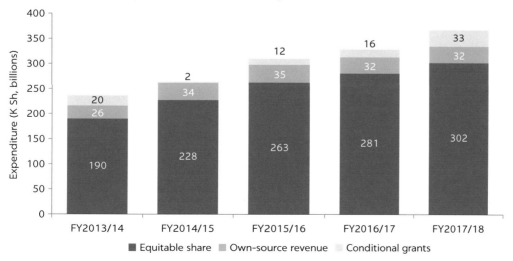

Source: Office of the Controller of Budget, annual county government budget implementation review reports, FY2013/14–FY2017/18.

FIGURE 4.4

Total county OSR in volume and as a percentage of GDP in Kenya, FY2013/14–FY2017/18

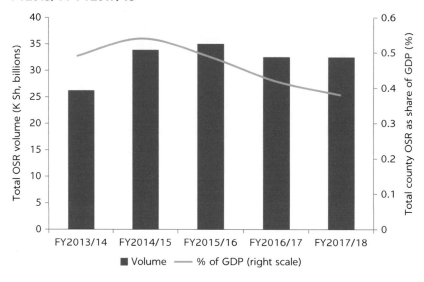

Source: DI 2018.
Note: OSR = own-source revenue.

The limited available evidence attributes the decrease in OSR mobilization to poor revenue collection practices and significant revenue leakages (DI 2018). There is clearly a good deal of room for improving revenue administration and management, but as mentioned above, the political incentives for counties to do so are weak.

Intergovernmental fiscal transfers

The third pillar of intergovernmental finance is the provision of intergovernmental fiscal transfers to fill the vertical fiscal gap between county expenditure needs and county OSR. The equitable sharing of national revenues accounts for roughly 80 percent of county funding, while conditional grants (from both government sources and development partner programs) account for an additional 10 percent of county funds (figure 4.3). As such, the current grant system provides considerable resources and decision-making space to county governments.

Equitable Sharing

Equitable sharing is distributed vertically (between the national government and county governments) as well as horizontally (among the counties) based on the advice of an independent constitutional body, the CRA, in a transparent manner (CRA 2012, 2017). Since the intergovernmental distribution of resources is expected to be decided in an intergovernmental allocation process that precedes the start of the annual budget formulation cycle, and since the distribution of grants is guided by a clear and transparent allocation formula, county governments are generally expected to prepare their annual budgets in the context of a clear budget ceiling if parliament approves the equitable allocation on time. Grants are generally released in a timely and complete manner each year.

However, over the past two fiscal years (2019/20 and 2020/21), there has been considerable debate and contention on the equitable share for counties between the Senate, National Assembly, Council of Governors, and other institutions, particularly the CRA and National Treasury. This has often resulted in delays, with the CARA only being passed weeks or months into the fiscal year. Because counties cannot pass their budgets before the CARA is finalized, these delays have a knock-on effect on counties' budgeting and ability to meet their financial obligations. The Constitution of Kenya of 2010 mandated that the CRA make recommendations for the basis (formula) for revenue allocation among county governments; the first two iterations would last three years and the third one, five years. The start of FY2020/21 saw a protracted lack of consensus on proposals for the third basis for county allocation of revenue formulas. With the previous formula having lapsed, the CARA could not be passed before a new formula was agreed upon. Moreover, in FY2020/21, the impact of COVID-19 on the national fiscal situation further negatively affected the timely release of the equitable shares for May and June 2020.

The equitable share has helped enable those counties that are lagging behind in service delivery, which are typically poorer and more sparsely populated, to start to catch up. Figure 4.5 provides an overview of the horizontal incidence of intergovernmental fiscal transfers—both equitable shares and conditional grants—across Kenya's 47 counties for the latest year available (FY2017/18). For completeness, it also shows the distribution of OSR across the counties.

Figure 4.5 instantly highlights the dominant role that the equitable sharing of national revenues plays in determining the overall horizontal incidence of county resources in Kenya. In contrast, conditional grants and county OSR (as already noted above) play a much more limited role in determining the overall horizontal distribution of county finances.

The horizontal allocation of the equitable share is determined by parliament, in line with the constitutional and legal framework, upon the CRA's

FIGURE 4.5

Per capita intergovernmental fiscal transfers and OSR in Kenya, by county, FY2017/18

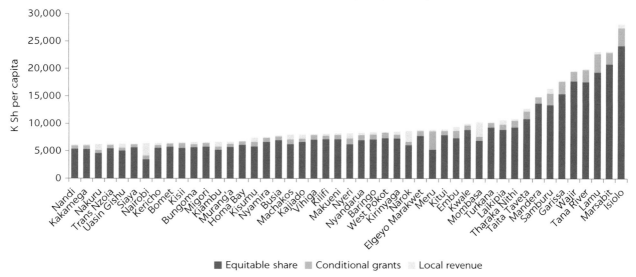

Source: Controller of Budget, annual county budget implementation review report, FY2017/18.
Note: OSR = own-source revenue.

recommendation (CRA 2012, 2017). Since the devolved governance system has come into being, the CRA has prepared three different allocation formulas, (or bases) that have guided the sharing of revenues among the 47 county governments from 2013 forward (table 4.1).

The formula apportions weight to various parameters, with the first two formulas having broadly similar parameters and weighting. In the second formula, the parameter with the greatest weight was population (45 percent), followed by equal shares (26 percent), poverty (18 percent), and land area (8 percent). The remainder of the equitable share allocations were distributed in accordance with a measure of revenue effort (2 percent) and a measure of county development (1 percent). Despite slight differences between the first and second formulas, the differences between these formulas—and in the resulting horizontal distribution—were quite minor.

Arguably one of the main shortcomings of the first and second bases for distributing equitable shares was the absence of a strong conceptual foundation of the allocation formula. Indeed, the structure of these formulas creates a disconnect between the vertical allocation of the equitable share revenues, on one side, and service delivery outcomes on the other side. During the preparation of the third basis, the CRA sought to develop a formula that links allocations more closely to the key service delivery functions assigned to county governments (table 4.1). The population parameter now has less weight, with parameters added to provide for the county burden in providing services or investments in the health, agriculture, and urban sectors.

The vertical allocation of equitable share resources is a binding constraint on the county governments' fiscal space and on their ability to spend more on frontline public services. It is particularly troubling that the CRA's advice regarding the vertical allocation of resources is habitually ignored, for reasons that are not fully understood.

TABLE 4.1 **Weighted parameters for equitable revenue sharing among county governments in Kenya under the first, second, and proposed third bases/formulas**

Percentage

OBJECTIVE	PARAMETER	FIRST FORMULA	SECOND FORMULA	THIRD FORMULA
Enhance service delivery	Population	45	45	18
	Health index[a]	0	0	17
	Agriculture index[a]	0	0	10
	Basic equal share	25	26	20
	Urban services[a]	0	0	5
Promote balanced development	Poverty level	20	18	14
	Land area	8	8	8
	Development factor[b]	0	1	0
	Rural access index[a]	0	0	8
Incentivize fiscal effort	Fiscal effort	2	2	0

Source: CRA 2017.
Note: Since the devolved governance system came into effect in 2013, the Commission on Revenue Allocation (CRA) has prepared three different allocation bases/formulas that have guided the sharing of revenues among the 47 county governments.
a. Added in the third formula.
b. Added in the second formula.

In the first six years of devolution, the resource allocation formula used to horizontally distribute equitable shares among the 47 counties was based on a rather generic index of expenditure needs. As a result, any link between the resource allocations to counties and the underlying county functions (for which counties are receiving national resources) was lost. The third formula has attempted to cure this.

The lack of timeliness in the release of funds is also causing budget execution challenges at the county level, which impedes their ability to deliver basic public services. An additional area of concern is that in some sectors, such as agriculture and water, there is limited use of conditional grants, and yet these are sectors where the national government has retained the most resources.

The inadequacy of county spending for service delivery is a concern in highly populous counties and counties that inherited greater staff, which are generally expected to do more with less. More-populous counties spend considerably less per capita across all sectors than less-populous counties, which tend to be more rural and less advantaged (figure 4.6). While it is important to enable previously neglected areas of the country, it is also important that the intergovernmental fiscal framework ensure the adequacy of resources for service delivery for all counties.

Conditional grants

In contrast to the allocation of equitable shares—which relies on a single horizontal allocation formula—each conditional grant scheme has its own vertical and horizontal allocation mechanism, typically tied to the grant's specific institutional or service-delivery objective. Some grants have been targeted to address specific financing gaps. For example, in FY2018/19, the Kenya Urban Support Program (KUSP) provided a major inflow of funding for urban infrastructure and services, reflecting a devolved sector that hitherto had been largely ignored since the commencement of county governments in 2013.

Other grants have targeted direct financing of service delivery in health, including allocations to Level 5 hospitals where there are spillover effects to

FIGURE 4.6

Per capita sector expenditure in the least and most populous counties in Kenya, FY2017/18

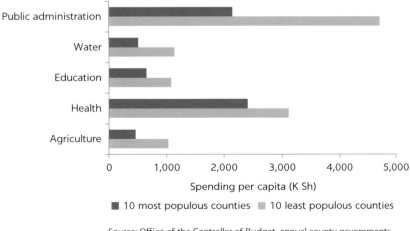

Spending per capita (K Sh)

■ 10 most populous counties ■ 10 least populous counties

Source: Office of the Controller of Budget, annual county governments budget implementation review report, FY2017/18.

other counties. Some grants have also been linked to county government and national government performance—such as the Kenya Devolution Support Program (KDSP) and the KUSP—and have shown potential in incentivizing improvements in institutional capability to deliver services while providing funding for service delivery (box 4.1). Conditional grants have also been an important modality for development partners to channel support in a way that is consistent with the financing framework for devolved service delivery.

From the analyses above, four areas of specific concern regarding the current intergovernmental fiscal transfer system should be flagged.

BOX 4.1

Performance-based conditional grants

The conditional grants made available to counties by the Kenya Devolution Support Program (KDSP) and the Kenya Urban Support Program (KUSP), both financed by the World Bank, are linked to county government and national government performance. The KDSP aims to strengthen national and county capacities under devolution, while the KUSP's objective is to strengthen urban institutions for the delivery of urban infrastructure and services. Through the KDSP and KUSP, counties can access program grants subject to meeting compliance-based conditions and achieving performance scores or standards. In meeting these requirements, counties demonstrate that their institutional performance has either improved or been sustained. In both programs, annual performance assessments are undertaken to verify compliance and to measure performance, thus determining grant allocations.

Kenya Devolution Support Program
The KDSP makes two types of performance grants available to counties. Modest capacity-building grants (Level 1 grants) are accessed by counties subject to meeting minimum access conditions (MACs). MACs are basic institutional performance benchmarks; all counties that comply with these can access Level 1 grants to finance capacity-building activities.

Larger, infrastructure grants (Level 2 grants, which can finance a wide range of county-level investment projects) are accessed by only those counties that meet both MACs and the more-demanding minimum performance conditions (MPCs) such as "clean" financial audits. The size of Level 2 grants varies according to the performance score of each county, measured against a set of performance measures (PMs). PMs are clustered into five categories, each of which corresponds to one of the five Key Results Areas (KRAs) that make up the National Capacity Building Framework (NCBF). The five KRAs cover public financial management (PFM), planning and monitoring, human resource management, civic education and participation, and social and environmental management for investment projects.

Kenya Urban Support Program
The KUSP provides Urban Institutional Grants (UIGs) and Urban Development Grants (UDGs) to counties on the basis of their performance in the urban sector. As with KDSP grants, counties qualify for UIGs and UDGs by meeting minimum conditions (MCs) and PMs. UIGs are relatively small grants, intended to finance institutional and capacity development activities in the urban sector (such as spatial planning or training) and made available subject to basic MCs. UDGs, which are much larger grants, are intended to finance investments in urban areas. Most MCs and PSs are related to institutional benchmarks (such as establishing and operationalizing urban boards for urban areas, appointing municipal managers, and so on) and to urban service delivery (such as solid waste management, urban planning, and so on).

KUSP grants, then, operate as incentives for counties to make progress in setting up effective urban institutional arrangements (as provided for in the Urban Areas and Cities Act 2011) as well as urban infrastructure and service delivery.

Sources: KDSP and KUSP program documents and reports.

Low grants relative to equitable share. Although the number and amount of conditional grants being allocated to the county level have been growing from FY2014/15 onward, they are still low relative to the equitable share (the unconditional transfer). Yet conditional grants can be a useful option to trigger performance in specific sectors. Under this heading, the national government provides a range of different (often sector-tied) conditional grants to county governments. The conditional grants contained in the 2017 and 2018 County Allocation of Revenue Acts are summarized in table 4.2.

Variable sectoral distribution of grants. The sectoral distribution of conditional grants, in terms of both the number of grants and the amounts being distributed—relative to overall sectoral spending—is highly variable. The health sector appeared to be more reliant on conditional grants than other sectors in FY2017/18, with five grants financing over K Sh 13 billion in health expenditures being funded from conditional grant resources, compared with total county-level health expenditures of K Sh 84 billion. Similarly, counties received a substantial allocation from the Road Maintenance Fuel Levy Fund in FY2017/18. Conditional grants available for agriculture are small and have yet to take off in the water sector, yet these are sectors where the national government has retained the most resources.

Fragmentation of grants. Although the National Treasury prepared a framework for conditional grants, in practice conditional grants have been developed and used in a fragmented and haphazard way. There are over a

TABLE 4.2 **Conditional grant allocations to counties, by type, FY2017/18 and FY2018/19**

	FY2017/18		FY2018/19	
GRANT TYPE	K SH, BILLIONS	SHARE OF TOTAL (%)	K SH, BILLIONS	SHARE OF TOTAL (%)
National government conditional grants				
Leasing of medical equipment	4.5	10.3	9.4	16.0
Level 5 hospitals	4.2	9.6	4.3	7.4
Road Maintenance Fuel Levy Fund	11.1	25.3	8.3	14.1
Compensation for user fee forgone	0.9	2.1	0.9	1.5
Development of youth polytechnics	2.0	4.6	2.0	3.4
Construction of county headquarters	0.6	1.4	0.6	1.0
Development partner grants				
World Bank–supplied financing of county health facilities	0.9	2.1	n.a	n.a
World Bank Kenya Urban Support Project (KUSP)	0.0	0.0	11.5	19.5
World Bank KDSP "Level 1" Grants	2.2	5.0	2.3	3.9
World Bank KDSP "Level 2" Grants	4.0	9.1	4.0	6.8
World Bank Transforming Health System for Universal Care project	2.8	6.4	3.6	6.2
World Bank National Agricultural and Rural Inclusive Growth project	1.1	2.5	2.9	5.0
DANIDA Support to Universal Health Care program	0.8	1.8	1.0	1.7
European Union (EU) grants	1.0	2.3	1.0	1.8
Other loans and grants	7.8	17.8	6.8	11.7
Total conditional grant allocations	**43.9**	**100.0**	**58.7**	**100.0**

Source: County Allocation of Revenue Act 2017, 2018.
Note: Percentages may not add up to 100 due to rounding. DANIDA = Danish International Development Agency; KDSP = Kenya Devolution Support Program; n.a. = not applicable.

dozen conditional grants. Development partners have contributed to this fragmentation, funding 9 out of 15 grants in FY2017/18.

Inadequate, inconsistent guidance for the use of grants. Counties complain of inadequate and inconsistent communication on the purpose of conditional grants. For instance, the national government made significant investments in the purchase of medical equipment for county health services through the Managed Medical Equipment scheme, but counties felt that this was not done in a consultative way, and some of this equipment is lying idle as a result. In addition, as currently configured, the Integrated Financial Management System (IFMIS) and the Standard Charts of Accounts (SCOA) do not adequately capture details on county budgeting and spending of conditional grant funds, which makes it impossible to track budgeting decisions and spending properly.

This means that counties allocate and use grants in different ways and that accountability is weak—a situation exacerbated by the lack of sectoral norms and standards for service delivery. In the absence of such sector-specific norms and standards, the expenditures financed out of conditional grants are likely to be inconsistent with wider sector policy objectives.

Funds delayed, services delayed

A key problem affecting county financing of service delivery is the late release of the equitable share and conditional grants—which together make up most county revenues—by the National Treasury. Although delay in the release of the equitable share does not explain variations in execution rates between counties, the lack of predictability is likely to affect the timelines of delivery of services and investments. It also is a source of tension between counties and the national government. Underlying this challenge are broader challenges to cash management at the national level, which include unrealistic revenue projections at the start of the financial year.

Although counties regularly receive unconditional equitable revenue sharing as well as conditional grants from the national budget, in practice, the national government has not exercised its option to disburse Equalization Fund resources to the county level as conditional grants.[2] Instead, the national government is generally implementing activities funded by the Equalization Fund through national government departments and projects. It is also important to note that the equitable share, itself, performs an equalizing function through its formula, which is inherently equalizing.

Alternative financing mechanisms for county services and infrastructure

Most intergovernmental financing systems typically include subnational borrowing and debt as well as alternative subnational financing mechanisms such as public-private partnerships. At this stage, although constitutionally and legally permitted to do so, Kenya has yet to operationalize a formal framework for local government borrowing because no county has formally engaged in borrowing yet. In practice, however, some county governments are thought to be engaging in short-term borrowing from domestic financial institutions for cash management purposes.

The absence of an operational borrowing framework should not necessarily be seen as an omission by the National Treasury. Instead, Kenya's devolved financing system has been prudently cautious with respect to debt financing. That county governments are not borrowing or taking on excessive debt loads should be seen as a positive effect of the current strategy. Unchecked and unsustainable subnational borrowing has the potential to undermine county and national fiscal sustainability, which is already at risk of high debt distress.

However, some counties in Kenya—especially those with relatively large urban infrastructure needs—lack access to adequate infrastructure financing. Whereas previously disadvantaged counties have benefited from a large increase in equitable share funding—and therefore have been able to fund considerable infrastructure projects from general-purpose resources—more-populous and densely populated counties have typically received much smaller equitable share allocations per resident. As a result, they have been unable to use general-purpose resources for meaningful infrastructure investments; moreover, their OSR is not sufficient for funding the quantum of urban infrastructure needed. As such, there is a need for a suitable mechanism that will allow county governments that have adequate repayment potential to access long-term financing in an accountable manner. One such mechanism is the County Creditworthiness Initiative (box 4.2).

BOX 4.2

County creditworthiness

The County Creditworthiness Initiative (CCI) is a collaboration between various partners, including the National Treasury, the Commission on Revenue Allocation (CRA), the Capital Markets Authority (CMA), and county governments, with support from the World Bank Group. The overarching objective of the initiative is to improve the creditworthiness of county governments and enable them to access market-based financing for public infrastructure and overall development through capital markets. The CCI aims to strengthen financial management systems in counties, assess the readiness of capital markets to facilitate county borrowing, address any known bottlenecks, develop a fiscal structure that supports responsible borrowing, and develop an institutionalized framework that will oversee sustainable borrowing by county governments.

The World Bank Group, in partnership with the CRA, has been providing training, capacity building, and technical assistance under the CCI. Nine county

governments were prequalified by the CRA to serve as the pilot cohort under the initiative. In January 2019, the nine counties participated in the first County Creditworthiness Academy, an intensive one-week capacity-building workshop for county government financial officials and the central government staff to master the underlying principles of creditworthiness. Out of the nine counties, three (Bungoma, Kisumu, and Makueni) were selected by the CRA to undergo a shadow (private) credit rating, which was later publicly disclosed at the request of the three rated counties.

The next phase of the initiative is expected to include provision of technical assistance to (1) address weaknesses identified through the credit rating and diagnosis of the three counties; (2) develop capital investment plans, climate-smart investments, and public-private partnerships; (3) help the National Treasury strengthen the county borrowing framework and approval processes; and (4) scale up creditworthiness training to other counties.

Source: World Bank.

ALLOCATION AND USE OF RESOURCES AT THE COUNTY LEVEL

Kenya's devolution reform offers the opportunity for counties to plan, budget, and spend far more effectively for local services than in the past. Previously, responsibility was fragmented between deconcentrated districts, local authorities, and constituency-based funds operating parallel mechanisms of service delivery (World Bank 2012).

County governments can improve local service delivery by better coordinating planning and budgeting for service delivery. They have greater autonomy to manage their finances than in the predevolution system where both deconcentrated districts' offices and local authorities had far more circumscribed authority over financial management than counties did.

County planning and budgeting

Under devolution, how and on what basis are counties allocating resources for service delivery? Is the process sound, and does it lead to budgets that underpin adequate access to services and good-quality services? The degree to which this has been the case is varied.

Improvements in service delivery are often not commensurate with increased resource allocations for public investment. Stakeholders lack adequate capacity and access to relevant information on budgets, service delivery, and public investments, which undermines effective decision-making and accountability for the use of those resources. The National Treasury has prepared public investment management (PIM) guidelines and manuals and initiated the development of an automated system titled Public Investment Management Information System (PIMIS). A stocktaking exercise of national government projects has commenced, and the adaptability of the PIM guidelines and manuals to various sectors is planned. The rollout of PIM to counties will be informed by this process, but timelines for this have not been provided. Support will be provided for this on a pilot basis (including capacity building to both the national agencies and counties) through the Kenya Accountable Devolution Program.

A comprehensive framework for county planning and budgeting has also been established through the County Governments Act 2012, the Public Finance Management Act 2012, and associated regulations. As outlined in box 4.3, these prescribe in detail the processes and documents for planning and budgeting—from a five-year County Integrated Development Plan, Annual Development Plans, County Fiscal Strategy Papers, and annual program-based budgets to County Budget Review and Outlook Papers (CBROPs).

Counties are also required to establish participatory planning processes. The regulatory framework also includes "fiscal responsibility" principles that guide resource allocation and spending at the county level. At a basic level, counties are planning and budgeting for a wide range of service delivery functions and thus taking on, *grosso modo*, their constitutionally mandated responsibilities.

Counties are fully responsible for their own budget processes and have extensive autonomy to manage their finances. Counties enjoy almost full discretion over resource allocation within the broad parameters set by the national government. Budget processes at the county level mirror the system at the national level, where there is full separation between the Executive (the governor and the county executive committee or cabinet) and legislature (the County Assembly).

BOX 4.3

County fiscal responsibility principles (for resource allocation and spending)

- Recurrent expenditure shall not exceed total revenue.

- Over the medium term, a minimum of 30 percent of the budget, and of actual expenditure, shall be allocated to the development expenditure.

- Expenditure on wages and benefits for its public officers shall not exceed a percentage of the county government's total revenue as prescribed by the County Executive member for finance in regulations, and approved by the County Assembly, and this shall not exceed 35 percent.

- The approved expenditure of a County Assembly shall exceed the lower of either 7 percent of total county revenues or twice its personnel emoluments.

Source: Public Finance Management Act (No. 18 of 2012), s. 107(2); Public Finance Management (County Government) Regulations, 2015, reg. 25(1).

Although the county executive prepares the various county plans and budget documents, the County Assembly approves those budgets and provides oversight of county spending (table 4.3).

Counties have used much of their autonomy to good effect; they have increased allocations to education, health, and urban services by over 50 percent between FY2014/15 and FY2017/18 (figures 4.7 and 4.8). Even though some believe that counties spend considerable resources on road construction projects, their spending on works, infrastructure, and information and communication technology (ICT) make up only the third-ranking sectoral share of county expenditures. This typically represents slightly more than 10 percent of county spending and expenditure and only a 10 percent increase in budget allocation during the same period. County health services, which is the largest county service delivery function, accounts for about 24 percent of county expenditure.

Issues with county budgets

Although counties are more or less following prescribed planning and budgeting steps, there are clearly aspects of county-level resource allocation processes that could and should be improved to strengthen service delivery.

Structural deficiencies

County budgets are not of sufficient quality to effectively show what should be and is achieved with the allocated funds and are thus not connecting spending to results as intended. A range of deficiencies compromise the utility of county-level program budgeting as currently practiced (box 4.4). For example, salaries are typically allocated to administrative or support services budgets rather than being tied to service delivery. Budgets also do not provide specific allocations to facilities and geographical areas within counties. This makes it hard to judge whether resources are well allocated or whether the desired

TABLE 4.3 **County budget cycle in Kenya after devolution**

ANNUAL TARGET DATE	ACTIVITY
August 30	**County Budget Circular Issued** • Budget Circular is issued by the CEC-MF from each county. • The Budget Circular must outline procedures for inviting the public to participate in the process.
September 1	**County Integrated Development Plan Submitted** • The CEC-MP submits the Development Plan to the County Assembly (CA) for approval. • A copy of the plan is sent to the CRA and National Treasury (NT).
September 30	**CBROP Submitted** • The County Treasury (CT) prepares and submits the C-BROP to the CEC. • CEC must review and approve the C-BROP within 14 days of submission.
December 31	• CRA makes recommendations on revenue sharing (vertical and horizontal).
February 28	**C-FSP Submitted** • The CT prepares and submits the C-FSP to the CEC, allowing enough time for review and approval before submission to the CA by February 28. • The C-FSP is submitted to the CA for approval by February 28. • The CA must review and adopt within 14 days of submission.
February 28	The CT submits the county's debt management strategy to the CA.
April 30	**Budget Estimates Submitted** • The CEC-MF submits the budget estimates to the CEC for approval before submitting it to the CA by April 30. • Budget estimates must be submitted with all supporting documents and draft bills. • The CEC-MF, with approval from the CEC, submits the County Finance Bill to the CA, which sets out the revenue-raising measures for the county government, together with a policy statement expounding on those measures. • The CEC-MF prepares and presents comments on the budget estimates (by May 15).
June 15	The CG prepares and submits annual cash flow projections for the county to the CoB with copies to the IBEC and NT.
June 30	**Budget Estimates Approval** • The CA considers budget estimates and approves them, with or without amendments, in time for the relevant appropriation law or laws required to implement the budget to be passed by June 30. • The CA approves the Finance Bill by June 30 of each financial year.
June 30	• The CA approves the budget estimates and passes the Appropriation Bill. • After approval of the budget, the CEC-MF is expected to consolidate, publish, and publicize the budget within 21 days.

Source: World Bank 20202b.
Note: CA = County Assembly; CBROP = County Budget Review and Outlook Paper; CEC = county executive committee; CEC-MF = CEC Member for Finance; CEC-MP = CEC Member for Planning; C-FSP = County Fiscal Strategy Paper; CG = County Government; CoB = Controller of Budget; CRA = Commission on Revenue Allocation; IBEC = Intergovernmental Budget and Economic Council.

FIGURE 4.7

Average sectoral shares of county expenditures, FY2014/15–FY2017/18

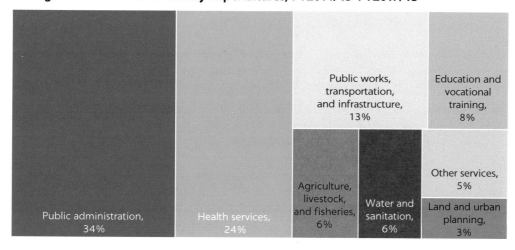

FIGURE 4.8

Change in sector allocation of county expenditures, FY2014/15–FY2017/18

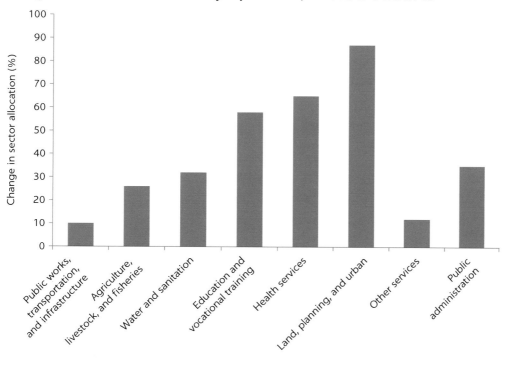

results are commensurate with the level of spending. The indicators used often relate to inputs rather than outputs (for example, "number of livestock feed centers established," rather than "number of farmers using livestock feed centers").

BOX 4.4

Weaknesses in the structure of budgets at the county level

County budgets are not able to answer four simple budgeting questions: What services are funds being spent on? Where are resources being spent? What are the resources allocated to service delivery facilities? What are the results of spending on services? These are discussed below.

The potential advantages of program-based budgeting are not yet being realized by counties, because their budgets are not of sufficient quality to relate funding allocations to planned services and the outputs of those services. Since FY2015/16, counties have been required to produce program-based budgets. The objective of this form of budgeting is to reduce the focus on inputs and increase the focus on outputs and outcomes—that is, what is being achieved in spending the funds allocated. However, a review of program-based budgets across five counties demonstrated major problems in how they were formulated, limiting their potential to bring any benefits.

Ministry salary and staffing reports are not program-specific enough. Within ministries, salaries are typically allocated to the administration and support services program and not the sectors, services, and administrative units they are supporting. This means that the budget allocations to the program do not reflect the real costs of service delivery, making it hard to judge whether resources are well allocated or the desired results commensurate with the level of spending. For example, county budgets do not show the allocation of staffing between primary health facilities and hospitals. One county even showed all staffing under the office of the county secretary.

Inconsistent budget formulations make connections to outputs and indicators difficult. There are inconsistencies in the subprograms (and even programs themselves in some cases) used to formulate budget allocations, which do not reflect the levels of service being provided and are not well linked to the outputs of those services. Furthermore, the outputs and performance indicators identified are often inconsistent with the subprograms to which they are assigned. This means it is difficult or impossible to relate the funds allocated to services and the outputs and targets proposed.

Indicators are inadequate for full program assessment. The indicators are not useful for assessing performance along the results chain and informing resource allocation decisions. Many of them relate to inputs, or to internal activities and work processes, and few relate to outputs and the quantity of services consumed by citizens. For example, an indicator for the number of "livestock feed centers established" is provided, but the number of farmers using the service is not. The "number of facilities supplied with health commodities and supplies" is provided, but the information on outpatient visits to health facilities is not. In addition, several departments have an excessive number of indicators. For example, Nairobi's health department has 160 indicators, and Kisumu's agriculture and health departments both have over 60, making it hard to work through which indicators are important for assessing performance and which are more tangential. A prioritized set of standard indicators to measure service delivery inputs, outputs, and quality would help inform decision-making.

Budgets are not facility- and location-specific. Finally, budgets are not structured in a way that enables explicit allocation of resources to service facilities and the location of services. This makes it challenging for counties to ensure an equitable distribution of resources. Salaries, operational, and other funding are not explicitly allocated to service facilities, subcounties, and urban areas. The budget structure does not enable systematic allocation of resources to facilities. Consequently, recurrent budgets do not reflect the geographical distribution of resources within a county for service delivery.

Source: World Bank 2020b.

Excessive focus on capital projects

Moreover, county planning and budgeting processes tend to focus on the selection of capital projects, not on recurrent spending and the delivery of services. This is true of both the executive-managed planning and budgeting stages and the legislative approval process by County Assemblies. In the latter case, scrutiny has focused on which ward-based capital projects to select rather than on the overall allocation of the budget to sectors to improve service delivery.

Elected officials in both the County Executive and the County Assembly often have electoral incentives to prioritize visible capital investments over less-tangible service delivery results. The result is that capital investments and recurrent services (to support those investments) are not effectively planned for, nor is much attention paid to how services are delivered. There are consequences for this inattention. For instance, in the agriculture sector, a focus on infrastructure investments and neglect of the operating budget has caused the quality of extension services to deteriorate in some counties. Similarly, in the rural water sector, the focus on distributing projects across wards is leading to a predominance of inefficiently small projects.

A focus on development spending in certain service delivery sectors may be distorting budget choices in some counties. For example, the requirement to spend 30 percent of the budget on development spending may be leading to poor budget choices in sectors such as health, early childhood development and education (ECDE), and agriculture. Development spending is effectively interpreted as capital spending. Counties are also constructing infrastructure without increasing the recurrent spending needed to operate them; for example, new health facilities are constructed, but no new staff are hired, and the medicines budget does not increase. At the same time, in other sectors that do need important infrastructure investments to expand services (such as water and urban, as discussed below), the 30 percent floor on development spending makes more sense.

The key issue here is that a blanket percentage floor on development expenditure does not make sense, and a more useful way forward would be to establish sector-specific guidelines that consider the characteristics of each sector. In all sectors, however, budgeting and spending guidelines need to encourage counties to allocate and spend more resources on operations and maintenance (O&M).

Inadequate resources for urban infrastructure

Related to the focus on capital spending, conversely, there is evidence that larger, more urbanized counties may not be allocating *enough* resources to urban capital investments because of their other spending needs. In general, urban development requires relatively high amounts of capital expenditure on urban infrastructure—which is not happening under devolution. Instead, county spending has, in general, been dominated by staff emoluments and related costs as well as O&M.

Of the five most urbanized counties (Nairobi, Mombasa, Kiambu, Kisumu, and Machakos), three spent below the average percentage of total expenditure on development in FY2018/19 (figure 4.9). This implies that they are allocating insufficient resources to investments in urban infrastructure. Although conditional grants (such as the KUSP's Urban Development Grant) make an important contribution to spending on urban infrastructure, counties are underspending on capital in urban areas. This does not promote urban development.

FIGURE 4.9

Development budget expenditure as a percentage of total county expenditure in Kenya, by county, FY2018/19

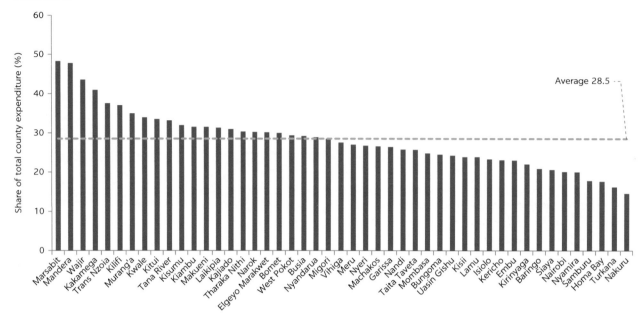

Source: Office of the Controller of Budget, "Annual County Governments Budget Implementation Review Report for FY2018/19."

Budgetary constraints from high salary and administrative spending

Operating budgets are squeezed in counties that inherited a large salary bill, leading to poor-quality service delivery. In FY2018/19, only 16 counties met the fiscal responsibility principle of spending less than 35 percent of total revenues on salaries (figure 4.10).

The inherited staffing structure in many counties has posed a considerable budgetary burden since the beginning of devolution (see chapter 5 on staffing). High payroll budgets continue to crowd out other spending choices and distort sectoral prioritization, providing an incentive to allocate funds to more capital-intensive but low-labor-input services (such as roads and water) and away from less capital-intensive but high-labor-input sectors (such as ECDE and health).

Sector budgets are also squeezed by the large allocations made to county administrative budgets. Spending on public administration is quite high as a proportion of county spending (figure 4.7). Measurement issues notwithstanding, it is the largest county spending category, accounting for over 30 percent of total county public spending. (This is quite high by international standards, since general public services globally average approximately 20 percent of total public spending.)

With over 70 percent of county resources being spent on the top three categories—administration, health, and infrastructure—relatively little remains by way of county resources for each of the other functional mandates assigned to the county level by the constitution. If Kenyan counties could reduce their spending on county administration by 5 or even 10 percentage points, this would free up considerable additional public resources for underfunded areas such as agriculture, water, and other services.

FIGURE 4.10

Public salary expenditure in Kenya, by county, FY2018/19

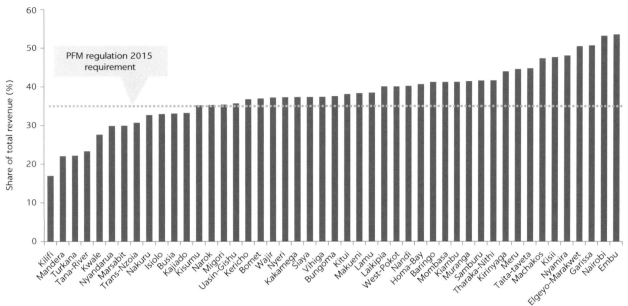

Source: Office of the Controller of Budget, "Annual County Governments Budget Implementation Review Report for FY2018/19."
Note: Under Public Finance Management (County Government) Regulations, 2015, reg. 25(1), counties are required to spend less than 35 percent of total revenues on salaries.

Questionable connections between sectoral spending and needs

Within some sector budgets, there are grounds for questioning decisions about resource allocation. In the health sector, for example, many counties seem to have prioritized curative care over preventive care (figure 4.11). High spending on new and relatively sophisticated equipment and greater numbers of staff in secondary referral facilities also attest to a relatively greater prioritization of curative over preventive and promotive health care. This is inconsistent with the facility construction, which has focused on hospitals over primary health care facilities.

At the same time, the extent to which increased county investments in health facility infrastructure correspond with health sector needs is unclear—given that, in many counties, health facilities serve relatively small populations—or with the county capacity to deploy staff and ensure operational expenditure for the new facilities. Also unclear is how the high priority on purchasing high-end medical equipment is consistent with health sector needs, given that some of this equipment is either not used or is underused (because technically qualified staff are not available and because such equipment is not always required).

Lack of sector-specific standards and expenditure guidance

Counties' sector planning and budgeting is hampered by the lack of sector-specific guidance on how they should budget for, manage, monitor, and report on funding for service delivery. Without clear county sector service delivery standards, results metrics, or sectoral expenditure norms, counties have little support to guide their sectoral expenditure decisions. Existing guidance on budgeting, planning, and financial management is generic even though the

FIGURE 4.11

Average health sector budget allocations in counties in Kenya, FY2019/20

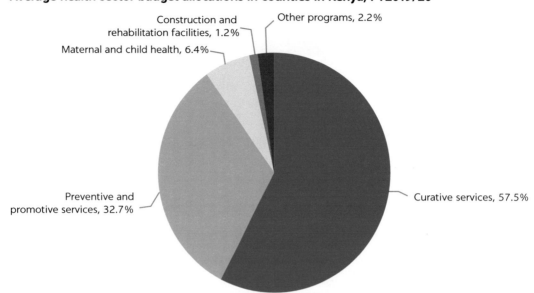

Construction and rehabilitation facilities, 1.2%

Other programs, 2.2%

Maternal and child health, 6.4%

Preventive and promotive services, 32.7%

Curative services, 57.5%

Source: Office of the Controller of Budget, "Annual County Governments Budget Implementation Review Report for FY2019/20."

services and investments in each sector are different and need to be allocated and prioritized in different and sector-specific ways to enable effective service delivery. In the absence of such guidance, counties are left to their own devices, without a grounded framework or set of principles for allocating resources within sectors.

In addition, the participatory planning processes required by legislation are only working effectively in a few counties. These processes are subject to capture and multiple parallel processes, leading to contested outcomes (box 4.5), and they are often driven by investment project prioritization rather than service delivery priorities. One cause of this may be that planning and budget documents are not always made readily available to the public. The challenge ahead is to move beyond the establishment of formal processes and toward improving their quality to ensure that they deliver on their underlying intent—which is to ensure that counties deliver quality services in a responsive manner to their residents.

This lack of sector guidance and weaknesses in participatory processes mean that county expenditure allocations across and within sectors and geographical areas vary significantly and appear to be influenced heavily by political and institutional considerations. In the absence of mature political and administrative processes at the county level, as well as sectoral norms and standards to ensure that resources are put to their best use, it is unlikely that county spending decisions will systematically prioritize public resources between and within sectors to put them to their highest use.

Weaknesses in asset and liability management

As part of the county planning process, it is important that asset management forms an integral part, but counties have typically not managed their assets well, and the transfer of assets and liabilities remains incomplete. County governments need to strategically plan to create or acquire, develop, operate, maintain, refurbish, and dispose of assets.

Participatory planning in public financial management

Participation processes can be problematic and ineffective. The constitution sets out public participation as one of the principles guiding public financial management (PFM). Although officials in all the counties visited during the Making Devolution Work for Service Delivery (MDWSD) study talked about their participatory processes, there was widespread feeling that these processes were not working as effectively as they should and were open to abuse.

County C, for example, struggled with inconsistent preferences being expressed at different stages of the budget cycle and when convened by different actors (for example, when the executive calls for participation in drawing up plans and when the County Assembly calls for input from the public as part of its scrutiny of documents). This was interpreted as the county having "three publics" and that the processes

may be leading to arbitrary outcomes or be vulnerable to manipulation or capture by certain groups.

Even where participation processes work effectively, they still pose challenges to counties. Makueni County provided evidence of an impressive level of ward-level engagement to select projects for the annual development plan. However, some interviewees felt that an annual consultation on ward projects may be excessive. Hundreds of projects are recorded for a single subward, yet only five projects are then selected for consideration in each subward and even fewer funded: "County officials struggle between upholding the constitutional right for participation and the necessity to impose some strategic selection on the overall portfolio of investments" (Moon and Chege 2018).

Source: World Bank 2020a.

Ultimately, asset management is about ensuring provision of adequate and sustainable public services. International experience has shown that good asset management can be a vital catalyst for accelerating urban development and for expanding assets and services in response to increased demand for public services from a rapidly growing population. As shown in Kopanyi and Muwonge (2020), modern asset and liability management (ALM) is not only an urgent need in Kenya; it is also feasible (box 4.6).

County expenditure management

The allocation of resources, however much it may (or may not) support service delivery, needs to be matched by actual spending.

Signs of progress

To that end, it is a significant achievement that the National Treasury's IFMIS has been rolled out to, and is used by, all 47 counties. It is also an achievement that issues with the operating system continue to be identified and resolved.

Overall, county management of public finances appears to be improving over time. The annual audit reports for each county, drawn up by the Office of the Auditor General, indicate a gradual improvement across counties in that the audit opinions are increasingly favorable (figure 4.12). Most county audit reports expressed in FY2013/14 (at the start of devolution) were either adverse or disclaimers. By FY2018/19, however, the majority of county audit reports provided either a qualified or unqualified opinion, indicating that county financial statements are more and more likely to accurately describe county finances.

BOX 4.6

Postdevolution asset and liability management remains incomplete

At the start of devolution, counties immediately took possession of assets, thereby enabling uninterrupted provision of basic services from day one of the transition to a devolved system. However, the transition of county assets and liabilities remains incomplete, as follows:

- Some assets are still left unattended, inherited financial assets are devaluing, and inherited liabilities are escalating, especially for Nairobi City County.
- County governments have not developed asset and liability frameworks, systems, policies, strategies, work plans, and procedures.
- There is incomplete verification, inventory, and registry of strategic assets, and no valuation of main fixed assets (including land, building, and networks) despite the requirements by law and regulations.
- Overall, there is inadequate financing capacity or allocation for development and maintenance of assets.

This situation is slowly changing. The National Treasury has established a National Assets and Liabilities Management (NALM) department, which is responsible for leading the strategic thinking and direction of managing assets and liabilities. The department has drafted an asset and liability management (ALM) policy and guidelines to support county governments. The NALM department is working in collaboration with the Intergovernmental Relations Technical Committee (IGRTC) to provide guidance to county governments on managing their assets.

Whereas the Transition Authority's model of asset transfer did not succeed, in 2017 the asset transfer by power of law (Legal Notice No. 858 and 2701) took place. Through technical assistance (TA) supported under the Kenya Accountable Devolution Program (KADP), the NALM department and counties are receiving support to develop asset and liability frameworks, systems, policies, strategies, work plans, and procedures. The KADP also provided TA to the IGRTC, leading to the preparation of the legal notice that directed the immediate transfer of assets owned by the defunct local authorities. In addition, County Asset and Liability Committees (CALCs) were established to assist in documenting county assets, a process that had proved cumbersome during the TA. The CALCs did decent but incomplete work.

Much more remains to be done. At the national level, the NALM department will require empowerment to start managing public assets as a regulator, guide, and as last-resort custodian of all public assets. In addition, it is important that the NALM policy, guidelines, and templates are approved and implemented. The NALM department will have to work closely with the IGRTC and other stakeholders to guide and capacitate counties on ALM systems and procedures. And the National Treasury will have to develop and implement a national program for the workout of inherited financial assets and liabilities and how these will be managed and settled.

Source: Kopanyi and Muwonge 2020.

Although counties are executing their budgets, the quality of spending is still an issue. Apart from the first year of devolution, average county budget execution has been fairly stable at about 80 percent. As discussed further below, however, execution of the capital budget has been much lower (at about 65 percent) than recurrent budget execution (of about 90 percent). Figure 4.13 shows budget execution rates across salary, operation, and development expenditure.

A key concern before devolution was that counties in marginalized areas might not have the absorptive capacity to spend the additional funds allocated to them through the equitable share formula. However, these fears have not been borne out, and counties with larger development budgets (per capita and as a

FIGURE 4.12

Decomposition of OAG audit opinions on county financial statements, FY2013/14–FY2018/19

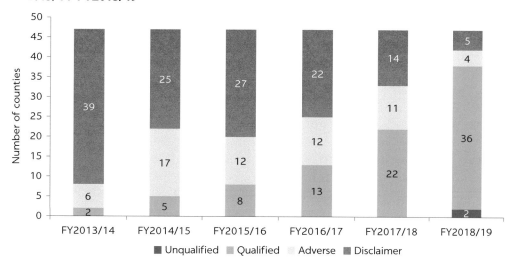

Sources: Annual Capacity and Performance Assessment Reports 2017–19, Kenya Devolution and Support Program (KDSP), Ministry of Devolution and ASALs, Republic of Kenya.
Note: ACPA = annual capacity and performance assessment; OAG = Office of the Auditor General.

FIGURE 4.13

Counties' budget execution rate, by type, FY2016/17–FY2018/19

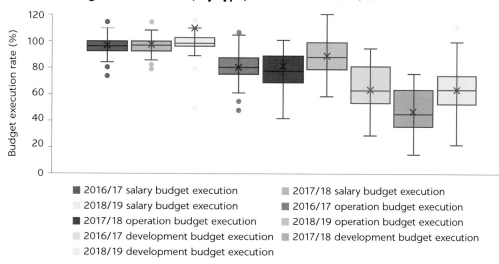

Source: World Bank calculations from BOOST dataset and Controller of Budget data.
Note: Each box shows the distribution from the 25th to 75th percentile; thus, half of the counties lie within the box. The horizontal line crossing each box shows the median, and the X shows the mean. The whiskers represent the rest of the data, with outliers shown separately as dots.

share of the county budget) are executing them more reliably. This suggests that counties have managed to rapidly put in place the staffing and systems to spend allocated funds. This is a major achievement, as failure to do so would have undermined one of the driving objectives of devolution—to better equalize access to services across Kenya.

A further success is that counties receiving higher allocations of the equitable share have used them to increase the number of staff to deliver those services. (For further discussion, see the section on staffing in chapter 5 of this report).

Persistent challenges

The downside to county expenditure management is that budget execution rates are highly unstable in many counties. Figure 4.14 shows these rates by county across FY2014/15–FY2018/19, with counties ordered by the standard deviation of their budget execution rates.

There are large differences in execution rates across counties but also large differences in the execution rates across years in the same county. The counties to the left of the figure spend a similar proportion of their budget each year, while those to the right perform very differently in different years. This instability in spending suggests weaknesses in PFM and is not likely to be conducive to the smooth running of public services if the funding available from year-to-year is fraught with uncertainty—meaning that sectors cannot plan on a sound basis. Development budget execution is the key driver of the variation.

Development budget execution rates are significantly lower and more unstable than salary and operating budget execution. Delays in the release of the equitable share do not explain variations in execution rates between counties, suggesting that some counties are coping with these late releases better than others. Even in years when the late release of the equitable share was not a major factor, development budget execution has been much lower, and much more variable, than overall budget execution.

Salary budget execution, on average, was close to 100 percent across all years and had low dispersion across counties. Operating budget execution averaged about 85 percent in FY2014/15 and FY2015/16, dropping slightly to 80 percent in

FIGURE 4.14

Budget execution rates, by county, FY2014/15–FY2018/19

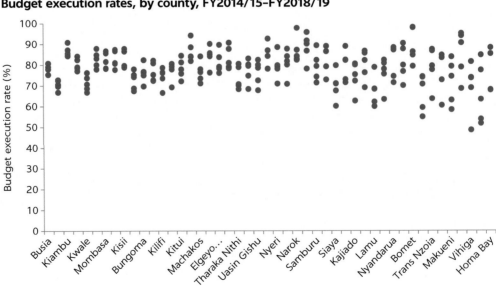

Source: World Bank calculations from Controller of Budget data.
Note: Each dot indicates the budget execution rate in a given year for each county. Counties appear in order (left to right) of the standard deviation of their budget execution rates.

FY2016/17. Development budget execution, however, averaged only about 65 percent across all three years and was more widely dispersed. In FY2017/18, because of late releases of the equitable share, the average development budget execution dropped to 47 percent.

The drivers of poor development budget absorption are not well understood. None of the commonly advanced reasons for the underperformance of development budget execution—such as delayed releases from the national government, cumbersome procurement processes, high personnel expenditures, underperformance of local revenue collections, and IFMIS connectivity—explains the variation in execution rates across counties and across years. The county public expenditure and financial accountability (PEFA) assessments conducted in 2018 in six counties, however, do suggest some reasons for the variation in county budget execution: fluctuations in revenue collection, monthly declarations on settlement of pending bills, stock of expenditure arrears, and limitations on in-year resource reallocations.

Manual exchequer processes also delay the transfer of funds from national to county governments. Once the equitable share has been released by the National Treasury to the County Revenue Fund (CRF), the current process involves each county manually requesting the Controller of Budget to approve individual requisitions for payments. These approved requisitions are then submitted to the Central Bank of Kenya (CBK) to honor. This process is cumbersome and extremely time consuming. Although some counties prepare this documentation in advance to save time (for example, Nakuru and Kwale), the manual process is still extremely slow. The National Treasury, Controller of Budget, and CBK have begun to automate this process, starting with the national government entities, and subsequently rolling it out to counties.

Poor cash management practices have also hampered service delivery. Sector departments do not reliably receive their operating budget allocations. Administrative county departments such as the Governor's Office, County Assembly, and county administration have higher operating budget execution rates than service delivery departments. From a sector department perspective, this situation leads to unpredictable and delayed access to operating budgets, the reasons for which are not well understood. Subcounty sector offices and frontline service delivery units have been affected by a further issue of concentration or resources and decision-making over resources at the county headquarters "recentralization within decentralization" and are not receiving operating funding on a reliable basis.

Furthermore, decisions for allocation of cash are centralized, and cash in many counties is not transferred to health facilities. Whereas all health facilities used to receive funds directly, now many hospitals and health centers do not receive a reliable flow of funds. Similarly, in the urban sector, decisions and financing are constrained by the tensions not to decentralize further beyond the County Treasury and urban department and to allow space for the newly established urban boards and committees to perform. These issues are also discussed chapter 3, on county management of service delivery. In addition, the incentive for health facilities to collect user fees is undermined by the requirement to transfer collections to the CRF, since facilities are not confident that those funds will be remitted back to them.

County budget reporting

County budget reporting is taking place. Counties are producing County Budget Reviews and Outlook Papers (CBROPs), as required by the Public Finance Management Act 2012. At the national level, the Controller of Budget provides quarterly and annual reports on county budget implementation. As with progress on county budgeting and planning processes, it is a significant achievement that these processes have been implemented within the first five years of devolution. However, as with county planning and budget processes, the focus now needs to be on improving the quality of reporting (particularly relating to service delivery outcomes).

Despite their progress, counties are not reporting on the results of their spending, and many sectors do not have functioning management information systems to support this. The basic idea behind program budgeting is that it should require counties to forecast and report not just on spending but also on the results being achieved with that spending. This is not currently occurring, because few counties are reporting against the indicators and targets that they set in their program budgets. Service delivery results are not routinely included in CBROPs, some of which do not discuss any detail of spending by county departments. Even if this were done, its usefulness would depend on the quality of the indicators included and the reliability of the data. Here, there is a clear role for the national government to set standards and systems for indicators and data collection.

In addition, county reports do not provide comparable expenditure data on county functions to support policy analysis and development. There is no common departmental structure across counties and so no common basis for comparing public expenditure on subdepartmental functions. This makes it hard to compare spending data across counties, thus hampering policy analysis of aggregate expenditures and spending across counties.

The accuracy and consistency of county expenditure data also vary between various sources, making it difficult to analyze and make conclusions about county spending. There are inconsistencies between data collected by the Controller of Budget and county reporting through IFMIS. While these differences are relatively small at the aggregate level, they can be large for individual counties and types of expenditure. The lack of a standard, authoritative dataset for county expenditure is a concern if different conclusions can be drawn for individual counties from the two datasets.

Oversight of county public financial management

Counties are largely complying with fiscal responsibility principles. Looking at the requirement to spend at least 30 percent of their budget on development, in FY2016/17 all but one county budgeted at least 30 percent of their budget for development, and all but two in FY2017/18 (figure 4.15).

National oversight bodies are effectively scrutinizing county spending. The Controller of Budget has refused to release funds when counties have not complied with the rulings of oversight bodies or when counties have tried to spend on areas it does not consider to be permitted by legislation.

Unfortunately, however, counties are not effectively tapping into some of the available technical support from key oversight institutions. As provided in the Public Finance Management Act 2012, institutions such as the CRA provide

FIGURE 4.15

Development budget expenditure in Kenya, by county, FY2017/18

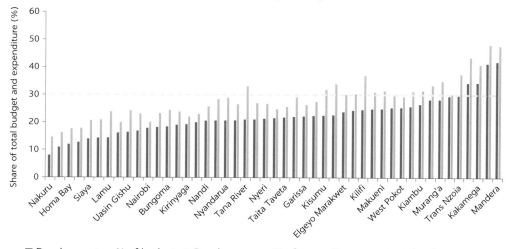

Source: World Bank calculations from Controller of Budget data.
Note: The "30% development target" refers to a requirement under the Public Finance Management Act 2012 that counties spend at least 30 percent of their budgets on development.

advice to the Senate on the allocation of revenue. The same law required counties to seek and consider the views of the CRA when preparing the County Fiscal Strategy Paper. However, few counties are doing this, missing the opportunity for independent technical input into their spending plans.

Similarly, the potential to use intergovernmental bodies to identify opportunities, address constraints, and build capacities for counties has not fully been used. IBEC functions effectively, especially relative to other sector bodies. However, it focuses almost solely on crisis management during the division-of-revenue process and does not effectively cover the broader range of fiscal and PFM issues that need discussion across national and county governments.

CONCLUSIONS

The key theme running throughout this chapter is that the establishment of a solid framework for fiscal devolution and for basic PFM functions and processes has been a major success. National fiscal resources are being shared between the national and county levels and distributed among counties in ways that are favorable to poorer and more disadvantaged regions. Counties have been able to put in place basic planning, budgeting, and expenditure management arrangements, enabling service delivery.

The challenge now, however, is to improve their quality to ensure that these frameworks and processes are effectively supporting improved service delivery. The financing of service delivery at the county level could be better, both in terms of the amounts allocated and the ways in which allocations are made across counties. OSR mobilization by counties has been weak. The quality of budget and expenditure processes has varied considerably. Resources are being allocated but not always in optimal ways. Use of resources has been moderately satisfactory but could be much more effective and efficient. In all, the ways in which counties allocate and use their resources to provide services is deficient and could be greatly improved.

Table 4.4 provides a summary assessment for fiscal devolution and for county-level resource allocation and use. Roughly speaking, the performance has been neutral-to-negative, indicating considerable room for improvement—and thus scope for improving service delivery.

TABLE 4.4 **Summary assessment of financing service delivery and county allocation and use of resources**

AREA	WHAT HAS WORKED	WHAT COULD BE WORKING BETTER
Expenditure assignment and vertical sharing of resources	• Counties are being allocated resources for basic service delivery. • Functional assignments to counties are largely in line with subsidiarity.	• The national share has been growing relative to the county share and may be disproportionately high. • A relatively high share of sector expenditure relative to functional assignments are made at the national level, especially in water and agriculture.
Revenue assignments	• Counties have been assigned own-source revenue (OSR).	• County efforts to mobilize OSR have been weak. • Counties have had limited incentives to mobilize OSR.
Intergovernmental transfers	• Allocations to counties are made ahead of the budget cycle. • Transfers to counties redistribute in favor of poorer and more disadvantaged areas. • Conditional grants have shown the potential to fill sector financing gaps and incentivize performance.	• Delayed release of equitable shares are due to poor national revenue projections and cash management. • Equitable share allocations do not sufficiently consider the service delivery needs of counties, especially those of larger and more urbanized counties. • There is limited reliance on conditional grants, which are fragmented, and a clear strategy for use of conditional grants is also lacking.
Alternative sources of finance	• There is a prudent approach to borrowing.	• Counties lack access to mechanisms for financing large development investments in urban areas.
Allocation of resources at the county level	• A comprehensive framework is established for planning and budgeting. • Counties are autonomous and exercise discretion in resource allocation.	• Budgets are not sufficiently linked to the types and location of service delivery and results. • The budget process is overly focused on capital investment projects. • Some sector budgets allocate insufficient resources to frontline service delivery. • Compliance with development spending thresholds may be distorting resource allocation. • Populous, more urbanized counties cannot allocate enough for infrastructure, and their budget choices are squeezed by large payrolls. • Allocations to service delivery are undermined by high administrative allocations. • Participation by citizens is often poorly structured and prioritizes projects rather than service delivery.
Use of resources at the county level	• IFMIS is operational in all counties. • OAG audit opinions of county finances are steadily improving. • Overall county budget execution rates average about 80 percent. • Counties in historically disadvantaged or marginalized regions are executing their budgets.	• County budget execution rates are unstable. • Development budget execution rates are relatively weak. • Some counties are not releasing budgets to their service delivery departments or delegating spending responsibilities to frontline facilities.

Note: IFMIS = Integrated Financial Management System; OAG = Office of the Auditor General.

NOTES

1. Despite persistent (and not unsubstantiated) criticism that Nairobi County substantially undercollects revenues, Nairobi by itself accounts for roughly one-third of county revenue collections. The top six counties (Nairobi, Mombasa, Nakuru, Narok, Kiambu, and Machakos) account for close to two-thirds of county revenues.
2. The Equalization Fund makes up 0.5 percent of all the revenue collected by the national government each year. Calculated on the basis of the most recent audited accounts of revenue received, as approved by the National Assembly, it was set up to provide basic services including water, roads, health facilities, and electricity to marginalized areas to the extent necessary to bring the quality of those services in those areas to the level generally enjoyed by the rest of the nation, so far as possible. It is an additional revenue source for the identified marginalized areas.

REFERENCES

CRA (Commission on Revenue Allocation). 2012. "Recommendations on Sharing of Revenue Raised Nationally Between the National and County Governments for the Fiscal Year 2012/2013 and Among County Governments for the Fiscal Years 2012/13–2014/15." Report issued August 8, 2012, CRA, Nairobi.

CRA (Commission on Revenue Allocation). 2017. "Recommendation on the Basis for Equitable Sharing of Revenue Between National and County Governments for the Financial Year 2018/2019." Report issued December 18, 2017, CRA, Nairobi.

DI (Development Initiatives). 2018. "Strengthening Subnational Government Own-Source Revenue Mobilisation in Kenya: Progress, Challenges and Opportunities." Report, DI, Bristol, UK.

Kopanyi, M., and A. Muwonge. 2020. "Managing County Assets and Liabilities in Kenya: Post Devolution Challenges and Responses." Unpublished manuscript, World Bank, Washington, DC.

Moon, S., and P. Chege. 2018. "Draft Report on Public Investment Management in Makueni: A Stock-take at the Time of Preparing the CIDP 2018/19–2022/23." World Bank, Kenya Country Office, Nairobi.

World Bank. 2012. "Devolution without Disruption: Pathways to a Successful New Kenya." Report 72297, World Bank, Nairobi.

World Bank. 2020a. "Politics and Accountability Background Study." Background study for this volume, World Bank, Nairobi.

World Bank. 2020b. "Public Finance Management Background Study." Background study for this volume, World Bank, Nairobi.

5 County Human Resource Management

KEY MESSAGES

Overall

- Devolution has resulted in a significant increase in frontline service delivery staff, especially in the harder-to-reach and historically underserved areas across the country.
- Weaknesses in the institutions, policy, and systems for human resource management (HRM) pervasively undermine capacity building, morale, and performance of personnel in many county governments.
- The national government should adopt a strategic, results-oriented, and coordinated approach to delivering capacity-building support to county governments.

Priority Interventions

- Introduce a national institutional framework and a comprehensive and sector-oriented set of principles, policies, norms, and standard procedures in pursuit of meritocratic, efficient, and effective HRM in county governments.
- Provide mechanisms (such as targeted conditional grants) to incentivize counties to establish nationally agreed-upon HRM standards and procedures.
- Install an institutional framework and program for coordinated, strategic, and practical capacity-building support to county governments by national institutions.

IMPORTANCE OF HUMAN RESOURCE MANAGEMENT TO SERVICE DELIVERY IN KENYA'S DEVOLUTION PROCESS

For counties to provide citizens with readily accessible and good-quality services, they need sufficient, appropriate, competent, and properly motivated staff. Sound human resource management (HRM) frameworks and practices ensure that counties can

- Identify service delivery staffing needs (profiles/skills mix, numbers);
- Hire, deploy, and retain competent staff in the numbers needed;
- Provide staff with incentives to sustain and improve their performance; and
- Effectively manage payrolls.

Getting service delivery staffing and HRM right has been challenging—and although some counties appear to have done reasonably well, others have not.

It is also important to bear in mind that the cost of human resources (the wage bill) is often the single largest budget item in every public service delivery system. In Kenya, counties continue to increase staff in the local public sector. By 2018, total employment in county governments was estimated at about 180,000, or more than 20 percent of total public sector employment. County governments have had by far the highest rate of growth in aggregate employment in the public subsector as a whole—an annual average of about 18 percent over the 2013–18 period, compared with about 5 percent for the aggregated public sector over the same period.

Despite some of these individual county efforts, by and large, the lack of public service restructuring means that the wage bill remains high in some counties and thus crowds out other spending (such as operations and capital). In fiscal year (FY) 2018/19, only 16 counties met the fiscal responsibility principle of spending less than 35 percent of total county government revenues on salaries (as shown in chapter 4, figure 4.10).

For the most part, new hiring is not a key driver of high wage bills as a proportion of total expenditure, because the counties that have hired the most are those with the fiscal space to do so. Although the correlation is weak, counties with high salary expenditure as a share of total expenditure are on average those with low employment growth and where the inherited staffing structure has posed a considerable budgetary burden since the beginning of devolution. Some of the largest wage bills are found in counties with below-average equitable share grants per capita (such as Baringo, Embu, and Nakuru), where new recruitment has been constrained.

COUNTY STAFF SIZE, TYPES, AND PRESENCE

Counties have generally increased staff in the local public sector, particularly the staff serving harder-to-reach and historically underserved populations. Before devolution, far-flung rural areas, especially in the arid and semi-arid lands (ASALs), were discriminated against in the supply of frontline service delivery personnel. County governments in these areas have increased the staffing of service delivery facilities—such as health centers and early childhood development and education (ECDE) centers—including those built since devolution.

Growth in county staff

Figure 5.1 shows the growth in county employment since FY2015/16 as a proportion of the current (FY2019/20) total. While most counties have added staff since the start of devolution, increases have been especially notable in the ASALs, such as Garissa, Mandera, and Wajir Counties. These increases in staffing reflect the extent to which counties are responding to demand for services as well as the increased funding available at the county level.

FIGURE 5.1

Growth in county employment on regular payroll since FY2015/16 as a share of FY2019/20 total, by county

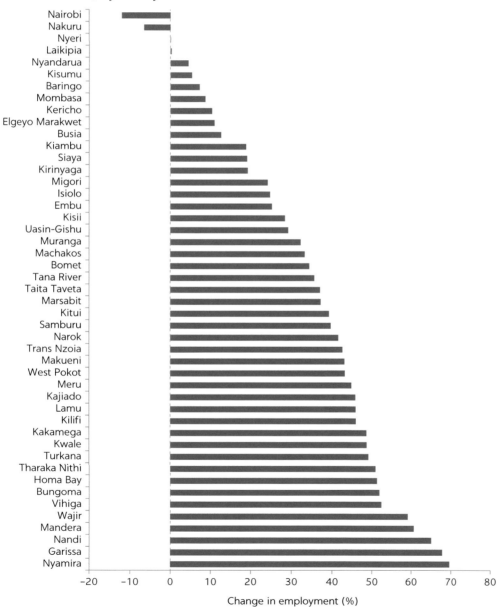

Source: Office of the Controller of Budget, annual county government budget implementation review reports, FY2015/16 to FY2019/20.
Note: County employment growth in Laikipia and Nyeri Counties was less than 1 percent.

The growth in salary expenditure since FY2014/15 is positively correlated with the size of the equitable share grant per capita, which is higher in poorer and more disadvantaged counties (figure 5.2). Counties receiving larger equitable shares per capita have, on average, been able to increase their wage budgets more rapidly through new hiring. Counties that have received greater per capita funding through devolution have thus been able to increase their workforces. These counties also tend to have a younger staff profile. In contrast, in those counties where the equitable share per capita is particularly low, the increase in salary expenditure has barely grown—and in the case of Nairobi, it has fallen.

Additional hiring has increased the frontline service delivery staff in the health sector (figure 5.3). In Garissa County, for example, the total number of doctors increased from 3 to 45, and the number of nurses and clinical officers rose from about 300 to more than 500 between 2013 and 2018. There has also been a general staff increase in county-managed health sectors, with employees increasing by 72 percent in Kilifi, 42 percent in Kwale, 28 percent in Makueni, 13 percent in Kisumu, and 5 percent in Nyeri.

In the devolved education subsector, the number of trained ECDE teachers increased by 54 percent between 2010 and 2018, from 73,012 to 112,703 (figure 5.4). However, the number of untrained teachers declined by 51 percent, from 21,418 to 10,452, within the same period.

The rapid rise in number of trained teachers may be attributed to Teachers Service Commission (TSC) regulations that all teachers be trained and registered.[1] The recruitment of only TSC-registered ECDE teachers by county governments has also motivated more untrained teachers to seek ECDE training opportunities.

In contrast to the education and health sectors, county-level agriculture staffs have declined since devolution owing to rationalization and attrition.

FIGURE 5.2

Correlation of growth in county salary expenditure since FY2014/15 with equitable share funding per capita in FY2018/19

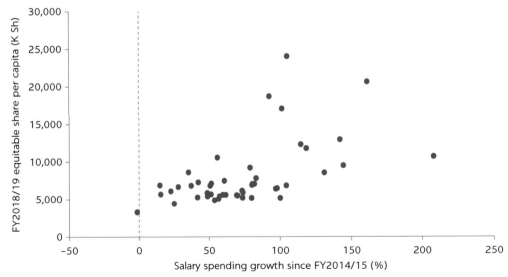

Source: Office of the Controller of Budget, annual county government budget implementation review reports, FY2014/15 to FY2018/19.
Note: Each dot designates a county.

FIGURE 5.3

Total number of health sector employees in six counties in Kenya, 2013–18

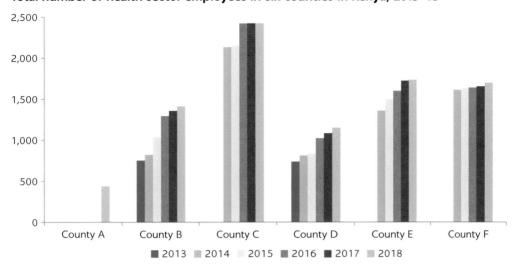

Source: National Human Resource Information System (HRIS) database.
Note: County A did not have up-to-date Human Resources for Health data in the National Integrated Human Resource Information system (NIHRSS) except for 2018. The NIHRSS did not have 2013 data for Counties C and E, and F did not have any data.

FIGURE 5.4

Number of trained and untrained ECDE teachers in Kenya, 2010–18

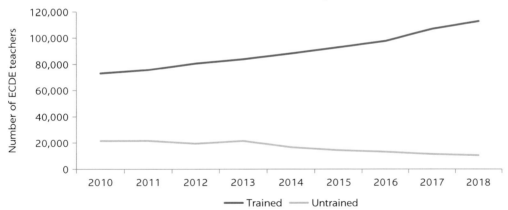

Source: Kenya National Bureau of Statistics (KNBS) Economic Surveys, 2010–19.
Note: Early childhood development and education (ECDE) teachers work in ECDE centers across the country, which enroll children aged four to five years.

County governments inherited national government staff who were working at the district level at the time of devolution. Many of the staff in the sector are approaching age 60 and will retire then.

In Kilifi County, for example, 40 percent of the agriculture staff will leave employment within five years (by 2024) upon attaining the retirement age of 60, and another 18 percent will follow in the subsequent five years (figure 5.5). Since devolution, the county has only managed to hire about 3 percent of the sector's total staff. A key challenge remains the lack of a clear succession plan to ensure that the older, more experienced staff can train the newer staff to ensure that

FIGURE 5.5

Years to retirement for agriculture staff in Kilifi County, Kenya, 2019

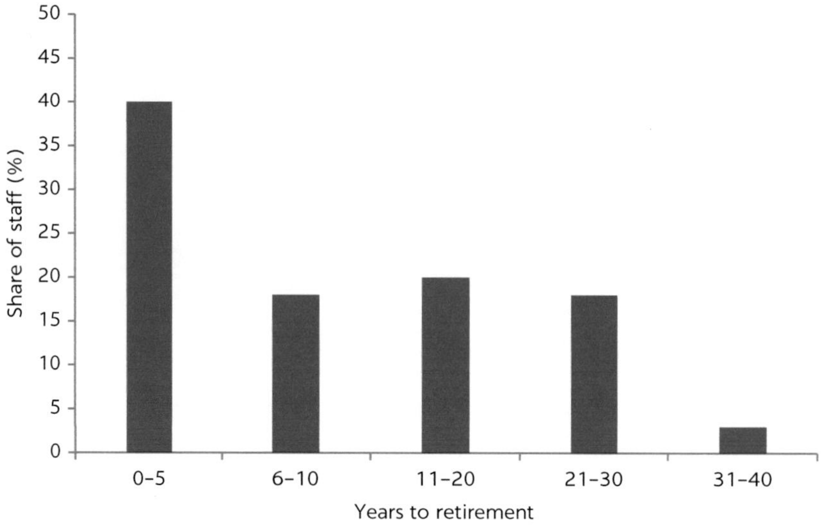

Source: World Bank 2020a.
Note: The retirement age is 60 years in Kenya.

services are delivered to the expected level. What is true of Kilifi is probably true of some other counties.

Changes in types of staff

At the same time, many counties may face shortages of frontline service delivery because they have favored the recruitment of more administrative and nontechnical staff. Poorly planned and prioritized recruitment results in too many administrative (rather than service delivery) staff being hired in some counties.

Administrative staff growth. Some data suggest that the imbalance of administrative to service delivery staff has affected many counties. In 2016, administrative staff averaged 56 percent of all county public service employees, and in 30 out of 47 counties they exceeded 50 percent (figure 5.6).[2] The administrative share is high even in counties with substantial new hiring, such as Mandera, Turkana, and Wajir.

In sectors such as agriculture and urban development, there are indications that administrative (rather than technical) staff are hired (or retained) more often and in greater numbers. This has almost certainly compromised the quality of some services.

Technical versus nontechnical staff. In the agriculture sector, new staff hiring since devolution has increased the proportion of nontechnical staff compared to technical staff at the county and subcounty levels. Positively though, the proportion of technical staff has increased at the ward level (figure 5.7).[3] The extent to which county and subcounty units in the agriculture sector are less and less technical may well be problematic in terms of wider sector decision-making as well as the support provided to ward-level staff.

Frontline versus higher-level staff. In certain sectors, staffing may become insufficient for frontline delivery purposes because more staff are employed higher up the service delivery chain. In the health sector, for example, counties

FIGURE 5.6

Decomposition of public service employees of counties in Kenya, by broad sector, 2016

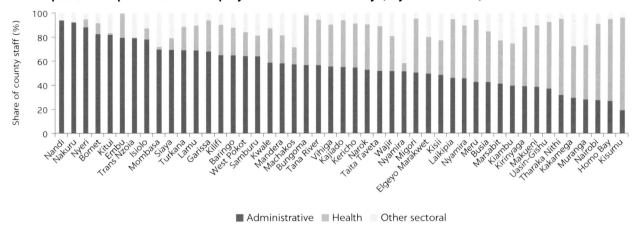

Source: World Bank 2020d.

FIGURE 5.7

Number of technical and nontechnical agriculture staff in Kenya, by jurisdictional level, 2013 and 2019

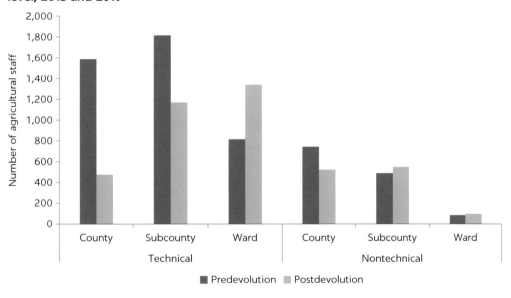

Source: World Bank 2020a.

have many more staff employed in the secondary referral facilities than in primary health care centers (figure 5.8). This mirrors a greater prioritization of curative (as opposed to preventive) care—which may result in poorer services and outcomes for much of the population.

In some sectors, however, frontline staffing has been strengthened (relative to county headquarters or subcounty offices). In agriculture—and despite an overall decrease in staffing since devolution and a growing number of nontechnical staff—there has been a greater shift toward increased ward-level staff, who are in close contact with rural producers (figure 5.9). Although overall technical staff

FIGURE 5.8

Distribution of health sector employees in Kenya case study counties, 2019

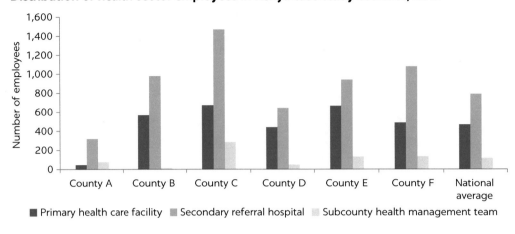

Source: World Bank 2020c.

FIGURE 5.9

Distribution of county agriculture sector technical staff in Kenya before and after devolution, by department and jurisdictional level

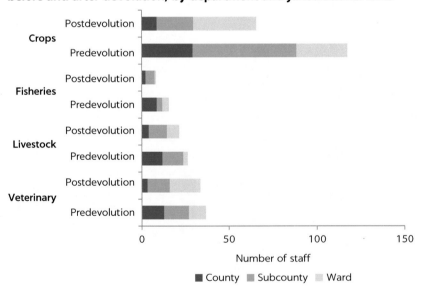

Source: World Bank 2020a.

numbers have declined in the sector since devolution, the numbers of ward-based frontline staff in the crops, livestock, and veterinary departments have increased. On the other hand, fisheries departments now have negligible numbers of frontline staff.

Staff presence in service delivery

Frontline staffing shortages

Despite increased hiring, overall staffing for some service delivery functions remains inadequate. Many counties claim that they lack enough staff for frontline service delivery and that this compromises their ability to deliver accessible, good-quality services.

ECDE teacher-pupil ratios averaging 1 to 28 in 2017 and 2018 (figure 5.10) are beyond the acceptable policy standard of 1 to 25 for many reasons—for example, a focus on infrastructure expansion without thinking of who will deliver the services, and a demand for ECDE teachers outstripping the supply—but this can also be attributed to the personnel expenditure ceilings that limit the options for recruitment. This potentially reduces the quality of ECDE as well as equity in learning.

Similarly, in the health sector, severe staffing shortages continue to be reported across counties. This could be attributed to a number of factors including recruitment limitations due to the budget cap on personnel expenditure. For example, in Seme Subcounty of Kisumu County, the authorized health care staff establishment is 397, but only 76 are in their posts. Of these, only 22 nurses out of the required total of 157 are in their posts.

In addition, blanket restrictions on the proportions of budgets that can be used for various development and recurrent expenditures have sometimes hindered the ideal placement of staff for service delivery in certain sectors. During the key informant interviews for some of the Making Devolution Work for Service Delivery (MDWSD) sector studies, the wage bill ceiling of 35 percent of total county revenues imposed by the broader Public Finance Management Act and regulations was blamed for restraining county governments' ability to hire more staff to close gaps in the priority service delivery. Many county health sector managers, for example, feel strongly that the need to keep payroll costs below the 35 percent ceiling and to ensure that at least 30 percent of the budget is allocated to "development" compromise their ability to take on more staff:

> You know, health worker salaries is currently considered a recurrent cost, but I have always been arguing with my colleagues in treasury that, to the health department, staff are a crucial input to service delivery, and investing in health workers has a longer-term benefit, that we should consider health worker salaries as a development cost. (senior county health department manager, World Bank 2020c)

At the same time, the 35 percent limitation on county wage bills is much less of a constraint in sectors (such as urban or water) where staff numbers are

FIGURE 5.10

ECDE pupils per teacher in Kenya, 2010–18

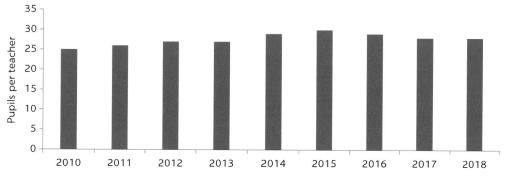

Source: Kenya National Bureau of Statistics (KNBS) Economic Surveys, 2010–18.
Note: Early childhood development and education (ECDE) teachers work in ECDE centers countrywide, teaching children aged four to five years.

somewhat less critical as inputs and where infrastructure development is as important. Moreover, the 35 percent rule does have the virtue of signaling the need to keep payroll spending under control.

The amount of time staff actually spend on their core service delivery tasks remains an ongoing challenge. In the early days of devolution, health worker industrial action and strikes increased because of the early teething problems of devolution, including salary delays and missing allowances. Salary delays for health workers persist in many counties including Bungoma and Vihiga.

High absenteeism

Another issue related to staffing in counties is absenteeism—which can obviously compromise service delivery. High staff absenteeism is an ongoing challenge in the health sector. A late-2018 nationwide survey showed significantly high numbers of health worker absenteeism, averaging 52.8 percent. Among the case counties, Nyeri had an absence rate of 65.0 percent, Garissa (58 percent), Kilifi (60 percent), Kisumu 48 percent), Kwale (51 percent), and Makueni (25 percent) (Ministry of Health and World Bank 2019).

The most significant cause of health worker absenteeism was official or permitted absenteeism, mainly for authorized reasons such as releases to attend short-course or long-term training, annual and maternity leave, and other absences approved by the workers' line managers (figure 5.11). County managers reported increasingly high numbers of Human Resources for Health (HRH) staff (particularly medical doctors) who had been released on paid study leave for long-term in-service training and hence were unavailable in the county to provide service while still crowding the county HRH payroll.[4] There is clearly a need to harmonize training between the national and county governments to address county priorities as well as the artificial shortage arising from the high number of county employees admitted for postgraduate training in relation to service delivery needs.

FIGURE 5.11

Reasons for health worker absence in Kenya, by job cadre, 2018

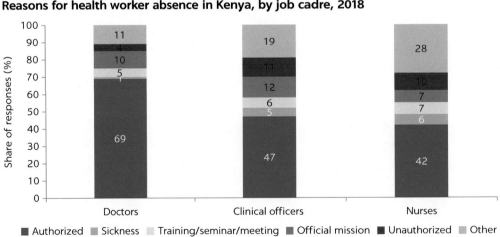

Source: Ministry of Health and World Bank 2019.

Overall trends

The staffing trends in counties reflect several factors. Increased ECDE and health sector staffing, for example, can be attributed to high demand from citizens for these services—and an appropriate and accountable response on the part of county governments. The decline in agriculture sector staffing, on the other hand, seems surprising given that many county economies are predominantly rural, with large farming and livestock-raising populations. This decline may represent either counties' failure to respond to demand or their inability to identify public sector responses to the need for agriculture services.

Meanwhile, budget constraints limit the maximum and absolute levels of staffing that counties can afford, making it difficult for counties to ensure that staffing norms (such as teacher-pupil ratios) are attained. At the same time, the fiscal responsibility limitation on county wage bills (no more than 35 percent of total revenues) may also limit counties' ability to afford enough staff.

Finally, county staffing patterns and practices have suffered from weak HRM systems and support. National sector staffing guidelines have not been available, leaving it to each county to work out what staffing is needed in each sector. At the same time, county governments have not benefited from guidance from the State Department of Public Service on how to authorize legitimate staff absenteeism without compromising service delivery. This is an HRM capacity issue at the county level.

STAFF PERFORMANCE

If service delivery staff are going to provide the public with good-quality services, they need to perform well, have incentives for improving and sustaining their performance, and face sanctions when their performance falls below expectations. In this respect, the postdevolution record at the county level has been mixed.

In a few cases, county administration of promotions, compensation, and incentives has raised morale and standards of performance by employees in basic social services. Before devolution, many employees outside the sector ministries' headquarters in Nairobi suffered discrimination and inordinate delays in securing promotions and other employment benefits. Although some employees still suffer discrimination, county governments have significantly improved the administration of promotions, compensation, and incentives for many employees engaged in the delivery of basic social services (especially in health and education). In Garissa County, for example, the health department offers newly hired staff comparatively attractive end-of-contract gratuities and provides staff with extra incentives such as sponsorship for training. As a result, there is anecdotal evidence that staff morale and performance in service delivery have improved.

Oversight by county executives and legislators has considerably enhanced the effectiveness of demand for performance and accountability on the part of local public servants. Following devolution, citizen engagement and empowerment have enabled service beneficiaries to more effectively alert local political leaders about the gaps in the discipline and performance of county employees.

Local citizens can more readily and effectively reach the county executives and their members of County Assemblies (MCAs) to demand performance and accountability. County government employees in service delivery centers are under continuous local pressure to improve their performance. However, the performance of service delivery staff in many counties is suboptimal for several reasons, as described below.

Low morale from poor HRM. In many counties, HRM has been poor, contributing to low morale. The failure to observe principles of meritocracy in staff appointment and deployment affects staff morale and performance at service delivery centers. In some counties, there is a perception of considerable politicization and patronage in deciding who gets promoted, who gets deployed where, who receives training opportunities, and so on. These decisions affect staff morale, discipline, and performance in the workplace.

Inadequate supervision. The absence of an intercounty transfer framework exacerbates the HRM issues. County staff often complain that their service delivery roles are unclear. Poor management of the county to subcounty to frontline relationship leads to centralization of management at the county headquarters level and unclear management responsibilities. County HRM has also been deficient in performance management (for example, regular appraisal) and career development management (such as staff development, career progression, and succession management schemes).

Poor coordination. County management of staff has been hampered by the fragmentation of county staffing across different types and classes of employees, which has undermined incentives and morale among staff and compounded the challenge of establishing sound HRM systems. Without any generalized cross-county process to create a harmonized structure for county staffing, county governments have a fractured staffing structure, typically consisting of five distinct employee categories, each of which has distinct terms and conditions of service (table 5.1).

County governments also lack effective control of terms and conditions of service for employees inherited from defunct local governments and those seconded from the national government. Legacy collective bargaining agreements confer superior employment benefits to employees inherited from the defunct local government councils.

OVERARCHING HRM FRAMEWORKS

Getting staffing and HRM right implies the need for some overarching institutional frameworks and the availability of support to use them properly. On this, Kenya's postdevolution track record has been uneven.

National structures, mandates, and support

An institutional framework for recruitment and oversight within counties has been established. The County Governments Act 2012 established County Public Service Boards (CPSBs) and County Assembly Service Boards (CASBs) in the executive and legislative arms of county government, respectively, with the mandates to establish and abolish offices, recruit and appoint staff, and enforce discipline of staff. The CPSBs and CASBs have been able to successfully recruit significant numbers of staff to the county public service.

TABLE 5.1 **Categories of staff on county payrolls in Kenya, FY2018/19**

CATEGORY OF STAFF	TERMS OF SERVICE	SHARE OF FY2018/19 COUNTY STAFF (%)
Employees *"inherited"* from the defunct local governments (county, city, municipal, town, or urban councils)	The terms and conditions of service of these employees remain much more attractive than those that the SRC has authorized for other categories of employees.	18
Employees *"seconded"* by the national government following the establishment of county governments	The terms and conditions of service of these staff are based on the national government's employment terms and schemes of service.	37
County public service staff newly recruited through the CPSB or CASB	Terms and conditions of service are specifically authorized by the SRC.	
Employees *"on contract"* with the County Executive or County Assembly	Generally, these types of employees make up the "personal" staff of the governor and speaker of the County Assembly. Although they are placed in job grades authorized by the SRC, in many cases their skills and other competencies are not up to the job grades bestowed by their sponsors.	45
Employees on *"casual or temporary or internship terms"*	This category of employee is often recruited by the executive of the county governments outside of conventional professional procedures, norms, and standards—sometimes on terms and conditions of service that are not aligned with those of other employees of equivalent competencies and responsibilities.	

Source: World Bank 2020d.
Note: CASB = County Assembly Service Board; CPSB = County Public Service Board; SRC = Salaries and Renumeration Commission.

However, this institutional framework for recruitment and staff management is not providing sufficient safeguards to ensure meritocratic recruitment and appointments. The CPSBs and CASBs in many counties have not been effective in this regard and in imposing checks and balances in HRM practices. This is because (1) CPSB and CASB membership is often shaped by political considerations that undermine the members' competencies and professional independence; and (2) the CPSBs and CASBs have fallen prey to political interference, and even blackmail,[5] by county governors and MCAs, respectively. Moreover, the CPSBs have not always relied on competent professionals to assist in the staff recruitment and contracting process, resulting in underqualified and incompetent hires. Finally, the national Public Service Commission (PSC) does not have a constitutional mandate to scrutinize, oversee, or supervise county HRM, CPSBs, or CASBs.

The national government has provided HRM guidance and training for county governments. Ministries, departments, and agencies—such as the PSC, the Ministry of Public Service and Gender (MoPSG), and Kenya School of Government (KSG)—have initiated early programs and projects to build the organizational and HRM capacity of county governments, often within the National Capacity Building Framework (as discussed in chapter 4, box 4.1). Some county governments have benefited from this support to adopt basic HRM policies, systems, and operating procedures, with some degree of success; however, many counties have yet to set up satisfactory HRM policies and systems.

County-level HRM efforts

Some counties have made efforts to restructure or rationalize their workforces and to manage personnel costs. Some counties have policy initiatives to control wage bill growth and improve the value for money of personnel expenditures.

BOX 5.1

Initiatives to improve HRM in Makueni County

Over the past few years, Makueni County has embarked on a wide range of initiatives to develop its HRM system. These initiatives (and their status of completion) include the following:

- A human resources manual for public service (complete), which was developed on the basis of updating a model manual provided by the Ministry of Public Service

- Policies on training and development (complete), recruitment (complete), performance management (drafted), gender mainstreaming (drafted), conflict management (drafted), and sexual harassment (drafted)

- Schemes of service and career progression (in progress), rewards and sanctions (pending), and skills inventory and competencies assessment (pending).

The county also wants to have an automated and integrated HRM information system. (Currently, only the payroll function is automated through the national government's Integrated Payroll and Personnel Database [IPPD] system.) To this end, the county government has sought technical assistance from development partners in pursuit of a strategic, comprehensive, and integrated program to implement a modern HRM information system.

Source: World Bank 2020d.

Some counties have carried out human resource and payroll audits; a few others have frozen new recruitment and taken measures to retrench staff. Box 5.1 outlines how one county has embarked on HRM reforms.

Missing elements

Fundamentally, there is no comprehensive set of standard policies, principles, procedures, norms, and practices to guide county HRM. Although the Ministry of Public Service has developed guidelines for counties to develop and implement HRM policies and systems, these are not sufficiently comprehensive.

Moreover, counties have not been given enough follow-up technical support in the use and application of HRM guidelines, which fail to cover standards and norms for establishment planning; budgeting and control; recruitment and appointments; staff development, appraisals, rewards, and sanctions; and linkage with the national, county, and department vision, with individual staff targets and clear job descriptions.

In addition, there is an absence of *sector-specific* standards, norms, and policy frameworks to guide compensation and staffing structures. There are disparities in staffing and salaries across counties. In the ECDE sector, for example, compensation scales vary from one county to another. A review of the compensation structure for ECDE teachers in the seven case-study counties found it ranged from K Sh 10,000 in Nyandarua County to K Sh 35,000 in Garissa County. Comparatively, the job grading scale for the ECDE teachers is very low compared with the TSC scale for primary teachers—whereby the lowest-paid teacher takes home approximately K Sh 30,000.

These disparities are large and known by teachers across counties. Some variation may be welcome as a consequence of counties responding to different local needs and priorities and adjusting pay and conditions to recruit workers in hard-to-reach and underserved areas. But an absence of sector-specific standards, norms, and policy frameworks makes this hard to evaluate.

Even if comprehensive general and sector-specific HRM norms and standards were in place, there is little evidence that counties would comply with them. No institutional framework is in place to ensure that counties follow nationally agreed-upon HRM standards and procedures. For example, the important recommendations made in the 2015 Capacity Assessment and Rationalization of the Public Service (CARPS) report[6] have never been systematically implemented at the county level. As a result, counties have generally failed to deal with HRM issues such as overlaps in functions, harmonized structures, job grading and compensation, equity in the distribution of scarce skills, and succession planning.

Finally, poor HR data continue to compromise informed decision-making. Decisions on HR planning and budgeting are difficult to make in the absence of complete, accurate, and disaggregated data on employment numbers, service delivery staff distribution, and skills mix in county governments. HR record management systems are underdeveloped, absent, or underused in most counties, and payroll fragmentation and system deficiencies are prevalent.

CAPACITY BUILDING

Capacity building has been something of a devolution mantra—and rightly so. Staff in all county departments need to have the skills and knowledge to plan and budget, to manage public finances, to organize service delivery, and to be technically competent in their respective sectors. Importantly, the Constitution of Kenya of 2010 (in its Fourth Schedule) explicitly recognizes capacity building as an important function and assigns the national government the responsibility for providing counties with capacity-building and technical assistance.

In some areas, capacity building has been effective. Counties have reported, for example, that the national government's capacity-building support has been effective across a variety of key public financial management functions but that there are areas where implementation could still be improved on both the national and county government levels.

To begin with, capacity building is fragmented. It is not well coordinated within and across sectors. As a result, the impact on county institutional and service delivery performance is unclear. The annual capacity performance assessment (ACPA) under the Kenya Devolution Support Program (KDSP) has been established, but it is not used sufficiently to assess cross-cutting institutional capacity-building needs. There are also no sector-equivalent performance assessment processes to identify sectors' capacity-building needs.

Capacity building has also suffered from being too classroom-based and insufficiently practical. County officials want to see less classroom training and more on-the-job support as well as capacity building that is better coordinated across the national government. However, counties also need to improve their management of capacity building by reducing staff turnover so those who are trained are also retained in their posts.

Many of the weaknesses of human resource and performance management in the county governments are also present within the national government. Although the constitution provided that national government agencies would build the capacity of the county governments, the former often lacks the requisite competencies, staffing, and authority to provide counties with appropriate support (box 5.2). Additionally, in the first years of devolution, neither the

BOX 5.2

National government support for county-level ECDE

The early childhood development and education (ECDE) section in the national Ministry of Education (MoE) is understaffed and inadequately financed. It has only three officers against an expected establishment of five officers to support service delivery in the 47 counties. Similarly, while the directorate collaborates with the education unit in the Council of Governors (CoG) to support service delivery in the counties, interviews with MoE officers indicated that the CoG's education department suffers from high staff turnover, affecting implementation of their planned activities.

In addition to human resource challenges, the MoE section is inadequately financed, thus limiting its capacity to coordinate and support ECDE services across the country. The national ECDE section relies heavily on support from donors, which results in delays in the implementation of planned activities due to mismatches between priorities and long approval processes.

Source: World Bank 2020b.

TABLE 5.2 **Summary assessment of county human resource management in Kenya**

AREA	WHAT HAS WORKED	WHAT COULD BE WORKING BETTER
Staffing levels	• Poorer and disadvantaged counties (with higher per capita equitable share allocations) have increased their staffing levels. • Staffing levels in the health and ECDE sectors have risen considerably. • The agriculture sector has significantly more technical staff at the ward level than at the county or subcounty levels.	• Staff numbers remain insufficient relative to norms and standards. • The 35 percent rule (wage bill ceiling relative to total county revenues) may be limiting staffing levels in labor-dependent sectors (such as health). • Agriculture sector staffing levels have declined. • There are increasing numbers of administrative and "back-office" (rather than technical) staff, except in agriculture. • In health, more staff are allocated to secondary referral subsectors than to frontline primary health facilities. • High levels of absenteeism in the health sector are due to poor management of authorized absences (such as for leave and training).
Staff performance	• Greater local accountability for service delivery has strengthened incentives for better staff performance. • Greater staff accountability to local political leadership has strengthened staff performance.	• Politicized appointments and promotions have undermined staff morale. • Fragmented staff structures and payrolls have undermined staff motivation.
HRM frameworks	• A basic institutional framework (CPSBs, CASBs) has been established. • National-level support for HRM has been available. • Some counties have tried to reform HRM.	• HR information management is weak. • Institutional arrangements do not provide for meritocratic HRM. • There is an absence of a guiding framework for norms and standards in general and across sectors. • There is no effective mechanism for oversight of county-level HRM.
Capacity building	• Some capacity building has been provided by the national government.	• Capacity-building support is fragmented. • The national government's own capacity to provide capacity-building support to counties is weak.

Source: World Bank.
Note: CASB = County Assembly Service Board; CPSB = County Public Service Board; ECDE = early childhood development and education; HR = human resources; HRM = human resource management.

leaders of county governments nor the professional and technical employees trusted the national government agencies to effectively support them in capacity building. Consequently, county governments took only limited advantage of the national government's capacity-building initiatives and programs. The overall assessment for county HRM under devolution is shown in table 5.2.

CONCLUSIONS

In striking contrast to public financial management, HRM under devolution appears to have been much less guided by national policy frameworks: When it comes to managing money, counties have been much more inclined to comply with norms and rules. When it comes to managing human resources, on the other hand, counties have enjoyed autonomy without sufficient checks and balances, and they have often not played by generally accepted professional principles, standards, and norms.

HRM in many counties is far from satisfactory—and this constitutes a serious threat to service delivery. Although the situation varies from sector to sector and from county to county, the overall picture is not encouraging for service delivery: many counties have too few technical staff, do a poor job of managing and motivating them, and are recruiting new staff on the basis of considerations other than merit. If these trends persist, county-level service delivery will suffer.

But improving HRM is no easy task. HRM is a complex and sensitive institutional and political process, characterized by a series of highly interconnected elements that must be carefully calibrated with each other to yield the right results. HRM is also highly vulnerable to clientelistic practices and abuses—with ramifications for staff quality, motivation, and performance.

NOTES

1. The TSC is an Independent government commission, established in 1967, with the mandate of registering, employing, disciplining, and paying teachers. It gives teachers one employer and uniform terms and conditions of service ("Brief History," TSC website: https://www .tsc.go.ke/index.php/about-us/brief-history). TSC manages all primary and secondary education, both public and private, but not ECDE (for children age four-to five-years-old), which is a function devolved to the counties.
2. Administrative staff are classified as those with designation codes starting with C, D, T, U, and V.
3. "Technical" staff are those officers with training or experience in crops, livestock, and fisheries and employed to work on those areas. "Nontechnical" staff refers to administrative staff (clerks, secretaries, watchmen, drivers, and the like).
4. Human Resources for Health (HRH) Kenya is a program funded by the US President's Emergency Plan for AIDS Relief (PEPFAR) and US population funds through the US Agency for International Development (USAID) and implemented by IntraHealth International, Inc. The program's purpose is to strengthen human resources for health management systems to achieve improved health outcomes (USAID 2021).
5. Board members often cannot withstand pressure from political leaders and their local or sectional communities to base decisions on patronage. There have been cases where a governor or MCA has threatened a CPSB with budget cuts, delayed cash disbursements, and dissolution in attempts to dictate the board's decisions.
6. CARPS, a joint national government and Council of Governors (CoG) initiative, was carried out in 2015 (Ministry of Public Service and Gender 2016). The CARPS report was adopted by the Council of Governors Intergovernmental Summit in 2016.

REFERENCES

Ministry of Health and World Bank. 2019. "Kenya Health Service Delivery Indicator Survey 2018 Report." Survey report published by the World Bank, Nairobi.

Ministry of Public Service and Gender. 2016. "Capacity Assessment and Rationalization of the Public Service (CARPS): An Inter-Governmental Steering Committee Report to the National Summit." Government of Kenya, Nairobi.

USAID (United States Agency for International Development). 2021. "Human Resources for Health Kenya." Fact sheet, USAID, Washington, DC. https://www.usaid.gov/sites/default /files/documents/HRH_Kenya_factsheet.pdf.

World Bank. 2020a. "Agriculture Sector Background Study." Background sector study for this volume, World Bank, Nairobi.

World Bank. 2020b. "Early Childhood Development and Education Sector Background Study." Background sector study for this volume, World Bank, Nairobi.

World Bank. 2020c. "Health Sector Background Study." Background sector study for this volume, World Bank, Nairobi.

World Bank. 2020d. "Human Resource Management Background Study." Background sector study for this volume, World Bank, Nairobi.

6 Citizen Engagement and Service Delivery

TRANSPARENCY, PARTICIPATION, AND ACCOUNTABILITY

KEY MESSAGES

Overall

- Basic provisions and mechanisms for transparency, participation, and accountability have been established and are, to various degrees, operating at the county level.
- The quality and effectiveness of participation and accountability is mixed and insufficiently focused on service delivery performance.
- For devolution to work for service delivery, a more integrated and institutionalized approach to citizen engagement is required, combined with a greater focus on strengthening the inclusion of minorities and marginalized groups.

Priority Interventions

- A more integrated and institutionalized approach to citizen engagement is needed to improve the quality of public participation.
- Measures that strengthen the inclusion of minorities and marginalized groups need to be implemented.
- Oversight and scrutiny of the County Executives in the delivery of services need to be strengthened, moving beyond their predominant focus on projects.
- Transparent and strategic resource allocation across the county should be promoted to achieve countywide sector service delivery objectives and avoid the fragmentation of resources toward their own wards.

INTRODUCTION

Calls for greater participation, accountability, transparency, and inclusion were central to demands for devolution as part of the 2010 constitutional reforms (Kanyinga and Long 2012). The Constitution of Kenya of 2010 sought to address public concerns over the skewed distribution of development resources and the concentration of power at the center, which had led to "winner takes all" politics. In this spirit, the constitution created a new tier of 47 autonomous county governments, but it also enshrined key principles of transparency, participation, and accountability. It was expected that devolution would bring government closer to the people, increasing the responsiveness of public services through greater citizen engagement as well as giving a voice to groups marginalized from the previous centralized system. However, new devolved systems, governance, and citizen engagement take time and effort and do not emerge overnight.

Whether devolution can deliver on its promise of improving service delivery hinges on the extent to which citizens have access to information on finances and service delivery performance, are empowered to participate in and contribute to decision-making, and have opportunities to hold their executives to account. County governments are more likely to deliver appropriate, accessible, and good-quality public goods and services when citizens can meaningfully inform decisions, scrutinize delivery, and incentivize or sanction good over poor performance.

In principle, devolution means that county governments, as service providers, are more proximate, making it easier for citizens to engage with them and to ask questions of them about what they are doing (or not doing). In practice, the scope, depth, and quality of citizen engagement depend on many factors, including access to accurate information and participatory mechanisms and systems, as well as citizen education and capacity.

There has been good progress putting in place the core laws and systems relating to budget transparency, citizen participation in county planning and budgeting processes, and implementing direct and indirect accountability systems, including elections. County governments have generally improved their compliance with planning and budget transparency requirements over time, with most of them publishing core documents. There has also been progress on participation mechanisms in relation to planning and budgeting, with some counties adopting innovative participatory budgeting as well as involving citizens in implementation through project committees. Furthermore, elections are competitive, and County Assembly (CA) oversight committees that provide horizontal accountability have been established.

The Senate also provides additional oversight with its powers to summon government officials, consider county government audit reports, and receive public petitions. In addition, it decides on the impeachment of county governors—and there have been several impeachment proceedings in the Senate, one of which in 2019 saw a governor impeached on issues that revolved around the management of county finances.

The constitutional commissions and independent offices created under Chapter 15 of the constitution also provide restraint in some areas. For example, the Controller of Budget has to approve county withdrawals from the revenue fund. The Salaries and Remuneration Commission has helped avoid arbitrariness in remuneration of public officers, while the Office of Auditor General has continued to produce audits of national and county governments.

The past two years have also seen a renewed focus on anticorruption efforts. Important institutions in this regard include the investigative agencies, the Director of Public Prosecution, and the judiciary. In addition, the judiciary has also played a role in reaffirming the Bill of Rights—for example, landmark decisions reversing various processes or documents that had not had sufficient public participation. The judiciary has protected devolution and adjudicated many intergovernmental disputes.

There has, however, been less progress on citizen engagement in relation to service delivery performance, and citizen engagement is often fragmented. The lack of accessible and timely information on service delivery performance is particularly notable. Citizens lack basic information on how their counties perform on key service delivery outcomes because the data is unavailable—and when it is available, it is often overly technical and fragmented. Similarly, citizens have few opportunities to participate in monitoring service delivery performance except for some small community scorecards and social audit pilots as well as pilots that encourage decentralization within counties by directly involving citizens in service delivery provision and oversight.

The experience is mixed as to whether the new accountability systems are creating incentives for improving service delivery. At the national level, devolution has arguably contributed to a more inclusive political settlement and helped reduce the stakes of the "winner takes all" politics that was a feature of the previous highly centralized state. There is also some evidence to suggest that the service delivery track record of governors may have contributed to citizens voting out about half of the pioneer governors in the first elections. But elections alone may be insufficient to orient governors and the county executives to improve services for citizens. More direct forms of accountability are not yet effective because of information and capacity constraints. Furthermore, in some counties, devolution could have exacerbated feelings of local-level exclusion among county minorities. There is also the risk that devolution may disproportionately benefit local elites at the expense of less powerful or marginalized groups.

Making devolution work for service delivery requires that all levels of government make a renewed effort to implement the next generation of citizen engagement initiatives—focused on holding counties to account for improving service delivery performances, not just for following rules and making investments. As detailed below, this will require information on outcomes, not just inputs; mechanisms that go beyond consultations on plans and budgets; and tools and increasing capacity that enable citizens to monitor service delivery outcomes. This will require an integrated approach.

CITIZEN ENGAGEMENT AND SERVICE DELIVERY

As noted in this report's analytical framework (see chapter 1), there are three requirements to maximizing the impact of devolution on service delivery and preventing accountability failures that would undermine devolution's promise to improve service delivery: transparency, participation, and accountability, as follows (World Bank 2012, 163):

- *The first element relates to information transparency.* To participate in decision-making and hold counties and service providers to account, citizens need reliable information about government programs, rules and standards, finances, and decision-making. They also need this information in formats that are accessible, timely, and relevant to citizens' needs and priorities.

- *The second element relates to citizen participation* in decision-making and service delivery oversight. Citizens need opportunities to participate in decision-making, articulate their needs and priorities, and provide feedback on service delivery outputs and quality.
- *The third element relates to accountability.* Ultimately county governments and frontline service providers will respond to citizen priorities and feedback if citizens have meaningful opportunities to hold them to account for their decisions and actions, as well as for their lack of action.

These three core elements underpin a virtuous cycle of strengthened citizen engagement and improved service delivery (figure 6.1).

Transparency. Transparent information across the full cycle of planning, budgeting, and implementation, as well as basic information about citizen rights and service delivery standards, is critical to meaningful and effective citizen engagement. This includes information about government plans, budget allocation, fiscal transfers, and service rules and standards, as well as comparative service access and quality metrics.

Transparency and the requirement to regularly publish information on government programs, finances, and performance is usually mandated in legal provisions (such as public financial management [PFM] laws) and in sectoral legislation (such as the Water Act or local government regulations). However, rules and regulations about information transparency are rarely sufficient in themselves in ensuring that citizens have adequate access to information about service delivery. National and local governments also require systems and the technical capacity to systematically collect and distribute this information in formats that are accessible, comprehensible, and timely.

It is often also critical to incentivize compliance by linking the collection and publication of information to fiscal transfers and the annual budget cycle. Civil society and other nongovernmental organizations (NGOs)—such as think tanks, the media, and academia—often play important intermediary roles in analyzing and presenting data in forms that are relevant and salient to ordinary citizens.

FIGURE 6.1

Elements of social accountability systems

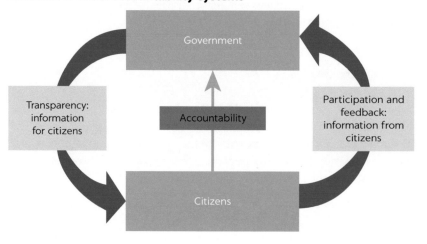

Source: World Bank 2012.

Participation. Although many participatory mechanisms span the full gamut of service delivery, from policy to outcomes, fundamentally they exist to provide an opportunity for citizens to express their needs, priorities, and preferences regarding government and service provider decisions and actions. Participatory mechanisms tend to focus on four stages in the service delivery cycle:

1. The first type of mechanism focuses on policy and project designs in which the objective is to seek citizen feedback and preferences regarding service delivery procedures and standards, project designs, and implementation arrangements, as well as broader development strategies. This mechanism includes public hearings, community consultations, and focus group discussions, as well as written and electronic consultations.

2. The second type of mechanism focuses on planning and budgeting, seeking citizen inputs on service delivery priorities and needs. This includes participatory planning, participatory budgeting, and rapid rural appraisal (RRA) methods as well as citizen committees or juries.

3. The third type of participatory mechanism focuses on implementation and the service delivery itself, including community implementation committees, integrity pacts or committees, and different types of user groups such as parent associations.

4. The fourth type of participatory mechanism focuses on service delivery outcomes, including whether a service delivery facility is operating, or the quality of the services themselves, such as complaint-handling systems, customer-satisfaction surveys, and community scorecards and social audits.

To be effective and fair, all these participatory mechanisms must be inclusive and open to the public, especially to poor and marginalized groups; relevant to citizen needs; and timely.[1]

Accountability. Devolution fundamentally changes the accountability relationships between the different actors and levels of government. Holding government to account for improving service delivery once required citizens to appeal to the national government, often via either members of parliament (MPs) or directly to the president and his entourage (figure 6.2, panel a). The need for citizens to aggregate their grievances and priorities in ways that would capture the attention of these national-level actors invariably required citizens to frame their grievances in local terms or to the use clientelist networks to resolve their complaints (EACC 2013).

There were also sector-level grievance mechanisms. For example, within the water sector before devolution, the Majivoice grievance redress mechanism was implemented by Athi Water Services and Nairobi Water Company. A framework also exists for complaint handling by the Kenya National Commission on Human Rights (KNCHR) (CAJ 2014).

Devolution (and the constitutional reforms more generally) fundamentally changed the accountability structure for service delivery for most services (figure 6.2, panel b). The new devolved governance arrangements effectively shortened the route for accountability and created multiple new formal and informal mechanisms for holding county governments and local service providers to account for service delivery.

The new devolved governance arrangements strengthened upward accountability, created new forms of horizontal accountability, reinvigorated diagonal

FIGURE 6.2

Power and accountability relationships in local service delivery: Centralized versus decentralized service delivery arrangements

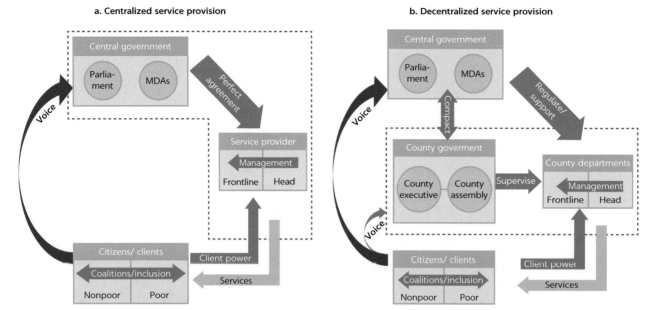

Source: Adapted from World Bank 2003. ©World Bank. Further permission required for reuse.
Note: Elements boxed within dotted lines designate MDAs = ministries, departments, and agencies.

accountability, and enabled new forms of social accountability. Accountability for county-level public services operates in four key ways:

- *Vertically,* through the ability of citizens to voice themselves by directly electing governors, deputy governors, and members of County Assemblies (MCAs) to represent their interests and provide public goods and services
- *Horizontally,* through the role of the County Assembly (CA) in holding the governor and county executive to account
- *Diagonally,* through oversight agencies, such as the Senate and judiciary
- *Varied social accountability mechanisms,* including citizen procurement committees and social audits.

Transparency and access to information

The national government has made significant progress ensuring legal provision of information on county development plans, budgets, and financial reports. The 2010 Constitution lays the foundation by designating access to information as a fundamental right. The County Governments Act 2012, the Public Finance Management Act 2012, and their subsidiary regulations include provisions for citizen access to timely and accurate provision of information on policy, decision-making, budgets, and oversight of service delivery.

These legal provisions require county governments to publish, within seven days of their passage, the County Budget Circular, the County Integrated Development Plan (CIDP), the Annual Development Plan (ADP), the County Budget Review and Outlook Paper (CBROP), the County Fiscal Strategy Paper (CFSP), program-based budgets (PBBs), and quarterly budget implementation reports.

TABLE 6.1 **Number of counties in Kenya that comply with planning and budget transparency requirements, FY2015/16—FY2019/20**

PLANNING AND BUDGETING DOCUMENT	FY2015/16	FY2016/17	FY2017/18	FY2018/19	FY2019/20
Annual Development Plan	4	11	22	25	30
County Budget Review and Outlook Paper	2	6	8	26	—
Program-based budget	—	—	—	6	11
Citizen budget[a]	—	—	6	13	—
Quarterly budget implementation reports	—	—	2	7	—

Source: Biegon and Wambui 2019.
Note: Kenya has a total of 47 counties. — = not available.
a. A "citizen budget" refers to a plain-language, user-friendly simplified version of the county budget that gives the public a general overview of the county's revenue and spending priorities.

County governments have generally improved their compliance with planning and budget transparency requirements. A study by the International Budget Partnership (IBP) Kenya examining the online availability of key planning and budgeting documents by counties has found that more and more counties are making their documents available online every year (Biegon and Wambui 2019). Table 6.1 shows the number of key documents published between FY2015/16 and FY2019/20—indicating that out of 47 counties, 30 publish their ADPs, 26 publish their CBROPs, 11 publish a PBB, and 13 publish a "citizen budget" in the most recent year for which data are available. Some counties publish approved line-item budgets, but these should be as additional supporting documentation and not as substitutes for the approved PBB.

However, citizen communication remains a challenge despite the publication of core financial information and the establishment of citizen communication units and frameworks (further discussed below). Key issues include the "one-size-fits-all" approach to communication, the lack of community segmentation of groups with different needs, and the presentation of information in formats that are often inaccessible to many citizens, as well as the timelines of publication. There is also scope to more systematically use digital technology and social media platforms to share information in accessible formats. This technology is mostly used to distribute information to citizens but is also used to elicit feedback from them (box 6.1).

More fundamentally, there has been little progress in ensuring transparency in the provision of information on service delivery performance, including basic information on access and quality of services by county. The Kenya Open Data portal was developed to consolidate and make accessible core data on service delivery across 10 sectors and all 47 counties. The first county fact sheets are comprehensive, including service delivery and socioeconomic indicators on agriculture, education, energy, finance and planning, forestry, health, land and climate, poverty, security, and trade and commerce, as well as water and sanitation. However, most data are from 2013 or 2014 and have not been updated. Indeed, updates have been sporadic in each sector and, as noted in chapter 2, service delivery performance information is simply not available for many sectors.

The lack of regular information on county service delivery performance fundamentally undermines citizen participation in decision-making as well as the effectiveness of the new accountability structures introduced with devolution. In many instances, citizens interact with budget information for the first time at public forums in formats that are long, technical, and in a language in which not all citizens are necessarily fluent. This is particularly problematic in rural

BOX 6.1

Digital technology and social media: New opportunities for citizen communication

The increasing use of social media and mobile phones are providing opportunities for citizens to engage with county governments on issues of service delivery. All county governments are leveraging social media platforms (such as WhatsApp groups, Facebook, and Twitter) to connect with their residents, respond to feedback, and identify issues that require attention. In some of the counties, governors have Twitter accounts and Facebook pages with hundreds of thousands of followers; at least one governor has about 2 million followers. They use these platforms to respond to criticism, showcase the county's performance, illustrate ongoing projects, or inform county residents about new government policies.

The use of social media platforms is enhanced by mobile phone penetration and growing internet use in the country. The 2019 population census shows that about 47 percent of Kenyans own a mobile phone, including 63 percent of city dwellers and 43 percent of rural residents. Mobile phone ownership increases with age: 86 percent of the population age 25 years and older owns a mobile phone. This is an important figure because this is the group of residents likely to use phones to discuss service delivery accountability. About 23 percent of the population uses the internet, while 10 percent has access to a computer. These figures, combined with ownership of mobile phones, suggest a growing opportunity for nontraditional civic engagement through the use of social media.

Sources: Nyabola 2018; Omanga 2019.

communities and negatively affects the quality of citizen participation. There is therefore a need for action at both the national and county level when it comes to transparency and access to information.

At the national level, the government needs to strengthen the requirements and systems for collecting and regularly publishing comparative information on basic county service delivery performance across the core devolved sectors. This could include reinvigorating the Kenya Open Data portal by requiring all sectors and counties to update core service delivery data annually.

At the county level, the governments must focus on ensuring that information provided to the public is published in plain, simple language (translated into local languages as necessary) and with sufficient lead time to provide citizens the opportunity to examine the information in advance of such mechanisms as participatory budgeting. There is also scope to more systematically use digital tools, including social media, to communicate relevant information to citizens.

Participation

County governments have made progress on implementing citizen participation mechanisms across the service delivery results chain. The annual capacity performance assessment (ACPA) synthesis report led by the Ministry of Devolution and the ASALs (Arid and Semi-Arid Lands), which looks at county performance in five Key Results Areas (including civic education and public participation), shows progressive improvement over the past few years.

Counties have improved performance on all seven indicators relating to civic education and participation (table 6.2). They achieved the highest average scores (above 90 percent) on three of the civic indicators: (1) the establishment of civic education units (CEUs), which are required by law; (2) the establishment of

TABLE 6.2 **Average county performance on ACPA civic education and participation indicators, FY2016/17–FY2018/19**

PERFORMANCE AREA		ACPA 2 (FY2016/17) AVERAGE COUNTY PERFORMANCE (%)	ACPA 3 (FY2017/18) AVERAGE COUNTY PERFORMANCE (%)	ACPA 4 (FY2018/19) AVERAGE COUNTY PERFORMANCE (%)
4.1	Civic education units established	63	86	94
4.2	Counties roll out civic education activities	40	70	75
4.3	Communication and engagement framework	65	93	97
4.4	Participatory planning and budget forums held	67	70	75
4.5	Citizens' feedback	20	32	40
4.6	County core financial materials published and shared	30	56	81
4.7	Publication of county assembly bills	75	88	94

Source: Ministry of Devolution and the ASALs 2020.
Note: ACPA = annual capacity performance assessment.

community communication and engagement frameworks; and (3) the publication of county assembly bills, which, as noted above, is a key precursor to meaningful citizen engagement.

Some of the most significant progress has been made on citizen participation in county planning and budgeting; however, there is large variation in the quality, effectiveness, and inclusiveness of these mechanisms. Public participation in the planning and budgeting of development projects and public service delivery is one of the main avenues through which the counties engage with citizens.

All county governments periodically facilitate public participation forums to allow for citizens' inputs into the different planning and budgeting instruments that determine the allocation of resources across the county. There is, however, large variation in the quality and effectiveness of participatory budgeting. Typical county budget consultations in Kenya consist of few meetings and limited inclusivity, which tend to be captured by elites rather than being gender or ethnically inclusive. In contrast, an increasing number of counties have adapted participatory budgeting as an innovative mechanism to engage local communities in making decisions on the priorities and spending for a defined amount of their development budget. Participatory budgeting in counties such as Makueni, West Pokot, Baringo, Kwale, and Elgeyo Marakwet has expanded opportunities for citizens to participate in government decision-making, increased budget allocations for citizen-identified projects to over 35 percent on average, and made the budget process credible and citizen-centric.

There has been only modest progress putting in place mechanisms that empower citizens to participate in service delivery implementation. Some counties have established project management committees (PMCs) to oversee county investment projects (for example, a building project). These PMCs are composed of citizens from the community in which the investment project is being implemented. The committee members are usually selected by the community, and many have quotas for women and other special interest groups.

The main responsibility of these PMCs is to follow up daily with the contractor and verify that the construction follows the agreed-upon bill of quantities to ensure that the final product meets the expected quality standards. Similarly, one county has established sustainability committees to help manage certain services, especially in the water sector. These committees comprise regular service users and play a hybrid role of management and oversight.

Similarly, there has been little progress toward institutionalizing participatory mechanisms focused on monitoring such service delivery outcomes as social audits, community scorecards, or grievance redress mechanisms (GRMs). Some civil society groups and innovative counties have, however, supported pilots that demonstrate the potential of these mechanisms (see box 6.3 on Makueni County). For example, the World Bank has supported piloting of citizen social audits as well as the development of a Citizen Accountability Audit Framework. The Office of the Auditor General will be spearheading the implementation of the framework. There have also been efforts to pilot community scorecards for various sectors, including on health (Machira 2015) as well as on livelihoods, infrastructure, and security (KAS 2017), but these have not yet been systematically integrated, institutionalized, and brought to scale across counties.

Another key challenge is the reconciliation of bottom-up priorities articulated by citizens with the need for strategic prioritization for service delivery, including decisions regarding the recurrent costs of operations and maintenance. The quality of participation is often low, with local citizens limiting themselves to the identification of small-scale "brick and mortar" projects, such as community health centers or dispensaries, irrespective of whether such facilities can be properly operated. These projects need to be part of an overall planning framework that ensures investments can be properly leveraged to improve service delivery.

To counteract this small-project bias, some counties have started to steer citizens' choices away from these types of projects by more narrowly defining the type of choices they are given and the kind of inputs they are asked for. If done well, this can be an effective way of guiding citizens' inputs in a way that helps express their needs and priorities regarding the delivery of public services. This is particularly important, because there is a risk of waning participation if citizens do not see evidence of that participation.

There is also a concern that devolution has not enabled inclusive participation by all, has created new political losers, and has increased ethnic tensions in counties that are dominated by one large ethnic group (Burbidge 2019; D'Arcy and Cornell 2016; Nyabira and Ayele 2016). Devolution may also create incentives for greater ethnic balkanization in political appointments and civil service recruitment, since majoritarianism at the county level can allow unrestrained ethnic preference in appointment and hiring decisions. Box 6.2 discusses representation in the civil service.

Variable progress on citizen participation is a result of leadership, capacity constraints, and incentives. From the side of county governments, the quality and effectiveness of participation appears to be a function of county leadership and incentives, technical capacity to facilitate participatory processes, and opportunities for learning about what does and does not work.

The extent to which the leadership considers public participation a genuine priority as opposed to a box-ticking exercise plays a key role in the strength of participatory processes, particularly given that most performance indicators relating to civic education and participation remain largely at the input level. Leadership and incentives determine support for the structures and resources allocated to carry out public participation exercises at the county level.

Technical capacity to facilitate participation forums in a way that engages citizens successfully is also critical. Interviews with county officials suggest that some counties have gone through a considerable learning curve since the onset of devolution and have been incrementally improving their practices over time. For example, the director of planning in one of the core counties described how they started off holding participatory planning sessions at the subcounty level

BOX 6.2

Devolution and inclusion: An example of ethnic representation in the civil service

The rules and policies to limit overrepresentation of ethnic majorities include the national policy for rotating civil servants and the County Governments Act 2012 requirement that new appointments by County Public Service Boards (CPSBs) constitute less than 70 percent of employees from any single ethnic group. In practice, many counties contravene this regulation: more than two-thirds of counties have hired more than 70 percent of staff from the county's majority ethnic group.

However, noncompliance with this rule does not necessarily mean that ethnic majorities end up being overrepresented: in 64 percent of counties, the largest ethnic group constitutes *more* than 70 percent of the county population, and in 42 percent of counties the majority groups exceed 90 percent of the population. Thus, although 32 of the 47 counties were found to be hiring more than 70 percent of new staff from the largest ethnic group, there were only 10 counties where the largest ethnic group was clearly overrepresented among new hires—and in many counties, this was in fact correcting for

underrepresentation of that group among existing civil servants in that county.

Although the data suggest that ethnic imbalances in public service are not severe in the aggregate, the government is right to continue actively responding to issues around county-level ethnic representation. In specific county cases, the ethnic recruitment balance is more seriously skewed. Even if there are structural reasons for these imbalances (such as migration, educational inequalities, or insecurity), this can still fuel grievances, as evidenced by numerous cases of intracounty conflict since 2013. However, the legislated quota would, if rigidly enforced, lead some counties to build a civil service with an ethnic composition that is very different from the populations that they serve, without necessarily protecting small, marginalized groups.

Affirmative action that promotes specific marginalized groups in a given county may prove a more effective means of addressing grievances related to representation, rather than blanket rules to limit overrepresentation of ethnic majorities.

Source: NCIC 2016.

but soon realized that ward- and village-level forums provided better opportunities for citizens to meaningfully and inclusively engage with the county's planning and budgeting processes.

Overall, the framework for transparency and participation exists nationally. In most counties, however, implementation remains piecemeal and fragmented—an approach that is unlikely to generate the incentives for counties to improve service delivery. Only through the integration and institutionalization of transparency and participatory public processes are county governments able to address endemic governance challenges. The example of Makueni County is illustrative (box 6.3). The County Executive made deliberate efforts to promote inclusive governance by integrating and embedding multiple participatory mechanisms—including participatory budgeting, a citizen-led project implementation committee, and the establishment of robust GRMs—that have enabled the county to address governance challenges and accountability across multiple dimensions, laying strong foundations for improving basic service delivery.

Accountability

Direct elections of governors (and deputy governors) and MCAs have offered an effective channel for citizens to hold county governments to account for their performance. Citizens have had the opportunity to directly elect the governor

BOX 6.3

Integrating and institutionalizing citizen engagement: The example of Makueni County

Through participatory development, Makueni County has transformed itself from a net recipient of food aid to food self-sufficiency. This was acknowledged by the Cabinet Secretary (CS) for Devolution and the Arid and Semi-Arid Lands during a structured peer learning exercise organized for governors and their technical teams in Makueni. "It is amazing that we can come for a visit to Makueni County and be gifted with food to take back. Previously, as the government, whenever we heard about Makueni, we would always think we needed to provide relief food," remarked the CS. The county has implemented impactful and value-for-money projects that cut across health, water, and agriculture, endorsed through public participation.

How has the county been able to achieve this? Development projects in Makueni undergo a citizen prioritization and validation process through a structured multiple-tier decision-making model that moves from the village level upward, to village clusters, subwards, wards, and finally the county forum. At each of these levels, a development committee comprising 11 citizens is selected by the community to represent the project priorities identified by the community at the next level of engagement. County officials conduct a technical evaluation on the feasibility of the projects before citizens arrive at final decisions on priority projects.

By shifting decision-making power to the citizens on the kind of projects they want to implement, Makueni County has significantly altered patronage politics in which elites exchange public resources and material goods for electoral support. Although the County Assembly members in charge of the wards approve the budget presented by the County Executive, it is hard for them to override citizens' decisions on the ward-level budget and introduce new projects given the elaborate participation structure that logically traces how projects emerged from the village level upward. At the county forum, which is attended both by governors and members of County Assemblies (MCAs), the citizens present their ward-level projects to the governor, who acknowledges by signing these as a true record of the citizens' choices. Citizens are also given an opportunity to verify that the investment projects reflect what they agreed upon.

Assigning a given portion of the county budget to citizens' decisions enables citizens to budget with a specific ceiling in mind, which manages their expectations and reduces the wish lists of projects that are often presented to governments operating on limited budgets. This builds the credibility of the budget process, resulting in increased trust between the county and citizens.

Citizens are further engaged in budget execution through democratically elected project management committees (PMCs), comprising community representatives who oversee the implementation of projects. This has greatly improved accountability in the use of county funds as well as of the county officials.

"The people of Makueni County do not just give us views; they must approve the projects and ensure that they have been completed to the people's desire before the county can process the payment," said Makueni County Governor Kivutha Kibwana.

During the public forum for the FY2020/21 budget, citizens took the county officials to task over what they termed slow implementation of some water projects. The citizens had also engaged their MCAs to report the slow execution by the County Executive, and the MCAs were able to make follow-up demands on the County Executive to address the matter. The County Executive responded by setting up a rapid results implementation committee comprising subward and ward administrators, subcounty administrators, and department heads. This committee evaluates how the budget is being implemented, reviews the progress of projects, identifies challenges, and addresses them to ensure projects are completed within the stipulated deadlines.

Source: World Bank 2020a.

and CA members in 2013 and 2017. Elections have been hotly contested and, as detailed in box 6.4, governors and MCAs are consistently perceived to be more important than the members of the national parliament (Cheeseman et al. 2019).

Citizens have shown themselves ready to vote out people occupying county political posts: less than half of incumbent governors retained their seats during

County elections matter: The hotly contested 2017 gubernatorial and MCA elections

County-level elections in Kenya allow voters to make a judgment on the performance of their elected governors and members of County Assemblies (MCAs), and can be hotly contested. The first county-level elections took place in 2013, at the start of devolution; a second set of county elections was held in 2017, four years into the process. Voter turnout for these elections (which take place at the same time as national elections) has been relatively high: 86 percent in 2013 and 78 percent in 2017.

The 2013 gubernatorial race attracted many professionals and technocrats. At the time, county governments were perceived as needing leaders who could plan and execute development programs. As a result, almost half of the candidates winning the elections had an administrative or managerial background, such as working for NGOs or bureaucrats in the public and private sector.[a] By 2017, however, perceptions had changed: governorships were now seen as being powerful political positions requiring candidates with political skills and the ability to negotiate for more resources for the counties. As a result, many elected leaders in the Senate and National Assembly began to show an interest in running for the office of county governor.[b]

Service delivery performance was an important campaign issue in the highly competitive 2017 elections. The challenge of service delivery—and how the first group of governors had performed in delivering development in their respective counties—informed the political campaigns for the 2017 gubernatorial elections. Those competing against the incumbent governors argued that their competitors' performance had been poor, and they often claimed that the incumbent governors misappropriated funds or spent them to implement projects that they had identified to help their reelection. Over half of the first-generation governors lost their seats in the subsequent election. As shown in 2017, governors need to perform if they want to stay in office.

Because MCAs are elected at the ward level and are expected to champion the priorities of their constituents at the county level, they also need to perform to ensure their reelection. The first generation of MCAs does not appear to have taken this responsibility seriously, preferring to use their positions to pursue narrower self-interests or reward political allies. Ward-based constituents, however, clearly saw things differently—and used the 2017 elections to vote out large numbers of MCA incumbents judged to have done a poor job of addressing ward needs and priorities.

Across all counties, about three-quarters (74 percent) of incumbent MCAs lost their seats in 2017; only 376 (26 percent) were reelected. In some counties, as many as 90 percent of incumbent MCAs lost their seats in 2017. This appears to have strongly incentivized the 2017 MCA cohort to take on a much more active representational role and to be much more responsive to the needs and demands of their ward constituents. MCAs now find that they must be perceived as taking the priorities of their ward constituents to heart if they are to seek and gain reelection.

The relative robustness of the accountability relationship between MCAs and their ward constituents is both encouraging and a cause for concern. In terms of the impact on service delivery, it suggests that MCAs—to the extent they can—must push to bring public goods and services to their electoral wards. Although positive, this somewhat narrow focus on the well-being of their ward constituents does not incentivize MCAs to address wider issues concerning neighboring wards or the county as a whole. As countywide institutions, County Assemblies do not seem to operate on the basis of countywide priorities and needs but remain much more focused on the narrower and more parochial interests of the MCAs' electoral wards.

Source: World Bank 2020b.
a. Some of the counties where a candidate with administrative or managerial experience in the running of private and public sector won in the 2013 elections include Tharaka Nithi, Siaya, Homa Bay, Kisumu, Isiolo, Turkana, Taita Taveta, Samburu, Kericho, Narok, Laikipia, Nyandarua, Kisii, Nyamira, and Murang'a.
b. Out of the 47 first-generation senators, 17 decided to run for governor in 2017 (only 6 of whom were successful), while one decided to return to running for MP (Hornsby 2018).

the 2017 election, and only 26 percent of all 1,450 incumbent MCAs were reelected in 2017. Interviews suggest that this has led the second generation of MCAs to be more responsive to citizens' needs than were their predecessors. These trends provide encouraging signs that electoral accountability is working relatively well.

County elections are not yet aligning the priorities of citizens and their representatives and generating incentives to focus on service delivery despite local elections shortening the "long route" of accountability and providing opportunities for local issues to feature in electoral platforms and campaigns. There are worrying signs that the county political establishment has suffered from a decline in credibility. Surveys show that public perceptions concerning performance, corruption, and trustworthiness of governors worsened between 2014 and 2016 (figure 6.3). Perceptions about MCAs on the same dimensions are not radically different from the local councils that preceded them (figure 6.4).

CAs and their committees hold significant powers to hold county executives to account; however, most offer only weak oversight and scrutiny. CAs have formal powers to approve some county executive appointments, legislate county laws, and scrutinize the work of the County Executive, and they have established a range of committees and units to do so in addition to hiring technical support staff (box 6.5).

The CA also has powers to remove a member of the County Executive Committee (CEC) and to impeach the governor, subject to approval from the Senate. Weak CA oversight appears to be due to capacity constraints among members and staff relative to the executive. MCAs tend to be less qualified than their counterparts in the executive and often lack crucial training on issues like budgeting and financial monitoring. Their support structures are also often understaffed and tend to lack the technical expertise necessary to scrutinize

FIGURE 6.3

Public perceptions of county governors in Kenya, 2014 and 2016

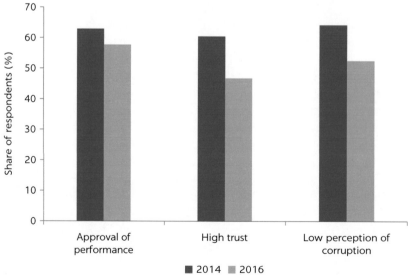

Source: Analysis of Afrobarometer data, rounds 3–7.
Note: Calculation excludes nonresponses, missing entries, and "don't know" responses. "Approval of performance" = percentage who "approve" or "strongly approve" of governor performance. "High trust" = percentage who have "a lot" or "somewhat" trust in governor. "Low perception of corruption" = percentage who believe "none" or "some" of office of governor is corrupt (as opposed to "all" or "most").

FIGURE 6.4

Public perceptions of county assemblies and local councils in Kenya, 2005–16

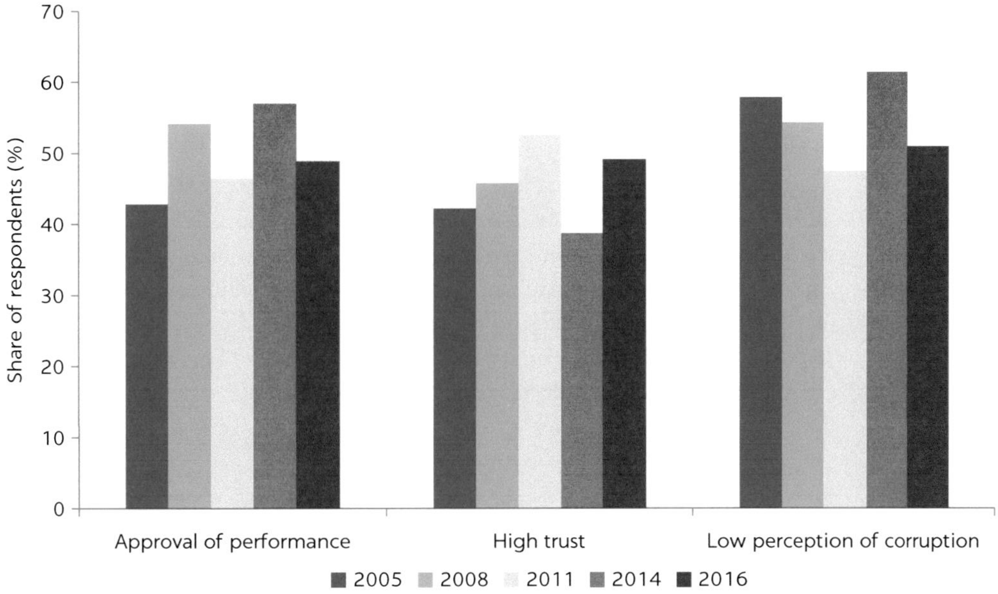

Source: Analysis of Afrobarometer data, rounds 3–7.
Note: Calculation excludes nonresponses, missing entries, and "don't know" responses. "Approval of performance" = percentage who "approve" or "strongly approve" of county assembly (CA) or local council (LC) performance "High trust" = percentage who have "a lot" or "somewhat" trust in CA or LC. "Low perception of corruption" = percentage who believe "none" or "some" of CA or LC is corrupt (as opposed to "all" or "most").

BOX 6.5

County assembly oversight

To fulfill their oversight mandate, the County Assemblies (CAs) have set up institutional bodies, as required by the legal framework. These include the County Public Service Board, the office of legal counsel, the fiscal analysis unit (budget office), various sectoral and select committees, and research departments and table offices.

As for overseeing service delivery, the sectoral committees take a central role, enabling the CAs to focus on such different sectoral issues as health, water, local economic development, youth, housing, tourism, and others. The committees, each comprising a subset of the members of County Assemblies, are charged with developing and deliberating county sector policies and other legislation in preparation of a plenary vote and holding public hearings on the proposed legislation to incorporate citizen feedback. They are also charged with scrutinizing the implementation of sector policies and plans by the County Executive, including the effective, efficient, and equitable provision of public services in the sector. To this end, each CA committee is assisted by staff who support committee management, strategic planning, research and analysis, and report writing.

executive actions and proposals. By limiting the information provided to their CAs, county executives do not help the situation. Finally, MCAs often lament their lack of financial autonomy from the executive since all CA expenditures must be approved by the CEC member in charge of finance.

One area of particular concern is the practice of giving each MCA direct control over a small share of the budget, primarily through the establishment of ward-level development funds. These practices echo the national Constituency Development Fund, which is managed by MPs.

Although interviews suggest that these ward-level development funds are used in a relatively responsive manner—which is good for accountability to citizens—they tend to result in the construction of small infrastructure projects without broader consideration for operational costs in the broader county budget. More importantly, there are suggestions that ward development funds further fragment CA oversight, diverting attention away from scrutiny of the county budget and service delivery as a whole.

All in all, many CAs are currently in a situation where their members have effectively given up their oversight role in exchange for the right to allocate a share of the budget to projects within their respective wards. This, along with the structural weaknesses of the CA relative to the executive and the lack of acceptance of this mandate on the part of the governor, dilutes horizontal accountability within the county government, with several problematic ramifications for efficient and effective service delivery.

Another opportunity for citizens to influence county-level services is to engage with local service providers directly. Although this practice predates devolution, counties have established participatory mechanisms (for example, the PMCs) through which citizens can influence the delivery of public investments and hold service providers accountable across a range of sectors (box 6.6). Another encouraging example of this kind of accountability at the local level is the use of sustainability committees for the water sector in one county, which has been an effective mechanism for ensuring cooperation between the ward and service users in the funding, maintenance, and operation of rural water services.

However, social accountability is insufficiently focused on actual service delivery outcomes. While the establishment of PMCs is a step in the right direction of strengthening direct bottom-up accountability, it restricts citizen involvement to overseeing infrastructure provision, reinforcing people's focus on

---

BOX 6.6

Project management committees

To fulfill their oversight mandate, some counties have established the practice of setting up citizen-led project management committees (PMCs) to oversee project identification, implementation, and monitoring. The committees oversee every investment project that the County Executive is carrying out. PMCs are made up of citizens from the neighborhood in which the investment project is being implemented. This ensures that community residents who live close by develop a sense of ownership of the project, which in turn motivates them to monitor implementation and ensure it is in line with their expectations.

The committee members are usually elected by the community, and many committees are inclusive; they

have quotas for women and other special interest groups. The main responsibility of these PMCs is to oversee the contractor on a daily basis and verify that the construction follows the agreed-upon bill of quantities to ensure that the final product has used the materials and other resources as per the contract and that the product meets the expected quality standards. In many instances, the PMC's formal approval is necessary for contractors to be paid in relation to the project. In one of the study counties, the governor has requested that all PMCs report directly to a unit in his office to ensure his direct and timely access to information about progress on the implementation of investment projects.

Source: World Bank 2020b.

projects. There is only limited emphasis on civic engagement in overseeing the actual delivery of public services such as health or early childhood education beyond hospital or classroom construction. Although the study has found only sporadic examples of effective citizen engagement in service delivery (for example, through one county's sustainability committees in the water sector), there is no clear evidence that these kinds of forums are effective for enhancing the quality of services.

CONCLUSIONS

Basic provisions and mechanisms for transparency, participation, and accountability have been established and are, to various degrees, operating at the county level. Most counties regularly publish planning and budgeting information. Almost all counties hold citizen consultations of some sort, with the more-innovative counties introducing more comprehensive participatory budgeting mechanisms as well as citizen implementation and oversight committees. Citizens are also using elections to hold local leaders to account, resulting in substantial changes to county-level political leadership. This has helped to engender a degree of accountability for performance and that counties spend on projects that are prioritized locally.

However, the quality and effectiveness of participation and accountability is mixed and insufficiently focused on service delivery performance. Gaps in information transparency are particularly glaring. There is practically no regular information available on county service delivery performance, with websites such as the Kenya Open Data portal hosting information from over five years ago (and before the previous elections). Most participatory and accountability mechanisms are also, therefore, largely focused on inputs and procedures and not service delivery outcomes.

Participation has been limited to expressing preferences about individual and small investment projects. The horizontal accountability exerted by the CAs has been weak and generally more concerned with ward-based priorities, not service delivery results and management. And despite the competitiveness of county elections, this shortened "long route" of accountability has, with exceptions, created incentives for a new generation of citizen- and service-oriented leaders to emerge.

Table 6.3 provides a summary assessment for citizen engagement under devolution. *Grosso modo*, citizen engagement is trending positive but is unlikely to help make devolution work for service delivery without greater focus on service delivery performance across all dimensions of citizen engagement and without more focus on the quality of information, participation, and accountability.

For devolution to work for service delivery, a more integrated and institutionalized approach to citizen engagement is required. Citizen engagement has been most effective when its three core elements—transparency, participation, and accountability—are integrated and institutionalized rather than fragmented. This requires local leadership capacity as well as an effort to further decentralize decision-making within counties so as to bring information, participation, and accountability closer to the experience and needs of ordinary citizens, including the poor and marginalized groups.

TABLE 6.3 **Summary assessment of citizen engagement: Transparency, participation, and accountability**

AREA	WHAT HAS WORKED	WHAT COULD BE WORKING BETTER
Transparency	• Legal provisions for transparency • Improved transparency of county budget and financial information • Comprehensive county data platform established	• Limited information on service delivery performance • Information formats often inaccessible • County open data platform not regularly updated
Participation	• Mandatory participation and improved county core civic community and participation indicators (ACPAs) • Participatory budgeting in some counties • Positive examples of citizen participation in project management committees and sustainability committees	• Participatory mechanism often token and ineffective • Limited county capacity and resources to facilitate • Little focus on participation in implementation and monitoring service delivery performance • Many mechanisms piloted but few implemented at scale
Accountability	• Strongly contested county elections • Significant changes in County Executive and County Assemblies in second elections • Oversight committees established by County Assemblies	• Declining trust in and credibility of county leaders • Weak oversight provided by County Assemblies • Insufficient County Assembly focus on cross-ward and countywide service delivery • Low quality of social accountability

Source: World Bank.
Note: ACPA = annual capacity and performance assessment.

This approach obviously implies action, not only at the county level but also at the national level. The national government must regularly publish comprehensive performance information on county service delivery and use county performance frameworks to generate incentives for meaningful participation. It must also expand capacity-building efforts focused on participation as well as accountability tools focused on service delivery (such as community scorecards, social audits, and grievance-handling systems), combined with a greater focus on strengthening the inclusion of minorities and other marginalized groups. Implementing measures that strengthen inclusion will improve these groups' access to public services that address their specific needs while also enhancing the equity of service delivery more broadly. Here, county-specific policy approaches to promote the inclusion of marginalized groups in a given county will offer a more targeted, and hence more effective, response to grievances related to ethnic representation and access to public services at the county level.

One approach that could help strengthen the inclusion of marginalized groups regarding access to public services is to continue to push for the establishment of village administrations across all counties, as stipulated by the County Governments Act 2012. This would help identify and communicate the needs and priorities of marginalized groups from within each village to the county governments, provide the foundation for an integrated approach to participation and accountability, and ultimately help ensure equitable access to public services.

NOTE

1. Local governments and community development projects will combine these different participatory mechanisms. For example, community-driven development programs often include all four mechanisms, including consultations on policy and procedures; participatory planning and budgeting; community implementation; and even community monitoring of service delivery quality through scorecards, social audits, or both.

REFERENCES

Biegon, K., and J. Wambui. 2019. "Are Kenya Counties Making Budget Documents Available to the Public? A Review of County Websites." Biannual study report, International Budget Partnership Kenya (IBPK), Nairobi.

Burbidge, D. 2019. *An Experiment in Devolution: National Unity and the Deconstruction of the Kenyan State*. Nairobi: Strathmore University Press.

CAJ (Commission on Administrative Justice). 2014. "The Commission on Administrative Justice Annual Report 2014." CAJ (Office of the Ombudsman), Nairobi.

Cheeseman, N., K. Kanyinga, G. Lynch, M. Ruteere, and J. Willis. 2019. "Kenya's 2017 Elections: Winner-Takes-All Politics as Usual?" *Journal of Eastern African Studies* 13 (2): 215–34.

D'Arcy, M., and A. Cornell. 2016. "Devolution and Corruption in Kenya: Everyone's Turn to Eat?" *African Affairs* 115 (459): 246–73.

EACC (Ethics and Anti-Corruption Commission). 2013. "Joint Public Complaints Reporting Centres Launched." Facebook post, June 25, 2013. https://zh-cn.facebook.com/EACCKenya /posts/211553098996645.

Hornsby, C. 2018. "Re-Election Rates for Kenya's Politicians." *An Occasional Kenya Blog*, April 16. http://www.charleshornsby.com/kenya-blog.

Kanyinga, K., and J. D. Long. 2012. "The Political Economy of Reforms in Kenya: The Post-2007 Election Violence and a New Constitution." *African Studies Review* 55 (1): 31–51.

KAS (Konrad-Adenauer-Stiftung). 2017. *Community Score Card on Livelihood Development, Infrastructure and Security: West Pokot and Baringo Counties of Kenya*. Report for the "One World, No Hunger" initiative of the German Ministry for Economic Cooperation and Development (BMZ). Nairobi: Konrad-Adenauer-Stiftung e.V.

Machira, W. Y. 2015. "Integrating Social Accountability in Healthcare Delivery: Lessons Drawn from Kenya." Kenya Devolution Working Paper No. 4, Kenya School of Government (KSG), Nairobi; World Bank, Washington, DC.

Ministry of Devolution and the ASALs. 2020. "County Annual Capacity & Performance Assessment (ACPA 4) 2019–2020." Report, Ministry of Devolution and the ASALs, Nairobi.

NCIC (National Cohesion and Integration Commission). 2016. *Ethnic and Diversity Audit of the County Public Service, Counties Vol. I*. Nairobi: NCIC.

Nyabira, B. C., and Z. A. Ayele. 2016. "The State of Political Inclusion of Ethnic Communities under Kenya's Devolved System." *Law, Democracy & Development* 20 (1): 131–53.

Nyabola, N. 2018. *Digital Democracy, Analogue Politics: How the Internet Era Is Transforming Politics in Kenya*. London: Zed Books.

Omanga, D. 2019. "WhatsApp as 'Digital Publics': The *Nakuru Analysts* and the Evolution of Participation in County Governance in Kenya." *Journal of Eastern African Studies* 13 (1): 175–91.

World Bank. 2003. *World Development Report 2004: Making Services Work for Poor People*. Washington, DC: World Bank.

World Bank. 2012. "Devolution without Disruption: Pathways to a Successful New Kenya.." Report No. 72297, World Bank, Washington, DC.

World Bank. 2020a. "Kenya Accountable Devolution Program (KADP) Completion Report: Second Phase (2015–2019)." World Bank, Nairobi.

World Bank. 2020b. "Politics and Accountability Background Study". Background study for this volume, World Bank, Nairobi.

7 Conclusions and Recommendations

INTRODUCTION

Kenya adopted a new constitution and began the process of devolution in 2010. The new constitution was the institutional response to longstanding grievances related to the overcentralization of state powers and public sector resources, regional disparities, and top-down service delivery. This radical restructuring of the Kenyan state has three main objectives: decentralizing political power, public sector functions, and public finances; ensuring a more equitable distribution of resources between regions; and promoting more accountable, participatory, and responsive government at all levels.

The first elections under the new constitution were held in 2013. Alongside the national government, 47 county governments were established. A new bicameral parliament was also elected, in which the National Assembly plays an oversight role with respect to the national executive, while the Senate protects and promotes the interests of the county governments. Each county government is made up of a County Executive, headed by an elected Governor, and works under the oversight of an elected County Assembly. County governments fulfill their constitutionally mandated responsibilities, financed by equitable shares of national revenues, conditional grants, and own-source revenues (OSR).

Devolution has led to the establishment of institutions and systems for delivery of devolved services. Stability of these institutions and systems will be critical for the reform to be assessed as a success. The basic institutional framework stipulated in the 2010 constitution has largely been put into place. County governments are now well established. National and county-level elections were held in 2013 and 2017, resulting in a successful transition of political power. Kenyans appreciate devolution as a major gain from the new constitution; however, the next phase will require stable, enabled, and effective institutions and systems to deliver more and better services to citizens and to further reduce regional disparities.

The constitution laid out a strong foundation for sharing responsibilities and resources between the national and county governments, with counties being assigned significant frontline service delivery functions and with the national government assuming a typical central mandate around policy, standards, and norms. With a constitutional guarantee of unconditional transfers from the national government, county governments were expected to have the means and the autonomy to begin to address local needs. Moreover, constitutional provisions ensure that transfers to counties are designed to address regional disparities and to favor historically disadvantaged counties.

Seven years after the "devolution train" left the station, this report takes stock of how devolution has affected the delivery of devolved basic services to Kenyan citizens. Whereas devolution was driven by political reform, the ensuing institutions and systems were expected to deliver devolved basic services to the people. The Making Devolution Work for Service Delivery (MDWSD) study is the first comprehensive assessment of Kenya's devolution reform. The study developed a simple analytical framework to assess the impact of devolution on service delivery. The framework lays out the envisaged inputs to the devolution process, the potential effects of these inputs on service delivery processes within and across sectors, and the potential impact of these effects on service delivery outcomes. The study draws on analyses of primary and secondary data as well as extensive literature reviews and interviews with officials from the national government and county governments. The study relied on input, output, and cross-sectional outcome data, where available; however, a major caveat concerned the paucity of data, especially on outputs and outcomes on some of the indicators used in the study.

Based on the currently available data, the study provides key messages regarding what is working, what is not working, and what could work better to enhance service delivery. It provides an independent assessment of service delivery performance in five sectors—health, education, agriculture, urban, and water services—and includes an in-depth review of the main pillars of devolved service delivery: public financial management, intergovernmental finance, human resource management (HRM), politics, and accountability. In addition to this synthesis report, each of the sector and cross-cutting background studies that underpinned this study had a distinct policy brief that we hope will provide further room for a conversation on tackling the challenges within specific sectors.

The study is the result of a coordinated effort by the government of Kenya and the World Bank, carried out under the guidance of a study task force comprising officials from the National Treasury, line ministries, independent commissions, the Council of Governors, and county governments.

MAJOR ACHIEVEMENTS AND CHALLENGES

Overall, this study concludes that the impacts of devolution on service delivery are mixed; however, there are promising signs. The glass is half full because devolution enabled the establishment of institutions and systems to support the delivery of devolved services and provided for a platform that is expected to enhance equity in Kenya. The glass is still half empty because of ambiguities in financing and provision—with the national government still heavily involved in the delivery of many devolved services, governance, and coordination; these challenges impede frontline service delivery. The picture is mixed regarding the level and quality of devolved services, since some sectors show positive trends in a few indicators but others do not. But also, it is not clear that overall inequities have been reduced across the country, in part because a lack of disaggregated data constrains the measurement of impacts. There is a general lack of data within and across sectors on service delivery outcomes, outputs, and inputs. Without regular and routine sector administrative data on service delivery and periodic and consistent surveys, it will prove even more challenging for the management, decision-making, and accountability processes to make devolution work for service delivery.

The promising sign is that since the "devolution train" left the station, the new county governments are growing up and becoming more responsive and accountable to deliver the devolution dividends to Kenyan citizens. Indeed, this study provides numerous examples in which counties have delivered transformative, world-class services and where high-quality county leadership is making the difference. Devolution has not led to a major disruption of service delivery. Counties have maintained and, in many cases, significantly expanded the levels of, and access to, services in some sectors, such as health, education, and water. In the health sector, for example, access to facilities has been expanded, deliveries by qualified birth attendants have increased, and immunization rates have been stabilized. In the agriculture and urban sectors, however, the picture is mixed. Core agricultural extension services appear to have declined since devolution, although counties have provided farmers with access to input subsidies. The newly created urban institutions are still weak, and many counties are slow to empower them to function as envisaged by the 2019 Urban Areas and Cities Act (UACA).

Counties have invested substantially in service infrastructure. For example, counties built 1,419 dispensaries and 821 early childhood development and education (ECDE) centers between 2013 and 2018. To underpin growth, counties have invested in rural water supply schemes and agriculture infrastructure, such as irrigation, markets, and rural roads. Urban investments have been focused on drainage, street lighting, and solid waste management, following renewed reform efforts to reestablish municipalities. However, across all sectors many counties are grappling with issues of infrastructure quality, with limited attention paid to issues of maintenance and proper project appraisal processes.

Counties have also invested in human resources, recruiting staff to deliver services, with the numbers of health workers and teachers for ECDE establishments increasing significantly. For example, the number of trained ECDE teachers increased by 54 percent, from 73,012 in 2010 to 112,703 in 2018. Between 2013 and 2018, in the health sector, human resource numbers increased by 72 percent in Kilifi, 42 percent in Kwale, 28 percent in Makueni, 13 percent in Kisumu, and 5 percent in Nyeri. Despite these increases, staffing shortages continue to be an issue, compounded by high rates of absenteeism, especially in the health sector, and sometimes low levels of staff motivation. The number of agriculture technical staff has declined, and extension services have suffered. In urban areas in some counties, such technical staff as planners, surveyors, economists, and municipal engineers are in short supply or misplaced and not working in the departments most relevant to their expertise. The overall allocation of staff by counties is inefficient because of the large share and growth of staffing in administrative departments and administrative staff within service sectors. Counties spend 60–70 percent of their operating expenses on labor, presumably in part because of inherited labor in administrations of the defunct local authorities. In short, human resource management is a major challenge to county service delivery.

In addition, disparities in economic, health, and education outcomes persist in Kenya, and addressing inequities is a long-term task. Poverty rates by county range from 17 percent to 78 percent in 2016. Gross domestic product (GDP) by county ranges from K Sh 48,000 to K Sh 350,000 per capita. Remote rural areas tend to have higher poverty and lower GDP, while more urbanized and populous counties have higher per capita GDP. Inequalities persist in health and education outcomes after devolution across poorer and richer Kenyans, and rural and urban counties. For example, maternal mortality varies from 187 to 3,795 per 100,000 births, while the percentage of pupils able to read a story varies from 21 percent to 67 percent.

There are still large disparities in health service delivery. Poorer and more rural counties continue to have access to fewer and lower-quality services than wealthier and more urban counties. Deliveries in health facilities vary from 33 percent to 100 percent; health worker density varies from 3.4 to 24 per 10,000 persons; the proportion of children fully immunized varies from 46 percent to 100 percent. Across many health outputs, inequalities between facilities in poorer and richer counties persist. Facilities in rural counties have worse availability for over half of the listed essential drugs and suffer from higher staff absentee rates than the more-urban counties. In possessing essential equipment, facilities in poorer counties fall behind those in richer counties. Likewise, in 2018, facilities in poorer and more rural counties tended to have fewer vaccines available than wealthier and more urban counties. ECDE enrollment rates are also lower in poorer and more rural areas.

Health services are improving, and disparities are shrinking in some health areas, such as access to vaccine availability and deliveries. Overall levels and disparities in skilled birth attendance have improved since devolution. The availability of measles vaccines has increased across all geographic areas since 2012; the same positive trend appears in the availability of polio vaccines. Essential drug availability has also improved, with one-third of these drugs available in facilities in poorer counties.

Similar degrees of disparity can be seen in ECDE, although overall disparities in preprimary gross enrollment rates have been reduced since devolution. For the water, agriculture, and urban sectors, the lack of data makes it difficult to identify tendencies and patterns regarding disparities between counties.

Financing service delivery

A notable achievement of devolution is that Kenya has put in place a fiscal framework for sharing national revenues between the national government and the county governments. At the apex is the Division of Revenue Act (DoRA), which stipulates how national government and county governments share national revenues. Between county governments, revenue sharing is enshrined by the County Allocation of Revenue Act (CARA). Both DoRA and CARA are enacted annually. But the actual amounts are set in a complex negotiated process, often heated with protests and disputes settled by the National and County Government Coordinating Summit ("the Summit"). This framework proposes a smooth flow of funding to support devolved service delivery in counties.

The constitution assigns significant functional responsibilities to county governments, but they currently account for only 13 percent of total public spending, down from a peak of 16 percent in FY2014/15. County spending has increased from an initial K Sh 229 billion in FY2014/15 to K Sh 327 billion by FY2017/18, representing an increase of 49.3 percent in nominal terms over the first four years of devolution. This is a significant increase, which has contributed to the observed increases in service delivery levels and investments.

In contrast, however, national spending nearly doubled, from K Sh 1,093.7 billion in FY2013/14 to K Sh 1,959.6 billion in FY2017/18. This increase has been driven not only by significant increases in debt servicing over time (a major driver of the Consolidated Fund Services line in the national budget) but also by growth in the national government's recurrent and development expenditures. Therefore, overall, the share of counties in total spending of both levels of government has declined. A higher share of fiscal resources is retained by the national government even where functions have been devolved.

The basic framework for county-level allocation and use of their financial resources is in place and functional. The Public Financial Management (PFM) Act (2012) provides a comprehensive framework for planning and budgeting; this is, by and large, used by counties. The national Integrated Financial Management Information System (IFMIS) has been progressively improved and rolled out to all counties. There have been significant achievements in ensuring minimum PFM standards; however, some counties use IFMIS halfheartedly and often in parallel with old systems.

County performance in planning and budgeting, however, has been suboptimal and has undermined the quality and sustainability of services. Plans and budgets do not focus sufficiently on service delivery, and budgets are not able to answer simple questions, such as how much is being spent in the county, and where, on different levels of services. Budgets tend not to show allocations to subcounties or facilities, and they tend to use input-linked results indicators rather than service delivery outputs or outcomes. This makes it difficult to link spending to services. In addition, operational expenditures are underbudgeted. Operating budgets for service delivery are also squeezed by high payroll costs and high administrative expenditures. As noted above, counties use 60–70 percent of operating expenses for labor, which crowds out spending on service delivery.

Although counties are executing their budgets, the execution rates are volatile and very low for development budgets. Some of this may be due to late releases of transfers by the National Treasury, although this does not explain why some counties do a much better job than others. At the moment, the reasons for low execution rates of development budgets remain unclear.

One aspect of county expenditure management that does compromise service delivery is the limited extent to which sector departments and service delivery facilities receive their operating budget allocations. In some counties, for example, where county treasuries operate in a very centralized way, hospitals and health centers do not receive a reliable flow of funds, which constrains their operations; in other cases, however, county treasuries have found ways of "decentralizing" operations spending to health sector facilities.

Citizen engagement in service delivery

Devolution has established electoral, horizontal, and direct accountability mechanisms at the county level, which have enabled citizens to exercise some degree of oversight of counties' service delivery performance. County-level elections—for both the executive and the County Assembly—have been competitive and enjoyed good voter turnout, at about 85 percent in 2013 and 78 percent in 2017. The performance of incumbents was a factor in the electoral choices made in 2017, when many incumbent governors and members of county assemblies (MCAs) lost their seats. However, MCAs are now seen as being more accountable to their ward electorates for the ward projects they support, rather than for what they do to improve service delivery on a county-wide basis.

Horizontal accountability, however, has been weak. MCAs offer only limited oversight and scrutiny of their respective County Executives. This is partly because of capacity constraints among the MCAs and staff relative to the executive. In addition, as noted above, MCAs' oversight and scrutiny in many counties is now strongly focused on ward-level investments and the funds allocated for ward-based projects rather than on countywide service delivery. Direct citizen accountability of county service delivery, through project management committees (PMCs), has in some cases tended to focus on the implementation of individual investment projects rather than on service delivery in a wider sense.

Counties are legally bound to ensure that citizens participate in a range of planning and budgeting activities, and all counties have tried to ensure that they consult with local citizens in one way or another. That said, citizen participation in county-level planning processes has been of relatively low quality, poorly coordinated, and inadequately facilitated by county governments. Moreover, citizens have tended to participate by advocating for particular local investment projects.

Coordination of service delivery

The normative framework for intergovernmental coordination, cooperation, and collaboration is in place, with the Summit at the apex, supported by a range of sectoral and cross-cutting intergovernmental forums. This is intended to ensure that the national government and counties work together to resolve the many issues that cannot be addressed unilaterally. These include functional assignments, PFM norms, HRM systems, sector-specific guidance, norms, and standards.

POLICY OPTIONS TO MAKE DEVOLUTION WORK FOR SERVICE DELIVERY

This study outlines a broad agenda for the future of devolution, which requires concerted action within, across, and between the spheres of government, their executives, and legislatures, as well as by citizens. There are several opportunities to start addressing the service-delivery issues now, and these opportunities should be taken. The study has identified policy options to make devolution work for service delivery and has proposed suggestions on how to start on and navigate the journey. Implementation of these policy options will require the national and county governments to walk together—learning to work together to overcome the hurdles met along the way and to trust each other.

A set of policy options emerges from the study that we hope will provide policy makers, technicians, and politicians with options to address the challenges impeding devolved service delivery in county governments. The study concludes by proposing the development of a joint plan of action between national government and county governments for making devolution work for service delivery and by identifying the initial entry points where county and national governments can start.

Policy Action 1: **Review functional assignments. Clarify service delivery responsibilities of various tiers of government and ensure that funding corresponds to responsibilities.**

The government has been applauded for a decisive devolution of functions at the outset of devolution. However, this study has shown that there is a continued dispute over some functional assignments in devolved sectors (for example, urban, water, health, and agriculture) between the two tiers of government and a lack of jointly agreed-upon, clear, and achievable norms and standards within sectors for service delivery. Policy options for bringing about further clarity in functional assignments and how services are to be delivered within each sector are extremely important to help the government tackle development challenges in terms of coordinating responses to COVID-19, managing recovery, and contributing to building resilient and sustainable county governments.

The study recommends that government address this challenge by tasking the intergovernmental coordination mechanisms with bringing together key stakeholders to develop an action plan.

Jointly, national and county governments should explore options such as these:

- Resolve disputes over functions in devolved sectors that exist or may occur from time to time. Alternative dispute resolution mechanisms can be used to resolve disputes over functional assignments.
- Establish norms for how services are to be delivered within sectors with clear roles across and within each tier.
- Address cross-sectoral bottlenecks in service delivery and strengthen systems and processes for use by county governments (for example, financing, PFM, HRM, and intergovernmental relations).
- Prepare guidelines for sector service delivery and cross-sectoral management of resources.

Policy Action 2: **Promote devolution beyond the county level. Counties can decentralize responsibility toward the point of service delivery and deliver predictable finance.**

The 2010 constitution laid a strong foundation of devolution in Kenya that has seen the creation of 47 county governments, which have stepped up to the task of providing meaningful service delivery to Kenyan citizens. The country is tackling the underdevelopment created by centralized tendencies of the past decades. The opportunity is now to deepen devolution beyond county government administrations. County governments need to further devolve responsibility to the point of service delivery by empowering lower levels of the devolution establishment, such as subcounties, wards, water service providers, municipalities and urban boards, and health delivery units. This will avoid centralization and the risk of underdevelopment within counties.

This study recommends that county governments take this bold step to empower the other levels of government and service delivery. Such empowerment will take the form of delegating or devolving responsibilities further, together with the finances, to these points of service delivery. With the support of the national government, county governments will need to develop and implement capacity support programs for these points of service delivery. This is not a decision to rush through but rather a cautious approach that counties need to take to ensure that they support these points of delivery to develop their capacity and to enable them deliver on their mandate by providing the necessary resources, support, and implementation monitoring.

County government-specific actions include the following:

- County governments commit to further devolution of responsibilities and finances to the points of service delivery. Sector departments devolve management responsibility to subcounty units, urban institutions (municipalities and urban boards), and facilities to enable them to respond to local needs and priorities. Such devolution should allow for autonomy in decision-making at those points of service delivery.
- Operational funding reaches the front line by allocating and channeling funding directly to service delivery units, enabling units to retain revenues collected, on time, and to enable management of funds at these levels.
- Counties ensure that the full costs of projects are budgeted and committed. Funds must be provided on time so that projects are completed before new ones are commenced.
- Sector departments monitor and provide capacity to support subcounties and frontline service facilities, focusing on the quality of service and investment delivery and service delivery results.

National and county governments can take the following enabling actions:

- Develop the necessary guidelines to support implementation at the point of service delivery. Such guidelines may help to operationalize specific legislation and will allow for further clarity in terms of devolved or delegated roles and responsibilities within counties to subcounties and service delivery units within sectors.
- Develop quality assurance and information management systems in all sectors and across counties.
- Strengthen processes for project implementation.
- Create cross-sectoral frameworks and systems for cash management and commitment control and for financing service delivery units, including the direct financing, retention, and management of funds within counties.

Policy Action 3: **Enhance the adequacy, efficacy, equity, and reliability of county financing in a way that follows service delivery functions within and across sectors.**

The government has established a strong fiscal framework that underpins devolution. This fiscal framework has enabled sharing of nationally generated revenues between the levels of government—first, vertically between the national government and the 47 county governments; and second, among the county governments. County government revenues come from the equitable share (an unconditional transfer), conditional grants, and OSR generated by the county governments. These revenues have enabled the delivery of critical services across the devolved sectors. Conditional grants have shown the potential to address sectoral funding gaps and incentivize sectoral and institutional performance.

However, as is indeed the case in other intergovernmental fiscal systems, there are fiscal challenges documented in this study that have an adverse impact on service delivery in counties. The share of national expenditure at the county level has declined in relative terms, and the share of national government expenditure in devolved sectors is relatively high. Conditional grants are fragmented, and the timing of central transfers is unreliable. This study recommends that the government consider the following policy options to tackle issues related to adequacy, equity, efficacy, and reliability that will need to be addressed to enable enhanced delivery of devolved services.

National government-specific actions include the following:

- Improve the targeting of the equitable share, as advised by the Commission on Revenue Allocation (CRA), and ensure that this equitable share keeps pace with growth rates in national expenditure.
- Increase the use of conditional grants in the devolved sectors, within a strengthened framework, to realign the vertical balance of resources and incentivize institutional and service delivery performance.
- Establish a sustainable financing mechanism for major infrastructure investments, especially for the urban and water sectors.
- Ensure that the equitable share and other transfers are made available to counties in a reliable and predictable manner.

County governments and the national government can take these enabling actions:

- Strengthen property tax collection through the devolution of valuation roles, strengthen cadasters in major urban centers, and explore the option of assigning "piggy-back taxes."

Policy Action 4: Adopt a strategic, results-oriented, and coordinated approach to HRM reforms to support county governments.

Human resources were devolved decisively to county governments, and one of the major achievements of devolution is that it has resulted in a significant increase in the number of staff working in frontline service delivery, especially in the harder-to-reach and historically underserved areas across the country. However, at the same time, devolution has exposed the inherent weaknesses in institutions, policies, and systems for HRM that have pervasively undermined capacity building, morale, and performance of personnel in many county governments.

Inefficiencies and inequity in the deployment of service delivery staff within counties means there is scope for better use of existing personnel. The share of administrative staffing is high relative to frontline staff. Efficiency in recruitment and deployment is undermined by a lack of sectoral norms and standards. Although recommended staffing structures exist in the health sector, they are unlikely to be affordable even over the medium term. In other sectors, there is little or no guidance on staffing norms and structures. The level of staff absenteeism at service delivery units, especially in health, remains high in many counties, and most of this absence is authorized. This undermines service delivery.

This study recommends that the government adopt a strategic, results-oriented, and coordinated approach to deliver capacity-building support to county governments. A key area of government action is to develop appropriate and affordable sectoral norms and standards for service delivery staffing and a comprehensive set of principles, policies, norms, and standard procedures in pursuit of meritocratic, efficient, and effective HRM in county governments. Several specific options emerged from this study.

County government-specific actions include the following:

- Deploy staff to the front line equitably within counties, rightsize administrative staffing, and align establishment structures and future recruitment plans with sectoral staffing norms.

- Strengthen the management of payroll by cleaning and automating county payroll systems.
- Effectively motivate staff and deal with absenteeism within their areas by addressing the politicization of recruitment, promoting meritocratic career progression within county services, and applying agreed-upon guidelines.

National and county governments can take these specific actions:

- Establish affordable minimum sectoral staffing norms and standards for service delivery in line with functional responsibilities and institutional structures for service delivery and appropriate norms for administrative staff.
- Support and incentivize counties to realign their staffing structures.
- Prepare a strategy and implementation plan for addressing absenteeism, particularly in the health sector.
- Streamline guidance on HRM to address staff motivation as well as establishment, recruitment, payroll, and performance management.
- Automate payroll and HRM systems for use by county governments.
- Establish independent oversight of HRM performance at the county level.

Policy Action 5: **Facilitate meaningful public participation in decision-making and strengthen the accountability of local politicians for service delivery.**
County governments have made significant efforts to involve citizens in the planning and budgeting process as well as in the selection and implementation of projects. However, such engagement does not always affect the decisions made in relation to service delivery. A greater focus needs to be placed on structures for community involvement in recurrent service delivery, including ECDE and health facilities, water schemes, municipal services, and extension. County Assemblies need to become more effective at overseeing service delivery by County Executives.

This study recommends the need to enhance public participation in decision-making and to strengthen the accountability of local politicians for service delivery. Several specific options can help achieve this goal.

County government-specific actions include the following:

- Build partnerships with civil society organizations (CSOs) to develop the capacity of citizen oversight groups.
- Improve the quality of participatory planning, which involves the public and the County Assembly.
- Strengthen the County Integrated Development Plan (CIDP) preparation and implementation processes to achieve efficient, equitable service delivery based on citizen needs and inputs.
- Develop and implement a broader set of county-specific policy approaches to improve ethnic inclusion within the County Executive and public service units, and exploit village-level information on the needs of marginalized groups to ensure inclusive and equitable access to public services.

County Assemblies can also take these actions:

- Strengthen the oversight and scrutiny of the County Executives regarding service delivery and move beyond their predominant focus on projects.
- Promote transparent and strategic resource allocation across the county as a whole to achieve countywide sector service-delivery objectives and avoid the fragmentation of resources toward the MCAs' own wards.

National institutions in partnership with counties can do the following:

- Prepare sector ministry guidelines on the structure and operation of sector-specific citizen groups for service delivery oversight.
- Provide capacity support to County Assemblies to enable them to oversee county service delivery.
- Undertake joint development of (cost-)effective tools for facilitating public participation in the planning and budgeting processes and ensure there is collaboration between national nongovernmental organizations (NGOs), CSOs, and counties in promoting participation and accountability.
- Strengthen peer-to-peer learning in inclusion of marginalized groups.

Policy Action 6: **Improve intergovernmental coordination. National and county governments need to cooperate, coordinate, learn, and build trust between and across levels of government and within sectors.**

Intergovernmental dialogue, coordination, and cooperation are fundamental to making devolution work for sector service delivery, with the spheres of government playing their roles effectively. The government is applauded for establishing intergovernmental coordination mechanisms (for example, the Intergovernmental Relations Technical Committee, Council of Governors, the Intergovernmental Budget and Economic Council, and the Summit) that are expected to help resolve policy and implementation disputes that arise from time to time during the devolution journey.

Effective service delivery is a joint (national and county) responsibility, and many of the challenges that have arisen—and will continue to arise—cannot be addressed "unilaterally." This is acknowledged and provided for in Article 189 of the Constitution of Kenya of 2010, which states that "Government at either level shall . . . assist, support and consult . . . the other level of Government" and that "Government at each level, and different Governments at the county level, shall co-operate in the performance of functions and exercise of powers." The COVID-19 pandemic has shown the importance of intergovernmental coordination, not only in health but also across all sectors and levels of government.

Despite the formation of various intergovernmental coordination bodies, this study documents the persistent weaknesses in intergovernmental coordination and the substantial tension and contestation within and across sectors. The intergovernmental mechanisms could work better by systematically setting out an action plan to clarify service delivery responsibilities among the various tiers of government and align these with national sectoral priorities to address the challenges set out in this study. Pursuing the following options will be critical to improve intergovernmental coordination.

National and county governments can take the following enabling actions:

- Strengthen existing coordination mechanisms with a renewed emphasis on cooperation and collaboration to make devolution work and with a strategic focus on service-delivery performance.
- Establish intergovernmental sector forums where they don't exist and make them operational.
- Use intergovernmental forums to monitor performance and reach mutual agreements at the technical and political levels so as to hold each other to account for performance.
- Strengthen the Senate's role in intergovernmental coordination in relation to devolved service delivery.

- Develop and implement standards and guidelines for how the relationship between county commissioners and county governments should function.
- Establish a strong, harmonized framework for sectoral and cross-cutting performance assessment and capacity building in managing and delivering services.

Policy Action 7: **Enhance county planning, budgeting, and execution. Realign and deploy resources within and across sectors in counties in ways that respond to local needs and national priorities for service delivery.**

County governments have allocated their resources in a way that has enabled the continuation and expansion of devolved services, especially in health and education. However, resources could be better oriented to service delivery, and this study recommends that counties could better balance resources within and across county sectors to better respond to local needs and national priorities.

The framework for budget preparation and reporting needs strengthening in ways that answer simple budget questions relating to expenditure on, and results of, service delivery in a consistent and comparable way. Decision-making and accountability processes need to be better structured, with a rationalization of planning and budgeting documents and stages to allow counties to focus on decisions to prioritize resources for operating and investing in services. A key area here is the quality of participatory planning, which needs to be more sharply focused and guided to be more meaningful.

Major priorities here start with developing explicit sector guidance for budgeting for service delivery. Such guidance should enable greater consistency within and across counties in how services are managed while allowing for counties to address their specific service delivery priorities. Linked to this is the need to reconsider how development spending is defined and incentivized in each sector, in ways that take into account the differences between infrastructure-focused sectors (such as urban and water) and service sectors (such as health and education) where delivery is more reliant on adequate staffing and operational expenditure. Planning and budgeting also need to become more focused on service delivery results as a whole, and less preoccupied with subprojects and activities.

This study proposes the policy options summarized below to enhance county planning, budgeting, and execution.

County government-specific actions include the following:

- Develop a strategy and plan to reduce county administration expenditure to allow for more resources to go toward the delivery of core services.
- Plan for and adequately cater to the staffing and operations of service delivery and prioritize financing frontline service delivery and primary levels of delivery within sectors.
- Prioritize capital projects through the appropriate appraisal processes linked to sector norms and local priorities identified through strengthened political and public participation.
- Improve equity in the location of services and investments within counties and prioritize urban services as well as those provided in rural areas.
- Report on the allocation and use of resources for service delivery performance in a way that is consistent with other counties in line with sector norms and standards.

National and county governments can take the following enabling actions:

- Develop and implement a unified framework for budget preparation and reporting, which answers simple budget questions relating to expenditure on, and results of, service delivery in a consistent and comparable way.
- Clarify decision-making and accountability processes, with rationalization of planning and budgeting documents and stages to allow counties to focus on decisions to prioritize resources for operating and investing in services.
- Prepare and disseminate sectoral budgeting guidelines to deliver sector objectives, norms, and standards and to respond to local priorities for service delivery.
- Provide capacity support to counties to focus on results-based budgeting and execution.

Policy Action 8: **Invest in data, information systems, and monitoring to build the evidence base for devolved sectors through increased focus on disaggregated sector data, development of service delivery norms and standards, disaggregation of financial reporting norms, and strengthened devolved monitoring for results.**

Assessing the impact of devolution requires specific, disaggregated data on inputs, outputs, and outcomes across sectors. Input data focuses on sector budgets and expenditures at different levels of disaggregation. Output data covers sectoral outputs produced by the inputs. For instance, in the health sector, output data might cover the availability of health equipment or essential drugs. Finally, outcome data provides information on indicators affected by the outputs. For example, health outcome data would cover indicators such as maternal and infant mortality rates.

In addition to disaggregated data, an urgent task is to improve the chart of accounts to address issues such as misclassification of some expenditures by counties—especially personnel—as public administration, which may artificially depress the level of sector expenditures and inflate administration expenditure.

The national government's policy-making function is being undermined in several sectors by the lack of routine monitoring data to compare county performance. This is, for example, a particular issue in the water sector (where there is no reliable system for monitoring the performance of rural water systems) and in agriculture (where data systems for commodities collapsed). It is also an issue for HRM data and fiscal data, where there is no standard sector or program classification that would enable comparisons of how much counties are spending on sector functions. Finally, it is an issue in the ECDE and health sectors. Weak county information management capacities in counties have been further stretched by the existence and use of multiple and fragmented monitoring systems, as well as a plethora of project-based monitoring and evaluation (M&E) systems.

National government can take the following actions:

- Develop a harmonized and simplified monitoring system at the county level.
- Prepare and roll out standard service delivery norms and standards.
- Enhance the current chart of accounts framework to allow for the reflection of source and use of funds at the disaggregated level and point of service delivery.

- Improve the quality of the BOOST dataset (which provides user-friendly access to granular county budget data) and its release to allow for timely assessment of trends in budgets and expenditures.
- Implement improved systems management at the county level, tracking budgets and expenditures to the subcounty level. This will enable the assessment of intracounty disparities in sectoral inputs, outputs, and outcomes.

National and county governments and jointly address the following:

- Implement systematic and coordinated service delivery surveys. Line ministries, working in close coordination with the Kenya National Bureau of Statistics (KNBS) and county governments, will enable the execution of systematic and coordinated service delivery surveys.

THE ROLE OF DEVELOPMENT PARTNERS

Development partners have played an important role in supporting the national and county governments in establishing devolved institutions, processes, and systems. Development partners have also channeled resources as conditional grants to programs that address financing gaps and encourage performance; these conditional grants programs have shown potential. However, the multiplicity of development partner engagements has also shown the potential to fragment county financing and support inconsistent approaches to service delivery.

In terms of future engagement to support devolution in Kenya, development partners will have to build on their current programs to address the service-delivery bottlenecks identified in this study and implement the recommended policy options. This will demand greater coordination among partners around a common agenda established by the government of Kenya and county governments.

Development partners can help the government to deepen devolution in the following ways:

- Provide national policy-level support and technical assistance for reforms to remove identified service-delivery bottlenecks and promote intergovernmental coordination within and across sectors. Special consideration is urgently needed to support the development of service delivery norms and frameworks; the establishment of a standardized evidence base for devolved sectors, particularly focusing on improving sector management information for service delivery; strengthening county service delivery, budget reporting, and monitoring for results; and addressing staff motivation and absenteeism.
- Support funding gaps for service delivery through jointly designed sectoral conditional grants in a way that provides incentives to address service delivery challenges and achieve sector policy objectives within a common framework. Performance-based programs such as the Kenya Devolution Support Program (KDSP) have shown the potential to catalyze institutional change in counties while financing service delivery investments.
- Align capacity-enhancement support to strengthen systems and institutions of both the national government and county governments in ways that address identified challenges to strengthening service delivery. Within this context, county-level support should be targeted toward addressing specific

constraints and challenges within this common agenda. Where a differentiated approach to tackle lagging counties is required, this should be coordinated through regional initiatives such as NeDi network-management software.

DELIVERING THE FUTURE PROMISE OF DEVOLUTION

The policy reform options outlined in this study have set out a broad agenda that requires concerted action within, across, and between the spheres of government, their executives and legislatures, as well as citizens. There are several opportunities to start addressing the issues relating to service delivery now. These opportunities should be taken. This study has highlighted the importance of a coordinated action collaboration. It is therefore proposed that a simple, high-level joint plan of action to make devolution work for service delivery be developed and endorsed by the Summit. Such a joint plan of action would include the following:

- A clear statement of the challenges facing devolved service delivery
- A limited number of high-level actions to address the challenges—actions that would be organized around (1) addressing sectoral service delivery issues through service delivery frameworks; and (2) addressing cross-sectoral issues in areas such as financing service delivery, HRM, and participation and accountability, with a strong message to tackle corruption in devolved service delivery
- The arrangements for implementation, including the key authorizers, stakeholder teams, and those actually responsible for leading the implementation of each action
- A process of mutual accountability in terms of jointly monitoring and assessing the progress of the implementation of the plan.

In conclusion, this study shows that the future of devolution is promising. The relatively new county governments continue to develop and become more responsive and accountable to citizens. Achieving the devolution promise will require both levels of government to play their part and, as envisaged in the Constitution of Kenya of 2010, to conduct their mutual relations on the basis of consultation and cooperation.

MDWSD Policy Options

This appendix brings together the principal policy and other options aimed at making devolution work better for service delivery. These are the most important options included in the Making Devolution Work for Service Delivery (MDWSD)'s background papers and policy briefs. (These papers and briefs include a much wider range of recommendations.) For the purposes of this synthesis, key policy options are grouped around the discussion in the final chapter of this report.

The MDWSD policy options are presented in a series of tables, each of which deals with one of the thematic areas, including functions and responsibilities; funding service delivery; county resource allocation and use; service delivery oversight, management, and systems; human resource management; politics, participation, and accountability; and intergovernmental coordination, collaboration, and cooperation. The tables consist of

- A first column spelling out the specific challenge or issue that is being addressed;
- A second column setting out some of the considerations for any response to the challenges identified;
- A third column presenting the policy options, with a description of measures or actions that could or should be taken to improve service delivery;
- A fourth column identifying who should take the lead in implementing recommendations and who should provide support to the leading institution or agency;
- A fifth column showing the time frame that will be needed to implement the recommendation, as follows: within the next 12 months (short term); within the next 3 years (medium term); and within the next 5–6 years (long term).

TABLE A.1 **Functions and responsibilities**

Review functional assignments. Clarify service delivery responsibilities of various tiers of government so that funding can follow responsibilities.

KEY ISSUES AND CHALLENGES	CONSIDERATIONS	POLICY OPTIONS	IMPLEMENTATION RESPONSIBILITIES	TIME FRAME
While Schedule 4 of the Constitution provides overall normative guidance on the two-tiered distribution of ser-vice-delivery responsibilities, in practice there remain ambiguities, overlaps, and contestation over the role of national and county government in some service-delivery functions. There continue to be areas where responsibility for service delivery between national and county governments is not aligned with the constitutional mandates, or where responsibilities are unclear, or disputed. This risks duplication or service-delivery "vacuums," which may arise when neither national government nor counties assume responsibility for a function for which responsibility is mistak-enly assumed to lie elsewhere. It can also lead to conflict between the two tiers of government. *Examples of disputes or lack of clarity over functions:* *Water:* In the water sector, county governments have taken owner-ship of urban water companies, however, responsibility for the urban water infrastructure investment remains disputed. The 2016 Water Act made this the responsibility of national water-works development agencies, but counties are challenging the constitutionality of this act in the courts. *Education:* It is not clear who is responsible for training teachers with respect to competence-based curricula. *Examples of where financing is not aligned with functional responsi-bilities:* *Health:* Under the Managed Equipment Scheme, the national government continues to make substantial investments in medical equipment for the counties, and over which counties have little control.	Functional roles and responsibilities in service delivery and associated arrangements for management and financing need to be jointly agreed by national and county governments through consultative processes.	*Identify cases where (1) there is a lack of clarity of responsibil-ity (for example, agricultural inputs) and (2) funds are not following functions (for example, in water, agriculture) and focus on resolving those.* *Clarify and codify functional responsibilities between counties and national govern-ment.* Ideally this should be done through intergovernmental forums (see the recommenda-tions on intergovernmental coordination) and endorsed by high-level authorities. Ambiguities, inconsistencies, and disputes over functional assignments should be addressed. This is important to ensure that accountability is clear, to reduce duplication and inefficiency, and to empower the level of government designated as being responsible. *The national government and county governments need to work together on drawing up sector service-delivery frame-works* to clarify roles and responsibilities, mechanisms for financing service delivery, county management of service delivery (PFM, HR, M&E), and identify joint actions to deal with service delivery issues. They should both set out the key responsibilities of each level, but also highlight the key challenges to improving service delivery. The aim would be to envisage these as joint challenges and identify the joint actions needed to address them. These frameworks should also identify if there is an appropriate role for conditional grants in the sector, and which policy function these might fulfil.	*Lead:* IGRTC Intergovernmental forums	Next 12 months

(continued next page)

TABLE A.1, *continued*

Review functional assignments. Clarify service delivery responsibilities of various tiers of government so that funding can follow responsibilities.

KEY ISSUES AND CHALLENGES	CONSIDERATIONS	POLICY OPTIONS	IMPLEMENTATION RESPONSIBILITIES	TIME FRAME
Urban: In the urban development sector (infrastructure, housing, and so on), the national government mandate is to provide policy direction and coordination. National government agencies continue to directly undertake projects in urban areas, both nationally and donor financed (for example, the Kenya Slum Upgrading Program, Kenya Informal Settlements Improvement Project, and Nairobi Metropolitan Services Project).		*Particular recommendations:* *The urban water and sanitation sector probably requires a major revision of the institutional framework. This issue may need to be dealt with directly by the Summit rather than by the sectoral forum.*		
Policy and regulatory functions are often poorly implemented Devolution has assigned policy and regulatory functions to the national government. These are important in terms of (1) ensuring that service delivery is consistent with citizens' constitutional rights; (2) ensuring that service delivery is guided by minimum standards and norms; and (3) ensuring that county "externalities" are managed. National MDAs are not finding it easy to fulfill their policy and regulatory mandates. They are accustomed to operating as command-and-control line ministries, with vertical assertions of policy and standards, rather than as national custodians who need to "negotiate" policy implementation and regulation with semi-autonomous county governments. These weaknesses in policy and regulatory functions apply to a range of sectors (ECDE, health, agriculture).	*National MDAs should strengthen their capacity to undertake "policy and regulatory" functions.* *National government "policy and regulatory" functions must become more effective through intergovernmental mechanisms*	National MDAs should ensure they have the organizational capacity to - Monitor, analyze, and publicize county performance and adherence to national policies; - Revise policies in light of this; and - Analyze when a conditional grant might be an appropriate policy response and be able to design this. This will require learning from counterparts in other highly devolved or federal states and being exposed to training. (See the recommendations on intergovernmental coordination.)	Lead: National ministries Involved: Sector ministries Intergovernmental forums	Next 3 years
Whether by constitutional design or because of institutional inertia, *the national government continues to retain considerable responsibilities for the delivery of infrastructure and frontline services.* It is unclear whether this is effective, efficient, or equitable.		*Expand county functional responsibilities for service delivery and limit national responsibilities.*	Lead: Intergovernmental forums	

(continued next page)

TABLE A.1, *continued*

Review functional assignments. Clarify service delivery responsibilities of various tiers of government so that funding can follow responsibilities.

KEY ISSUES AND CHALLENGES	CONSIDERATIONS	POLICY OPTIONS	IMPLEMENTATION RESPONSIBILITIES	TIME FRAME
Examples: - Most education sector functions and subfunctions - Rural, feeder, and urban roads In a short time, county governments have shown themselves capable of delivering a wide range of public goods and services. Although county performance has been far from perfect or ideal, subnational service delivery has not collapsed and, in many cases, has been improved. Given this relatively robust track record of counties, there are good grounds for arguing that counties should take on more responsibilities in the future, either by assuming responsibility for functions or subfunctions (such as education or school construction) that are currently an explicit part of the national government's statutory mandate, or through national government withdrawing from "devolved" sectors (such as urban roads or agriculture) in which it continues to play a direct role in service delivery, parallel to the statutory role played by counties.		Any further devolution of functions to counties should go hand-in-hand with the implementation of measures to strengthen and upgrade county-level capabilities, intergovernmental relations, and the policy and capacity support functions of the national government.		Next 5–6 years

Source: World Bank.
Note: ECDE = early childhood development and education; HR = human resources; IGRTC = Intergovernmental Relations Technical Committee; M&E = monitoring and evaluation; MDAs = ministries, departments, and agencies; PFM = public financial management.

TABLE A.2 **Funding service delivery**

Enhance the adequacy, efficacy, equity, and reliability of county revenues.

KEY ISSUES AND CHALLENGES	CONSIDERATIONS	POLICY OPTIONS	IMPLEMENTATION RESPONSIBILITIES	TIME FRAME
The vertical sharing of national revenue between the national government and county governments seems unbalanced and skewed in favor of the national level. The vertical allocation of equitable share resources is a binding constraint on the fiscal space of county governments and on the ability of counties to spend more on frontline public services.	Finance should follow function and continuously assess county against national functions and the vertical distribution of funds.	*Gradually alter the vertical fiscal balance in favor of county governments,* as well as explore the balance between unconditional and conditional grants in funding county services.	*Lead:* CRA *Involved:* NT CoG National sector ministries Parliament IBEC	Next 5–6 years
The national government currently absorbs the lion's share of national revenues and accounts for about 85 percent of total public expenditure, even though counties (which account for only 15 percent of the national fiscal pie) are constitutionally responsible for the delivery of many (if not most) public goods and services. A fairly strong argument can be made that the current vertical distribution of financial resources is (1) inadequate for counties and does not stand in proportion to the powers and functions that have been devolved to them and (2) more than adequate for the national government in relation to its constitutional mandates.		It should be possible to create the necessary fiscal space for further devolution by (1) increasing resources to counties faster than national government by allocating a larger share of national efficiency savings and revenue increases to counties and (2) transferring further resources for devolved functions from the national level to the county level within devolved sectors with high shares of national expenditure. Given that much of the responsibility for frontline service delivery lies with counties, allocating a greater share of resources to the subnational level would enable counties to expand and improve services. A first step in implementing this recommendation would be to undertake a thorough review of national government spending and budgets, linked to an analysis of the national government's functional mandates (as spelled out in the constitution).		
Sector ministries tend to retain budgets rather than devolve to counties in areas where there is a lack of clarity in functions, or areas of national policy priority.	Use conditional grants as a mechanism to finance mutually agreed-on priority functions and associated national policy objectives for sectors within a common framework.	Conditional grants can be identified and designed as mechanisms to fund counties to deliver functions and incentivize the achievement of national policy objectives and meet minimum sectoral standards and norms and responsibilities in service delivery.	*Lead:* NT Sector ministries *Involved:* MoDA CRA	Next 3 years

(continued next page)

TABLE A.2, *continued*

Enhance the adequacy, efficacy, equity, and reliability of county revenues.

KEY ISSUES AND CHALLENGES	CONSIDERATIONS	POLICY OPTIONS	IMPLEMENTATION RESPONSIBILITIES	TIME FRAME
Conditional grants are not used in purposeful or strategic ways. The 2016 framework has not resulted in a well-defined and coherent set of conditional grants. Conditional transfers have emerged in a more-or-less ad hoc manner from sectoral or political requests, rather than based on any coherent strategy or sound technical rationale. Many of the current conditional grants are simply a carry-forward of sectoral programs initiated prior to the new constitution, or specific earmarked programs funded by donors.	Conditional grants are the likeliest way of addressing vertical imbalances within sectors. Well-designed and well-managed conditional grants can have a direct impact on service delivery. A common and streamlined framework for conditional grants whereby sector grants support national policy objectives and service delivery. Conditional grants are used to incentivize sectoral as well as cross-sectoral institutional and service delivery performance.	*Strengthen the policy framework for conditional grants.* Provide standard design principles for (1) the purpose and rationale for grants, (2) a consolidated structure of grants, (3) the allocation principles for grants, (4) the framework for budgeting and reporting, and (5) the types of input and performance conditions to be used in grants. *Sectors rationalize and (re) design conditional grants within the new framework.* Sectors prepare grant guidelines within a common structure elaborating the design. *Sectors use conditional grants to incentivize performance in sectors.* Building on the experience of the KUSP and KDSP and results-based financing in health, increase the use of conditional grants to incentivize sector institutional performance and service delivery performance based on agreed sectoral norms and standards. Establish the role of IBEC in authorizing conditional grants within the agreed framework.	*Lead:* NT IBEC *Involved:* CoG National sector ministries CRA	Next 3 years
The equitable share and conditional grants are not released on a timely basis to counties by the National Treasury.	The NT provides timely releases for the equitable share and conditional grants	The NT releases the equitable share on time in line with an agreed-on schedule that is consistent with a national annual cash-flow plan, with transfers to counties prioritized in national cash flows.	*Lead:* NT *Involved:* CoB	Next 12 months

(continued next page)

TABLE A.2, *continued*

Enhance the adequacy, efficacy, equity, and reliability of county revenues.

KEY ISSUES AND CHALLENGES	CONSIDERATIONS	POLICY OPTIONS	IMPLEMENTATION RESPONSIBILITIES	TIME FRAME
County own-source revenues are low Given existing revenue assignments, counties are highly grant-dependent. This creates a situation in which county leaders only have a weak political incentive to collect own-source revenues. In most counties, even if the elected county leadership were able to double the level of county taxes and revenues collected (which would no doubt be a politically difficult decision), the corresponding increase in total county funding would only allow for an increase in county spending of about 10 percent. The reluctance (or hesitancy) of county leaders in trying to improve county revenue collections is further exacerbated by general weaknesses in county revenue administration (or in country revenue forecasting).	Urbanized counties and better-developed counties (with stronger economies) will benefit from strengthened revenue administration. Focus on land rates, property taxes, and licenses. Strengthen accountability through establishing a stronger link between services delivered and taxes in urban areas.	*Strengthen county revenues to improve service delivery,* by - *Improving county revenue administration* of existing county revenue sources. The greatest return to administrative efficiency of county revenue administration will naturally result in disproportionate revenue yields in counties with large economic bases. A focus could be placed on property tax collection in urban areas, through rationalization or devolution of valuation roles and strengthening cadasters in major urban centers. - *Expanding the revenue base;* for instance, it might be useful to explore the option of assigning certain "'piggy-back taxes." Piggy-back taxes are surtaxes where county governments would be able to place a surtax on a nationally collected tax, but where the collection of these taxes is handled by the national revenue authority. As such, it would be possible to provide greater own-source revenue autonomy and authority to the county level, while taking advantage of the typically more efficient national revenue administration.	*Lead:* NT&P *Involved:* CRA CoG	Next 3 years
Highly urbanized counties do not have adequate fiscal space to undertake major investments.	Highly urbanized counties have access to financing to undertake major investments.	*A financing framework for large infrastructure needs in major urban centers is established and functioning.* Alternative county-level financing mechanisms, such as public-private partnerships and debt financing should be explored as a mechanism for counties to fund major urban infrastructure. Any borrowing facility should be within macroeconomic limitations and clearly linked to future revenue streams.	*Lead:* NT UDD *Involved:* CoG CRA	Next 3 years

(continued next page)

TABLE A.2, *continued*

Enhance the adequacy, efficacy, equity, and reliability of county revenues.

KEY ISSUES AND CHALLENGES	CONSIDERATIONS	POLICY OPTIONS	IMPLEMENTATION RESPONSIBILITIES	TIME FRAME
		Investments that generate their own revenues downstream, such as tariff-generating water and sanitation infrastructure; market infrastructure; toll roads; or community investments where user fees or property rates (in the form of betterment levies) would be able to repay the upfront investment over time.		

Source: World Bank.
Note: COB = Controller of Budget; CoG = Council of Governors; CRA = Commission on Revenue Allocation; IBEC = Intergovernmental Budget and Economic Council; KDSP = Kenya Devolution Support Program; KUSP = Kenya Urban Support Program; MoDA = Ministry of Devolution and the Arid and Semi-Arid Lands; NT = National Treasury; NT&P = National Treasury and Planning; UDD = Urban Development Department.

TABLE A.3 **County resource allocation and use**

Enhance county planning, budgeting, and execution. Realign resources within and across sectors in counties that respond to local needs and national priorities for service delivery.

KEY ISSUES AND CHALLENGES	CONSIDERATIONS	POLICY OPTIONS	IMPLEMENTATION RESPONSIBILITIES	TIME FRAME
Planning and budgeting processes have not been sufficiently focused on the services counties are meant to finance. Budget documents do not transparently set out either the allocation of funding across the county or the results that are to be achieved with public funds, making it difficult to evaluate the effectiveness of public spending. Planning and budgeting processes focus on the selection of capital projects, not recurrent delivery of services. Participation processes are not working effectively.	*County planning and budget processes to focus more on the delivery of services and less on the selection of projects.* Budgets should answer the simple budget questions: 1. What sectors and services is the budget being spent on? 2. Where is the budget being spent? 3. How much money is being spent at a school/health facility/sub-county project? Clarity in decision-making and accountability processes, with rationalization of planning and budgeting documents to allow counties to focus on decisions relating to medium-term planning and then the annual budget.	Rationalize planning and budgeting documents to allow counties to focus on quality. Remove the requirement for counties to produce a CADP in addition to the CFSP. Provide more support and guidance to counties to improve the quality of their program budgets by improving the formulation and selection of the key outputs expected from each county department and identifying a few important results and indicators for each sector. By planning and budgeting in relation to service delivery results, counties may improve their allocation and monitoring of spending. The ways in which counties allocate resources to sectors also needs to be revisited if services are to be improved. Ensure subcounty structures and facilities (a subcounty agricultural extension team, or a health facility) are shown as a cost center in budgets to clearly show the funds they are allocated to provide services. This will help provide a greater results-orientation of the county budget. The key rules for participatory budgeting need to be clarified in many counties: What is the size of the allocation over which the participatory process is making decisions? How can residents make a proposal for consideration? What is the decision-making process for selecting projects? Counties must also provide significant administrative support if participatory processes are to be effective.	*Lead:* NT&P CECs (finance) *Involved:* MoDA National ministries County departments	Next 3 years

(continued next page)

TABLE A.3, *continued*

Enhance county planning, budgeting, and execution. Realign resources within and across sectors in counties that respond to local needs and national priorities for service delivery.

KEY ISSUES AND CHALLENGES	CONSIDERATIONS	POLICY OPTIONS	IMPLEMENTATION RESPONSIBILITIES	TIME FRAME
Counties are not currently reporting against results (indicators and targets set in program budgets) in their County Budget Review and Outlook Papers (CBROPs). Furthermore, many sectors do not appear to have the national data systems needed to produce reliable data for sector outcomes. County reporting is also not based on a common framework. This makes it difficult to compare county spending and outcomes for policy purposes.	Common program structure and indicators agreement. Reporting against program expenditures and outputs. Ensure reports are used in decision-making and accountability. County systems and dashboards linking performance and resources, linked to the sector MIS and IFMIS. National reporting comparing service delivery performance across counties in sectors.	*Counties need to report (in meaningful and comparable ways) on whether results have (or have not) been achieved.* *Good practices on reporting have been set that can be emulated by other counties.* Nyandarua has started producing a county annual progress report that reports against the targets set in its program budget. This should be emulated by all counties. However, ideally this information would be part of the CBROP, rather than separate, to ensure the results of spending are connected to the broader review of the budget and to the forecasts for the next fiscal year. The National Treasury should coordinate an annual report on county performance with each sector providing a chapter. *Develop a common program structure for all counties.* As all counties have the same functions mandated by the constitution, it should be possible to develop a common program structure and common key performance indicators connected to national sector information systems, which makes sense for all counties.	*Lead:* NT CoB CECs (finance) *Involved:* National sector ministries County departments	Next 12 months
There are inconsistencies between data collected by the Controller of Budget and county reporting through IFMIS.		*Move to a single data source for county expenditure.* To ensure there is a single data source, National Treasury, the Controller of Budget, and counties need to agree upon a common format for reporting through IFMIS, which may also require capturing some data from outside IFMIS.	*Lead:* NT CoB *Involved:* CECs	Next 3 years
There is no sector-specific guidance on how counties should budget for, manage, monitor, and report on funding for service delivery. Existing guidance on budgeting, planning, and financial management is generic but the services and investments in each sector are different.	*Develop explicit sector guidance for budgeting, management, and monitoring of service delivery within a common framework.*	*Sector budgeting guidance should be prepared in a collaborative way between the national government and counties* to ensure joint ownership. The National Treasury should coordinate this process, with national and county sector ministries and departments collaborating.	*Lead:* Intergovernmental forums Sector ministries CECs (sectors) *Involved:* NT MoDA	Next 3 years

(continued next page)

TABLE A.3, *continued*

Enhance county planning, budgeting, and execution. Realign resources within and across sectors in counties that respond to local needs and national priorities for service delivery.

KEY ISSUES AND CHALLENGES	CONSIDERATIONS	POLICY OPTIONS	IMPLEMENTATION RESPONSIBILITIES	TIME FRAME
The 30 percent development spending rule is distorting budget allocations. This is leading to "development" spending on infrastructure, crowding out spending on operations and maintenance, which includes essential health commodities and inputs for agricultural extension. In addition, the cap on payroll spending can constrain HR-dependent services (for example, health).	*The policy objective underlying fiscal rules should be clarified.*	*Reconsider the division between recurrent spending and development spending at the county level.* This currently adds little or no value. Flexibility is needed in the determination of spending for service delivery needs, shifting from a focus on compliance to performance (for example, the 70 percent/30 percent "development spending" rule is one size fits all for all counties).	*Lead:* CoB NT *Involved:* National Assembly Senate	Next 12 months

Source: World Bank.
Note: CADP = County Annual Development Plan; CBROP = County Budget Review and Outlook Paper; CECs = County Executive Committees; CFSP = County Fiscal Strategy Paper; CoB = Controller of Budget; HR = human resources; IFMIS = Integrated Financial Management System; MIS = management information system; MoDA = Ministry of Devolution and the Arid and Semi-Arid Lands; NT = National Treasury; NT&P = National Treasury and Planning.

TABLE A.4 **Service delivery oversight, management, and systems**

Promote devolution beyond counties. Devolve responsibility toward the point of service delivery and deliver predictable finance.

KEY ISSUES AND CHALLENGES	CONSIDERATIONS	POLICY OPTIONS	IMPLEMENTATION RESPONSIBILITIES	TIME FRAME
Centralized management structures within counties concentrate decision-making and resources at county headquarters, undermining service delivery.	Counties need to delegate responsibilities and authority to the subcounty level, urban boards, and facilities.	Counties and sector ministries need to jointly agree and clarify respective roles and responsibilities (potentially as part of the proposed SDF process), which involves appropriate delegation to the following subcounty structures and facilities:	*Lead:* MoDA MoTIHUD MoH MoE MoALF CoG	
Counties have not delegated enough operational responsibilities to their "agents." County departments have not delegated operational autonomy to their frontline service delivery units to the degree necessary. This means that local service delivery can be paralyzed or cumbersome. This is the case in: - Health, where health facilities do not have budgets for operations - Water supply and urban development, where the *principal-agent relationship* between county governments and various "semi-autonomous" subcounty institutions is not always clear (for example, water supply companies, urban boards)		- Urban boards - Subcounty health offices and health facilities - Subcounty education offices and boards of management for ECDE centers - Subcounty agriculture offices.	*Involved:* MoPSYGA	Next 12 months
Data and performance monitoring systems are not functioning effectively in many sectors. Poor information management is a threat to county service delivery. It weakens the basis for decision-making, programming, and resource allocation, makes it difficult or impossible to assess service delivery results, and undermines intracounty and intergovernmental coordination. Good information management underpins good service delivery.	National government departments need to take a more proactive role in supporting information management systems.	*Establish or strengthen information management systems in all sectors and across counties.* National government MDAs need to consult with counties on MIS and survey data that will both meet counties' management needs as well as national government. Sector MIS need to be developed or strengthened to meet agreed-on data needs and rolled-out with training for counties in each sector. Survey instruments, including the household survey, are strengthened to provide periodic countywide data on service delivery outcomes and socioeconomic indicators.	*Lead:* NT&P National ministries County departments KNBS	Next 12 months
Counties do not appear to ensure enough in the way of oversight, supervision, quality assurance, and on-the-job support for frontline service delivery units.		*Oversight, supervision, and quality assurance of service delivery need to be strengthened at the county level.*	*Lead:* CECs	Next 3 years

(continued next page)

TABLE A.4, *continued*

Promote devolution beyond counties. Devolve responsibility toward the point of service delivery and deliver predictable finance.

KEY ISSUES AND CHALLENGES	CONSIDERATIONS	POLICY OPTIONS	IMPLEMENTATION RESPONSIBILITIES	TIME FRAME
These "meso-level" (or "back-up") functions appear to be poorly assured by county departments. This weakens their ability to track performance and thus to ensure quality. This is of particular importance in sectors such as health, ECDE, and agriculture.				
Operating spending is not effectively supporting service delivery. Sector departments and frontline service delivery units do not reliably receive the funds they need (and were promised in the budget) to deliver services. In many counties, county-level financial management has been over-centralized (by county treasuries), depriving frontline service delivery units of spending authority and slowing down day-to-day operations. This has not only impeded service delivery; it has also had a negative impact on budget execution.	*Counties to improve cash management, ensuring operational funds for service delivery projects.* *Clarify modalities for ensuring funds get to and are available at facility or subcounty level.*	*Ensure operating funds reach the front line.* *Counties need to improve cash management processes to ensure that all county departments can reliably receive the operating funds they are promised in budgets and to ensure that funding reliably reaches the front line.* *County cash management practices need to become more decentralized to ensure that service delivery facilities receive budget resources regularly and on a timely basis. Counties need to find ways of providing their service delivery units with more spending authority. Options include imprest-type arrangements.*	*Lead:* CECs (finance) NT	Next 12 months
County performance on development budget execution has been poor. There are also large variations in performance between counties.	*Develop a common understanding of the reasons for variable performance.* *Improve project appraisal, prioritization, and budgeting.* *Improve contract management and oversight of project implementation.*	*There is not a clear understanding of the reasons for variable performance. Better understanding the bottlenecks to improved county public investment management should thus be a priority through a diagnostic study to identify different bottlenecks to project implementation.* *Develop PIM guidelines and systems for appraising and prioritizing of projects and management of project implementation for counties.* *Promote peer learning between better- and worse- performing counties based on the findings of the diagnostic study.*	*Lead:* National Treasury CECs (finance)	Next 3 years

Source: World Bank.
Note: CECs = County Executive Committees; CoG = Council of Governors; ECDE = early childhood development and education; KNBS = Kenya National Bureau of Statistics; MDAs = ministries, departments, and agencies; MIS = management information system; MoALF = Ministry of Agriculture, Livestock, Fisheries and Cooperatives; MoDA = Ministry of Devolution and the Arid and Semi-Arid Lands; MoE = Ministry of Education; MoH = Ministry of Health; MoPSYGA = Ministry of Public Service, Youth and Gender Affairs; MoTIHUD = Ministry of Transport, Infrastructure, Housing, Urban Development and Public Works; NT = National Treasury; NT&P = National Treasury and Planning; SDF = Service Delivery Framework.

TABLE A.5 **Human resource management**

Adopt a strategic, results-oriented, and coordinated approach to HRM reforms to support county governments.

KEY ISSUES AND CHALLENGES	CONSIDERATIONS	POLICY OPTIONS	IMPLEMENTATION RESPONSIBILITIES	TIME FRAME
Despite increased hiring, overall levels of staffing remain inadequate in some service delivery sectors.	*Develop sector-specific guidance on affordable and achievable minimum staffing standards* to guide recruitment and deployment decisions. Sectors may also show aspirational or international norms for staffing but should prioritize setting minimum standards.	State Department of Public Service to coordinate a process, with the *PSC*, to ensure that national ministries work together with counties to *develop sector-specific guidance such as minimum staffing standards, norms, and policy frameworks that can support identification of recruitment needs, and the equitable and efficient deployment of staff within the county.* This is particularly important for sectors with the largest staffing numbers: agriculture, health, administration, and urban services formerly carried out by local authorities. The PSC and State Department of Public Service should coordinate this with national sector ministries and counties.	*Lead:* MoPSYGA PSC Sector ministries CoG	Next 12 months
Inefficient or inequitable deployment of service delivery staff within counties means there is scope for better use of existing personnel in some counties.		Counties should align establishment structures to minimum standards and transparently deploy staff in line with minimum staffing standards.	*Lead:* CECs CPSBs	Next 3 years
Budget or resource constraints to service delivery staffing (35 percent wage ceiling, crowding out due to excessive numbers of administrative staff).	*Improve payroll management to ensure control over wage bills.* In particular, there should be transparency and reporting on staff engaged on contract, casual, and temporary terms and paid outside the IPPD system.	*Counties should implement a hiring freeze on administrative cadres* and make internal transfers between departments. *The State Department of Public Service to finalize GHRIS enhancement and rollout to counties.* Counties should clean and then automate payrolls, including payments to casuals through the proposed submodule for casuals under the recruitment and selection module of the enhanced GHRIS. National government oversight institutions should introduce sanctions for counties that use nonautomated payrolls.	*Lead:* MoPSYGA CoG CECs	Next 12 months

(continued next page)

Adopt a strategic, results-oriented, and coordinated approach to HRM reforms to support county governments.

KEY ISSUES AND CHALLENGES	CONSIDERATIONS	POLICY OPTIONS	IMPLEMENTATION RESPONSIBILITIES	TIME FRAME
	Allow flexibility for counties to recruit where they can show it will benefit service delivery even if fiscal rules are not met.	*Establish procedures whereby counties can be given flexibility on the 35 percent wage ceiling if a county government can show that this is in the interest of improved service delivery. The procedures should include the evidence that a county is required to submit and how the NT, CoB, and CRA will assess any such submission. In any process, the county submission and the NT, CoB, or CRA response should be public.*		
Demoralization and indiscipline among the service delivery personnel caused by the failure of many counties to comply with generally accepted principles, policies, standards, and norms for professional HRM management. For example: - Failure to adhere to meritocratic principles, public service values, and integrity in recruitment and deployment of personnel; - Inefficiencies and ineffectiveness in management of the service delivery personnel. Staff complain that their roles in service delivery are unclear. Poor management of the county to subcounty to front-line relationship leads to centralization of management at the county HQ level and unclear management responsibilities; - Poor human resource performance management (for example, lack of regular appraisal) and career development management (for example, lack of staff development, career progression, and succession management schemes).	*Guidance on basic principles and standards of HRM should be developed for counties.*	Develop and support the use of HRM guidelines for counties that cover: - Basic staff discipline procedures, including electronic clocking in and out of the workplace - Simple, basic integrated performance management systems, including frameworks for rewards and sanctions - Model staff development, career progression, and succession management schemes.	*Lead:* PSC MoPSYGA CoG *Involved:* KSG	Next 3 years

(continued next page)

TABLE A.5, *continued*

Adopt a strategic, results-oriented, and coordinated approach to HRM reforms to support county governments.

KEY ISSUES AND CHALLENGES	CONSIDERATIONS	POLICY OPTIONS	IMPLEMENTATION RESPONSIBILITIES	TIME FRAME
	Establish sector-specific guidance for counties on model organizational structures. This will also address the challenge that management structures at the county level can be top heavy and poorly organized.	State Department of Public Service to coordinate a process to ensure that national sector ministries work together with counties to develop sector-specific guidance on model organizational structures to improve their management performance.	*Lead:* MoPSYGA National MDAs CoG *Involved:* PSC	Next 3 years
	Counties should implement a simple, basic performance management system that covers all staff.	The national government should support counties to establish a performance management system, implemented through the performance management module in the enhanced GHRIS.	*Lead:* MoPSYGA CoG CECs	Next 3 years
	Model staff development, career progression, and succession management schemes to be adapted by sectors and by county governments.	The national government should support counties to adopt the model guidelines that have been developed by the State Department of Public Service.	*Lead:* MoPSYGA CECs *Involved:* KSG	Next 3 years
The level of staff absenteeism from work at service delivery centers remains high in many counties, and most of this absence is authorized.	Counties should establish systems to better track and manage absence to ensure adequate levels of time at task achieved.	The National government is to ensure the enhanced GHRIS can be used to track absenteeism. Where absence for training is a legitimate reason for absence, counties will need to strengthen training policies, such as increasing the amount of training carried out within facilities.	*Lead:* MoPSYGA CECs	Next 12 months
County governments do not have effective control of job grading and compensation of the staff inherited from defunct local governments and seconded from the national government, and the resulting inequities give rise to resentment, demotivation, and indiscipline of some staff in the service delivery centers.	Job grading and compensation across former civil service, former local authority, and county public service staff needs to be harmonized and rationalized.	*Rationalize county staff structures and payrolls.* This would entail - Formulating a program to harmonize job grading and compensation in the county governments and - Developing model policy framework and strategy for rationalization of staffing structures and payrolls - Providing demand-driven support to counties to rationalize their staffing.	*Lead:* SRC CoG MoPSYGA *Involved:* PSC	Next 3 years

(continued next page)

TABLE A.5, *continued*

Adopt a strategic, results-oriented, and coordinated approach to HRM reforms to support county governments.

KEY ISSUES AND CHALLENGES	CONSIDERATIONS	POLICY OPTIONS	IMPLEMENTATION RESPONSIBILITIES	TIME FRAME
The overarching HRM institutional framework of CPSBs and CASBs is *not* working as CPSBs and CASBs are not immune to political interference and influence, both in terms of their own membership and in terms of their decision-making. For example: - The institutional framework for recruitment and appointments is not providing sufficient safeguards to ensure adherence to meritocratic principles, which results in hiring or promotion of inappropriate staff and demoralizes other staff in the county.	*Establish independent oversight of County HRM performance.* *Review and reform the county-level Public Service Board model to make county-level HRM more technocratic and more independent of county government patronage or influence.*	Either (1) establish a national-level County Public Service Advisory Authority (as recommended in the Socio-Economic Audit of the Constitution undertaken by the auditor general) to oversee human resource management performance in counties; or (2) accord the PSC the mandate to regularly audit county governments' compliance with laid down principles, standards, norms, and practices in HRM, and to present an annual report to the senate on the same.	*Lead:* PSC CoG MoPSYGA Senate	Next 5–6 years
- CPSBs and CASBs do not always have the technical capacity or sector knowledge to assess and recruit candidates for some technical positions. Consequently, there have been instances of staff without requisite skills or other competencies being recruited.	Enhance the technical and operational capacities of the CPSBs and CASBs for sectoral recruitment.	Train CPSB members and secretariat staff and provide inputs from sector specialists in CPSB and CASB recruitment and appointment processes.	*Lead:* PSC MoPSYGA CoG *Involved:* KSG	Next 12 months
Incentives and support for county government engagement in HRM reforms and improvements.	*Ensure counties have sufficient support to undertake HRM reforms.*	*Provide counties with focused and demand-driven TA and capacity building for HRM.* This should include support to - Conduct HR audits and implement recommendations, - Build capacity for use or application of HRM guidelines, and - Rationalize staff structures or payrolls.	*Lead:* MoPSYGA Development partners CoG	Next 12 months
	Provide counties with incentives to undertake HRM reforms.	*Explore the options for providing counties with financial incentives or additional funding to initiate HRM reforms and adjustments.*	*Lead:* MoPSYGA NT CoG	Next 3 years

Source: World Bank.
Note: CASB = County Assembly Service Board; CECs = County Executive Committees; CoB = Controller of Budget; CoG = Council of Governors; CPSB = County Public Service Board; CRA = Commission on Revenue Allocation; GHRIS = Government Human Resource Information System; HQ = headquarters; HR = human resources; HRM = human resources management; IPPD = Integrated Payroll and Personnel Database; KSG = Kenya School of Government; MDAs = ministries, departments, and agencies; MoPSYGA = Ministry of Public Service, Youth and Gender Affairs; NT = National Treasury; PSC = Public Service Commission; SRC = Salaries and Renumeration Commission; TA = technical assistance.

TABLE A.6 **Politics, participation, and accountability**

Enhance structures for meaningful public participation. Facilitate the participation of the public in decision-making and strengthen accountability of local politicians for service delivery.

KEY ISSUES AND CHALLENGES	CONSIDERATIONS	POLICY OPTIONS	IMPLEMENTATION RESPONSIBILITIES	TIME FRAME
Struggles over mandates and functions between national institutions and county governments continue to prevail in certain service sectors, resulting in tensions and disruptions in the provision of public services.	Focus on the systematic unbundling and costing of service delivery functions, with the aim to establish clarity about the roles, responsibilities, and resources available to all actors within the intergovernmental framework.	Strengthen the role of the IGRTC in mediating between line ministries and counties for dispute resolution by transforming it into an independent commission.	*Lead:* MoDA *Involved:* The Summit Parliament IGRTC	Next 12 months
		Identify cases of dispute over mandates at the sector level; push counties and sector ministries to clarify functional assignments:	*Lead:* CoG *Involved:* Counties Sector ministries	Next 12 months
		Agriculture: Address the overlap of functions devolved to county governments on the one hand and assigned to SAGAs and numerous multipurpose projects implemented by the national government on the other.	*Lead:* Intergovernmental forum for Agriculture *Involved:* JASCCM, CoG, Counties Ministry of Agriculture SAGAs	Next 12 months
		Water: Revise the institutional framework for delivery of the urban water and sanitation sector. Here, focus should be on the development of a coherent and sustainable financing model for the urban water and sanitation sector that integrates the current two poorly coordinated parallel systems for asset creation.	*Lead:* CoG *Involved:* Counties Ministry of Water and Sanitation WWDAs	Next 12 months
		ECDE: Develop a framework to clarify roles and responsibilities of county governments and MoE in the provision of quality assurance in ECDE and dissemination of findings.	*Lead:* NEB/CEB CoG *Involved:* Counties Ministry of Education	Next 12 months
		Urban: Improve coordination of financing for larger urban infrastructure investments controlled at the national level, despite policy and management authority being in the hands of the counties.	*Lead:* CoG *Involved:* Counties SDHUD	Next 3 years

(continued next page)

Enhance structures for meaningful public participation. Facilitate the participation of the public in decision-making and strengthen accountability of local politicians for service delivery.

KEY ISSUES AND CHALLENGES	CONSIDERATIONS	POLICY OPTIONS	IMPLEMENTATION RESPONSIBILITIES	TIME FRAME
County Assembly oversight and scrutiny of the operations of county government executives is weak.	Strengthen the capacity of County Assemblies, in particular their technical committees and their support structures through systematic training, and reinforce the links of the County Assembly with national oversight bodies to strengthen their oversight and scrutiny of the County Executive.	Use the Center for Parliamentary Studies and Training (CPST) and SOCATT to build the technical capacities of CA support staff.	*Lead:* CAF *Involved:* CPST SOCATT CAs	Next 3 years
		Call on online ministries to train respective county assembly sector committees on sector policy making, regulation, and oversight.	*Lead:* CAF *Involved:* Line ministries CAs	Next 12 months
		Develop processes and instruments for CA oversight by drawing on the type of technical and fiscal analyses conducted by the national parliament.	*Lead:* CAF *Involved:* NP CAs IGRTC	Next 12 months
		Provide new MCAs with orientation through the dissemination of guidance publications to prepare them for their roles.	*Lead:* CAF *Involved:* CAs DPs	Next 12 months
		Strengthen formal relations between CAs and national oversight bodies such as the Office of the Auditor General to allow CAs to leverage the technical expertise and analytical capacity of the former.	*Lead:* CAF *Involved:* CAs OAG Senate	Next 12 months
The practice of providing each MCA with resources through a ward development fund (WDF) has reinforced their focus on the needs and demands of their ward constituents only and resulted in an overemphasis on small-scale infrastructure projects, to the detriment of countywide priorities and service delivery as a whole.	Create systems and incentives for MCAs to collaborate with other members to promote coherent and equitable planning and resource allocation across the county.	Explore county (for example, Makueni and West-Pokot) and international good practice for WDF-type mechanisms to help shift the focus of MCAs away from implementation to oversight.	*Lead:* CAF *Involved:* CAs DPs	Next 3 years
		Design WDF project selection criteria to encourage project development planning across more than one ward, including maintenance and operation requirements, and comprising components fostering equity and inclusion.	*Lead:* CAF *Involved:* CAs CoG NP	Next 12 months
		Ensure implementation of WDF projects by the County Executive and limit MCAs' role to planning and providing oversight of implementation.	*Lead:* CoG *Involved:* CAF NP	Next 12 months

(continued next page)

TABLE A.6, *continued*

Enhance structures for meaningful public participation. Facilitate the participation of the public in decision-making and strengthen accountability of local politicians for service delivery.

KEY ISSUES AND CHALLENGES	CONSIDERATIONS	POLICY OPTIONS	IMPLEMENTATION RESPONSIBILITIES	TIME FRAME
Citizen oversight groups have not always been effective or sufficiently autonomous. Even when citizen groups have been put in place, for example, PMCs to oversee investment projects, they tend to be initiated and orchestrated by the county administration, weakening their independence.	Encourage civil society organizations (CSOs) to organize and build the capacity of citizen oversight groups for holding counties accountable for the quality of service delivery.	Build partnerships between CSOs and county governments for developing capacity of citizen oversight groups.	*Lead:* Counties *Involved:* CSOs	Next 12 months
		Encourage collaboration (possibly through national funding) between national and local CSOs in places where local structures are weak.	*Lead:* MoDA *Involved:* CSOs CBOs	Next 3 years
		Encourage support from DPs in this area.	*Lead:* MoDA *Involved:* DPs	Next 12 months
		Encourage peer learning on various models or approaches.	*Lead:* CSOs *Involved:* CBOs	Next 3 years
		Develop guidelines on the structure and operation of citizen oversight groups (for example, PMC, water user groups, market user groups, community health committees, PTAs, and so on) within each sector, including: - Selection of members, - Reporting to the wider community, - Source and management of finances, and - Safeguards against perverse incentives (for example, PMCs being paid by contractors).	*Lead:* MoDA *Involved:* CSOs Counties Line ministries	Next 12 months
		Develop guidelines for civilian anti-corruption committees, including a mechanism for submission and review of their reports by a national oversight body (for example, EACC or CAJ).	*Lead:* EACC/CAJ *Involved:* CSOs Counties	Next 12 months
		Establish formal reporting links between citizen oversight groups and county assemblies, in particular with sector committees, so as to support oversight of sector service delivery.	*Lead:* CAF *Involved:* CAs CSOs Sector ministries	Next 12 months

(continued next page)

TABLE A.6, *continued*

Enhance structures for meaningful public participation. Facilitate the participation of the public in decision-making and strengthen accountability of local politicians for service delivery.

KEY ISSUES AND CHALLENGES	CONSIDERATIONS	POLICY OPTIONS	IMPLEMENTATION RESPONSIBILITIES	TIME FRAME
One-size-fits-all national provisions for protecting minority rights and fostering ethnic inclusion within counties have so far proven ineffective in addressing individual county circumstances and resulting grievances. (For example, the policy to impose ethnic quotas in public sector hiring at the county level may lead to perverse outcomes.)	Consider a broader set of county-specific policy approaches to improving ethnic inclusion within the County Executive and public service, possibly informed by further research.	Develop county-specific policies and laws, for example, for affirmative action, which promote ethnic inclusion in line with the individual county's social or ethnic profile and issues.	*Lead:* Equalization Fund Board Counties *Involved:* Senate National Assembly NCIC	Next 3 years
		Strengthen grievance redressal and response mechanisms for effective and equitable service delivery to all citizens, in particular to marginalized and minority groups.	*Lead:* CAJ/NCIC *Involved:* NCIC, CoG, NP IGRTC	Next 12 months
		Develop a sanctions framework to take disciplinary measures against counties consistently violating minority rights.	*Lead:* MoDA *Involved:* NP	Next 3 years
		Develop an approach to take the needs of marginalized groups into consideration in CIDP planning, drawing on the framework developed by the CRA.	*Lead:* CRA *Involved:* CoG, CRA, IGRTC NCIC	Next 3 years
		Refocus and restructure the equalization fund to target marginalized groups or areas at the subcounty level.	*Lead:* Equalization Fund Board *Involved:* COG CRA	Next 3 years
Within-county marginalization of small ethnic groups and minorities appears to have consequences for the equitable distribution of county services. This is reinforced by the fact that most county governments lack reliable village-level information about the needs and priorities of minorities.	Exploit village-level information on the needs of marginalized groups to ensure inclusive and equitable access to public services.	Advance the establishment of village administrations, or (in light of the financial ramifications of expanding the county civil service) volunteer village councils across all counties, as stipulated by the County Governments Act 2012.	*Lead:* CoG *Involved:* CAs MoDA IGRTC	Next 3 years
		Use village-level structures to identify and communicate the needs and priorities of marginalized groups from within each village to the county governments.	*Lead:* Counties	Next 3 years
		Develop county-level policies to promote the equitable distribution of resources below the ward level.	*Lead:* Counties	Next 3 years

(continued next page)

TABLE A.6, *continued*

Enhance structures for meaningful public participation. Facilitate the participation of the public in decision-making and strengthen accountability of local politicians for service delivery.

KEY ISSUES AND CHALLENGES	CONSIDERATIONS	POLICY OPTIONS	IMPLEMENTATION RESPONSIBILITIES	TIME FRAME
Many county governments still lack the technical approaches, skills, and tools to facilitate effective participation forums; for example, with regard to the format or type of engagement asked of the citizens.	Provide county governments with (cost-) effective tools for facilitating public participation in planning and budgeting processes.	Develop practical guidelines or manuals with hands-on tools and templates to support the implementation of public participation forums.	*Lead:* MoDA *Involved:* IGRTC, CSOs, Counties	Next 3 years
		Train country planning and finance staff in moderation techniques so they can better facilitate public participation forums.	*Lead:* MoDA *Involved:* Universities, CSOs, Counties	Next 12 months
		Prioritize engaging vulnerable and marginalized groups, as they will require the most support in making their voices heard.	*Lead:* MoDA *Involved:* Counties	Next 12 months
		Encourage counties to seek out partnerships with CSOs to benefit from their expertise and their mobilization capacity for strengthening civic education and engagement activities.	*Lead:* Counties *Involved:* CSOs MoDA	Next 3 years
The CIDP process (and all planning and budgeting documents derived from it) tends to be fragmented, resulting in planning outcomes that overemphasize small-scale projects without considering implications for recurrent costs.	Strengthen the CIDP preparation and implementation process to achieve objectives of efficient and equitable service delivery based on citizen needs and inputs. This is closely linked to the need to make county planning and budgeting more focused on service delivery results.	Ensure that the preparation of the CIDP is informed by a systematic analysis and needs assessment.	*Lead:* COG *Involved:* CRA	Next 3 years
		Restructure the CIDP process to balance bottom-up participatory inputs with sectorwide service delivery inputs.	*Lead:* MoDA *Involved:* CRA, IGRTC, CoG	Next 3 years
		Define and communicate the parameters within which citizen inputs can and will influence county planning and budgeting outcomes; that is, by providing clarity about: (1) the size of the allocations over which public participation is making decisions,	*Lead:* MoDA *Involved:* CRA, IGRTC, CoG	Next 3 years
		(2) what form citizen inputs and proposals should take for consideration, and (3) the decision-making process based on which projects are ultimately selected.	*Lead:* MoDA *Involved:* CRA, IGRTC, CoG	Next 12 months
		Develop a checklist for CIDP to ensure it addresses issues around inclusion of marginalized groups.	*Lead:* MoDA *Involved:* CRA, IGRTC, CoG	Next 12 months

(continued next page)

TABLE A.6, *continued*

Enhance structures for meaningful public participation. Facilitate the participation of the public in decision-making and strengthen accountability of local politicians for service delivery.

KEY ISSUES AND CHALLENGES	CONSIDERATIONS	POLICY OPTIONS	IMPLEMENTATION RESPONSIBILITIES	TIME FRAME
		Develop guidelines on how to derive short-term planning and budgeting documents (ADP, program budget) from CIDP.		
		See PFM policy note for further recommendations on strengthening the county planning and budgeting processes.		

Source: World Bank.

Note: ADP = Annual Development Plan; CAs = County Assemblies; CAF = County Assembly Forum; CAJ = Committee on Administrative Justice; CBOs = community-based organization; CEB = County Education Board; CIDP = County Integrated Development Plan; CoG = Council of Governors; CPST = Center for Parliamentary Studies and Training; CRA = Commission on Revenue Allocation; CSO = civil society organization; DP = Development Partner; EACC = Ethics and Anti Corruption Commission; ECDE = early childhood development and education; IGRTC = Intergovernmental Relations Technical Committee; JASCCM = Joint Agriculture Sector Cooperation and Coordination Mechanism; MCA = members of county assemblies; MoDA = Ministry of Devolution and the Arid and Semi Arid Lands; MOE = Ministry of Education; NCIC = National Cohesion and Integration Commission; NEB = National Education Board; NP = National Parliament; OAG = Officer of the Auditor General; PFM = public financial management; PMC = project management committee; PTA = Parent Teacher Association; SAGAs = semiautonomous government agencies; SDHUD = State Department of Housing and Urban Development; SOCATT = Society of Clerks At the Table; WDF = Ward Development Fund; WWDA = Water Works Development Agency.

TABLE A.7 **Intergovernmental coordination, collaboration, and cooperation**

Improve intergovernmental coordination. National and county governments need to cooperate, coordinate, learn, and build trust between and across levels of government and within sectors.

KEY ISSUES AND CHALLENGES	CONSIDERATIONS	POLICY OPTIONS	IMPLEMENTATION RESPONSIBILITIES	TIME FRAME
There are weaknesses in intergovernmental coordination to foster cooperation and collaboration and resolve conflicts between levels of government. This means that a range of challenges and problems (which require both levels to work together) are not adequately addressed or resolved. Key types of challenge include: - Clarifying and assigning functional responsibilities - Capacity building, technical, and logistical support - Policy formulation and implementation - Regulatory functions. For example, the failure to effectively agree on how to manage conditional grants reflects the shortcomings of the IBEC, with counties complaining of inadequate and inconsistent communication on the purpose of conditional grants. IBEC should provide the consultative machinery that would allow conditional grants to be discussed, clarified, and agreed on.	Strengthen forums where national and county governments can reach mutual agreements at the technical and political levels.	Make sure that these mechanisms are operational, properly resourced or funded, and used on a regular basis; this may require, for example, establishing a full-time secretariat for each sector forum, accessing donor support to finance forum interactions, and so on. Strengthen technical inputs to the Summit so that it can move away from a current focus of "fire-fighting" or "conflict resolution" and toward a more agenda-driven and systematic approach. Many MDWSD findings and recommendations could be used to establish sector or cross-cutting agendas: - Strengthen the technical-level county secretaries meeting convened by the Intergovernmental Relations Technical Committee so that it effectively prepares the ground for the Summit. - Ensure it functions as a regular working-level meeting between the twice-annual meetings of the Summit. - Ensure that sector political and technical level committees feed into the county secretaries meeting and that sectoral reports are produced regularly to feed into the Summit. Ensure that independent commissions provide recommendations to intergovernmental forums, modelled on the way the CRA provides inputs to the IBEC.	*Lead:* IGRTC MoDA National Sector Ministries County Secretaries *Involved:* County CECs and principal officers	Next 12 months

(continued next page)

TABLE A.7, *continued*

Improve intergovernmental coordination. National and county governments need to cooperate, coordinate, learn, and build trust between and across levels of government and within sectors.

KEY ISSUES AND CHALLENGES	CONSIDERATIONS	POLICY OPTIONS	IMPLEMENTATION RESPONSIBILITIES	TIME FRAME
Sector coordination mechanisms could work more effectively in many sectors.	*Sector intergovernmental forums need to be established and operational.*	*Sectors can follow the model of agriculture.* This sector has set up four coordination mechanisms: - A ministerial-level, Intergovernmental Forum for Agriculture - A Joint Agriculture Steering Committee to replicate this on a technical level - The Joint Agriculture Sector Cooperation and Coordination Mechanism (JASCCM), which brings together all stakeholders in the sector, including the private sector, civil society, and development partners - The Agriculture Sector Caucus for County Executive members in charge of agriculture to enable counties to coordinate. An equivalent forum at the technical level for county chief officers should also be established. In addition to the formal committee structures, sector ministries should establish technical working groups to resolve specific issues. Such a group could be established to develop service delivery frameworks.	*Lead:* National sector ministries *Involved:* County CECs and principal officers	Next 3 years
	The CoG and the Senate should have a stronger role in coordinating sectors.	The sector standing committees of the Senate should be strengthened to enable them to play a stronger oversight and accountability role on intergovernmental coordination. Strengthen the sector committees of the CoG to enable them to play a stronger role in coordinating the county position with national government MDAs.	*Lead:* Senate CoG	Next 3 years

(continued next page)

TABLE A.7, *continued*

Improve intergovernmental coordination. National and county governments need to cooperate, coordinate, learn, and build trust between and across levels of government and within sectors.

KEY ISSUES AND CHALLENGES	CONSIDERATIONS	POLICY OPTIONS	IMPLEMENTATION RESPONSIBILITIES	TIME FRAME
Implementation of measures identified through intergovernmental coordination mechanisms has not been effective. Their recommendations and resolutions are often not implemented or complied with by either the national government or county governments. Example: The Intergovernmental Sectoral Forum for Public Service Management has met regularly to discuss issues and identified ways forward for tackling some of the deficiencies in HRM. Despite this, few agreed-on actions have been rolled out or complied with.	*When intergovernmental forums for coordination and cooperation identify ways forward, these need to be implemented and enforced.* Intergovernmental coordination and cooperation mean little if they do not result in binding decisions and compliance, on the part of both the national government and counties. Recommendations and resolutions from sectors and other intergovernmental groups need to be given weight by being endorsed by the Summit.	The Summit needs to (1) agree on what the NG and CGs must do to make service delivery work more effectively; and (2) what sanctions will apply if the NG or CGs do not comply with collective decisions reached by the Summit. The IGRTC needs to play its mandated role of ensuring that the discussions, findings, and recommendations of the cross-cutting and sector intergovernmental forums are fed into and discussed at the meeting of county secretaries and then into the Summit. The IGRTC then needs to follow up on any Summit resolutions, through the meeting of county secretaries and through sector intergovernmental forums to ensure that they are taken seriously and adhered to by both national MDAs and county governments.	*Lead:* The Summit IGRTC CoG *Involved:* National ministries County governments CECs	Next 3 years
Coordination between county governments and county-level national government structures is inconsistent.	Set standards and guidelines for how the relationship between county commissioners and county governments should function.	The State Department of Interior, State Department of Devolution and the ASALs, and the CoG need to develop standards and guidelines for regulating the relationship between county commissioners and county governments.	*Lead:* IGRTC *Involved:* MoDA CoG SDoI	Next 3 years
Capacity building is fragmented within and across sectors, and the impact on county institutional and service delivery performance is unclear. The ACPA and NCBF have shown promise in assessing and supporting cross-cutting institutional capacity but have not reached their full potential.	Establish a strong and harmonized framework for cross-cutting and sectoral capacity building and assessment of institutional performance in the management and delivery of services.	*Institutionalize and strengthen the NCBF* and develop sector capacity-building frameworks that address key functions in county management and delivery of services, linked to the implementation of the SDF.	*Lead:* MoDA	Next 12 months

(continued next page)

TABLE A.7, *continued*

Improve intergovernmental coordination. National and county governments need to cooperate, coordinate, learn, and build trust between and across levels of government and within sectors.

KEY ISSUES AND CHALLENGES	CONSIDERATIONS	POLICY OPTIONS	IMPLEMENTATION RESPONSIBILITIES	TIME FRAME
		Institutionalize and strengthen the annual county performance assessment (ACPA) and align performance measures to broader government PFM and HR reform strategies.	*Involved:* Sector ministries Intergovernmental forums NT MoPSYGA	
		Establish county sector performance assessments linked to the ACPA.		
		National government and counties need to strengthen collaboration on capacity building. As improvements are needed on both sides, it would make sense for county and national governments to agree on a set of actions that together will improve the impact of capacity building.		

Source: World Bank.
Note: ACPA = annual capacity and performance assessment; CEC = County Executive Committee; CG = county government; CoG = Council of Governors; CRA = Commission on Revenue Allocation; HR = human resources; HRM = human resources management; IBEC = Intergovernmental Budget and Economic Council; IGRTC = Intergovernmental Relations Technical Committee; MDAs = ministries, departments, and agencies; MDWSD = Making Devolution Work for Service Delivery; MoDA = Ministry of Devolution and the Arid and Semi Arid Lands; MoPSYGA = Ministry of Public Service, Youth and Gender Affairs; NCBF = National Capacity Building Framework; NG = national government; NT = National Treasury; PFM = public financial management; SDF = Service Delivery Framework; SDoL = State Department of Labor.